BRUNG UP PROPER

JASON MANFORD

BRUNG UP PROPER

EBURY
PRESS

1 3 5 7 9 10 8 6 4 2

First published in 2011 by Ebury Press, an imprint of Ebury Publishing
A Random House Group company
This edition published 2012

The Random House Group Limited Reg. No. 954009

Addresses for companies within the Random House Group can be found at
www.randomhouse.co.uk

A CIP catalogue record for this book is available from the British Library

The Random House Group Limited supports the Forest Stewardship
Council® (FSC®), the leading international forest certification organisation.
All our titles that are printed on Greenpeace approved FSC® certified paper
carry the FSC® logo. Our paper procurement policy can be found at
www.randomhouse.co.uk/environment.

MIX
Paper from
responsible sources
FSC® C016897

Printed and bound in Great Britain by CPI Group (UK) Ltd,
Croydon, CR0 4YY

ISBN 9780091939069

To buy books by your favourite authors and register for offers visit
www.randomhouse.co.uk

For RJ, MG and AN

Contents

Chapter 1
Christmas

11.43pm, Christmas Eve, 1990

I'm lying in bed trying not to think about what was said – hoping that it somehow isn't true. I'm more tired than I've ever been but still I can't sleep. My eyes are stinging like a thousand tiny golf players are walking across my eyeballs. The room's freezing – it's December, after all – and although my Manchester City curtains are shut tight, they're so paper-thin that the colours from the neighbour's Christmas lights are shining through the otherwise dark and silent night outside.

My room is tiny and my single bed (the one my Auntie Kathleen gave us when she got a new one in the MFI winter sale) is pushed up to the wall, so sometimes in the night I roll over and the ice-cold wall wakes me from whatever dream I was having. Not that there's any chance of that tonight as in between me and the pale blue wall are my two younger brothers, Stephen, seven, and Colin, five. Stephen has decided to leave his bed free in case Father Christmas needs somewhere to rest, and Colin has presumed that at least one of his reindeer will be knackered too.

But behind the usual Christmas excitement is another feeling, a feeling I'm trying to block out. It's not a nice feeling. My thoughts drift back to earlier in the week…

I was in the front room winning my way through a game of Megaman 2 on the Nintendo when I heard my dad shout from the kitchen.

'Jason! Stephen! Colin! Come in here please.'

I knew something was up straight away. He never said 'please'.

In unison, from all over the house three young boys' voices shouted back, 'Aww, Dad, what is it, can't it wait?'

Then my dad did something unprecedented. He gave up home advantage and came in to the living room.

'No, it can't wait, turn that bloody thing off, it's not a life support machine.'

Colin and Stephen hurtled down the stairs, jumped on the sofa and settled either side of me as we all waited impatiently to find out what was so urgent. It had stopped me defeating the main boss on Megaman 2; Dr Wily had got away for the last time, damn you, Dad!

I'd presumed it was the usual mannish inquisition about who'd left wee on the seat or broken one of Mum's fake china dolls on the wall unit, but one look at my mum nervously eyeing my dad told me this was something different.

'Look, there's no easy way to say this,' my dad started.

There was a long pause. There really was no easy way of saying it.

My mum took over. 'Listen, boys, we're really sorry but me and your dad have had a struggle these last few months and, well –' tears were filling her eyes ' – we're not going to be able to get you any presents this year.'

We sat there, gobsmacked. I'm not sure Colin even understood at first. Had we been bad? Had they found out that one of Mum's china dolls' heads was actually just balanced on its body, or that Dad's Desmond Decker LP had actually been snapped in two and carefully slid back into its cardboard sleeve?

'No, no, don't be daft.' Mum cut short our questions. 'We would never do anything like that. We'd love to buy you presents. But things are just a bit tight at the moment, money-wise. But, hopefully when the January sales kick in and your dad gets paid, we'll go and get a few bits.'

My brothers both burst into tears and my mum joined in soon after.

My dad looked at the ceiling and then the floor, then ruffled Colin's and Stephen's heads to try and cheer them up.

I kept it together. In fact, I'd had a Eureka moment. I'd had the idea that was going to save our Christmas.

'Don't worry, Mum, you don't need to get us anything this year,' I said.

A look of relief and humbling pride spread across my parents' faces as I, their first-born, had got it. Even though I was only nine years old, I'd understood that times were tough and we couldn't always get what we wanted.

'You don't need to get us anything – Father Christmas will bring us all the presents we need.'

Their faces fell. This is the one moment in life that the Father Christmas myth really backfired.

CHRISTMAS WAS ALWAYS a big deal in the Manford house. We loved it. The tree always went up at the beginning of December, the Phil Spector Christmas album was blasting from the hi-fi, in every room we had more decorations than wall space, and the fridge was full to bursting with the most brilliant stuff, as if someone had robbed Iceland and brought the frozen swag round to our house. That was because someone *had* robbed Iceland and brought it round to our house. My Uncle Stephen, to be exact, and despite the fact that he was usually high as a kite on drugs, he always seemed to have no problem finding their boxes of mini quiches and tiny vanilla slices just when we needed them.

If my mum had had her way the tree would have been up even earlier but Christmas decorations were a major and time-consuming operation; it took two weeks alone to detangle the lights. The opening event in all this was getting up to the attic. Only Dad could manage it, of course. He was over six foot and only ten stone. If you look up 'lanky streak of piss' in the dictionary, there's a picture of my dad there. He was the only one allowed to climb into the loft, because, as he confidently put it, 'I've got a system, love.'

His system was dangerous. He'd get his left foot on the rickety wooden banister at the top of the stairs, then use his hands on the wall to hoist himself up, often with an 'ooompah' type noise. I don't know why he made that noise when he exerted himself – he made the same noise when lowering himself onto the toilet – but it seemed to help. From the banister he'd reach across with his spindly right leg and use the landing light switch as a foothold like a rock climber. I'm not an electrician but that can't be safe, can it? For nearly twenty years he honed it to a fine art, but how on earth he never fell or killed himself – it pained me to even watch – is beyond me. He was like a kind of Mancunian Spiderman. Or Spidermanc.

For me and my brothers, though, Christmas started even before all that – with the magical arrival of the Littlewoods catalogue mid-October. Thank God for catalogues. Every year me and my brothers would sit down to carefully circle the things we wanted in the hundreds of toy pages. Then every year without fail my dad would cut the pictures out and hand them to us.

'There you go, I got you a little something. I know you wanted it.'

My mum loved Christmas more than any of us, and every December she would go through the Littlewoods catalogue and order way more stuff than we could afford, and then spend the next eighteen months paying for it. But as a year only lasts twelve months she would still be paying for last year's presents (I'd got a Hot Wheels set and we'd all got a Nintendo to share) when this year's Christmas rolled along. You see the catch here? That sort of payment scheme can only last so long before a catalogue company decides that actually it'll have its money back this year and suddenly you haven't got enough credit to order a refill for last year's Mr Frosty.

The only present I wanted as a kid was a Scalextric. I'd seen the adverts come on the telly during *Wacaday* and I was in love with the cars and the speed, but more than anything – the crashing. A kid called Tim who lived at the top of our road for a few months had one and I became his best mate for a brief time. Every Saturday morning I'd get dressed, go to his house and we'd play with his Scalextric until the street lamps switched on and my mum knocked on to tell me I'd missed tea.

It was only a basic model but I loved it. He'd have the red controller and I'd handle the blue and our gold and silver Porsche 934s (with working lights, by the way) would go whizzing past the crowds of cheering plastic fans in a figure of eight before careering off the side through the plastic safety barriers and getting stuck in his mum's shagpile carpet. When he moved house I was more sorry to see the back of the Scalextric than I was Tim. I begged my mum and dad for one every Christmas but to no avail.

To be fair to Dad, he never wrote 'from Father Christmas' on any presents, although Mum liked to sneak it onto a couple. I asked Dad years later why he never signed a present from Santa.

'Why would I? I work hard all year round – why would I give the credit to some made-up fat bastard?'

When I say we loved Christmas, my dad really just went along with it to keep my mum and the rest of us happy. It's not that my dad disliked Christmas, it was just a time when money worries would come to a head. You can get by living hand to mouth just fine the rest of the year, but at Christmas, when it's compulsory to go to town with food and toys, it's easy for things to go wrong. I suppose it was hard for him to forget, as the unpaid bank holidays mounted up and his family overate and overspent, that January's brown paper envelope was the thinnest of the year.

Where Dad worried, my mum, as I've said, bloody loved it. She's just a big kid at heart. Whereas in most houses the cliché was for the kids to go running into their parents' room at 4am, bouncing on the bed until they got up, in our house it'd be Mum making as much noise as possible until everybody woke up and we could start Christmas properly. My mum is top. I know everyone says that about their mum but everyone says it about my mum too. Every person she meets becomes her best friend within seconds.

Like most families, we had a set routine on Christmas morning. With Boney M on the radio singing 'Mary's Boy Child', all the presents would be in individual piles like a festive Jenga and we'd all sit round the room taking it in turns to open a present each. Including the dog. It used to take bloody hours.

My dad would be clock-watching and my mum would accuse him of being a miserable sod.

'What's up with you?'

'It's 6am, love, and I've been up for an hour that's what's up with me.'

'Well, why are you so tired? Were you visited by three ghosts again?'

My dad would be sat on his usual spot on the couch with a black bag, collecting wrapping paper. We'd open a present, screw up the paper and throw it over at him, aiming for his head like a basketball player bouncing the ball off the backboard before it slips into the net. He'd sit there muttering to himself: 'I only stopped wrapping these three hours ago.'

He was never a massive drinker, but his one concession was that he'd crack open his annual can of breakfast Carling.

Dad joined in with the festivities but he would never instigate them; he did just enough to get through the holiday period. We would pop to church for a sing-song but his heart wasn't in it. He wasn't a religious man and we didn't go to church every Sunday religiously. Well obviously we went religiously but not, you know, religiously! I enjoyed church as a kid mainly because they gave us free Bourbon biscuits and a glass of Vimto. He came to my first school nativity play though, when I got the part of the penguin. What, you've never heard of the Christmas penguin? Oh, very integral to the whole nativity story is the Christmas penguin. It's in the Bible like. Check it out, Luke, Chapter 5, Verse 7.

'...and lo the three wise men did get lost after Balthazar turned to Melchior and said unto him, "What did that Shepherd say, Melch? Was it left or right at the Pyramids?" And Melchior said unto Balthazar, "I wasn't listening, mate, I thought you were listening, we can't be that far away from Bethlehem, let's ask this penguin."'

It's a classic scene.

My dad couldn't resist asking the priest stupid questions at the end of the service.

'But, Father, why did the three wise men bring such odd gifts for a child? I don't know if you've been to a maternity ward as a visitor recently, mate, but it's mainly flowers and babygros.'

Dad was an odd atheist in that he knew the Bible inside out, he once asked our local priest, 'If Jesus drove the traders out of the temples and said, "Do not make my father's house a house of merchandise," why have you got a little shop at the back of church selling plastic Virgin Marys and bottles of holy water?'

He's not really welcome at St Jude's any more.

Like a lot of families, Nana and Granddad would come over for a massive Christmas dinner. I've never been a huge fan of Christmas dinner. My mum only had one way of cooking the turkey: leave it in the oven until it's so dry you'd need a mug of Vaseline to swallow it down. And sprouts, come on, they're evil. My dad calls them the 'Devil's haemorrhoids'. They sort of have the taste of a full cabbage concentrated into a little pocket of wickedness. My mum loves them and will actually get two pieces of white Warburtons and have a sprout butty for her supper. All famous chefs give tips for Brussels to take the taste away – 'cook them in butter', 'wrap them in bacon'. If you have to try that hard to mask the taste then don't have them; no one says 'here's the roast potatoes – I know they're horrible so I've cooked them in chocolate'. But my dad loved being the head of the table at Christmas dinner, it was the only bit of the day he seemed to really enjoy. Maybe not the actual dinner but doing all the turkey jokes to a roomful of family.

'Do you want stuffing, love?'

'Who'd like a bit of breast? Or are you more of a leg man?'

'Who wants a slice of this dirty turkey whore?'

Sometimes he went too far.

DAD WASN'T QUITE as bad as Scrooge, mainly because he didn't have Scrooge's money, but he did have his moments. Though we had endless Christmas decorations, he wouldn't let my mum put any Christmas lights in the windows.

'Why should we pay electricity to entertain the neighbours?'

He hated the fact that the house across the road was virtually flood-lit and it wound him up no end that they would still be flashing away around a semi-inflated Santa come the start of February.

When it came to wrapping presents, they'd always be in the shape of a cracker so he didn't have to do corners – just screw the end up and whack some gaffer tape round it. There was nothing he couldn't make look like a cracker. Jigsaws, chocolate orange, a puppy, the man was a genius. Although, like most men, he hated the shopping part of it all – doing most of his present buying on Christmas Eve at Manchester Arndale.

'Jesus, I was trying to get out of Debenhams against a stream of people. I felt like that bleeding Mufasa in *The Lion King*. I was only after a Lynx gift set for Uncle Tony.'

One year my mum asked him what he wanted for Christmas. He gave us all a huge smile and said lovingly, 'Sweetheart, I don't need any presents off any of you, I've got everything I could possibly want. This year my only Christmas wish is that my whole family, every last one of you, from you, Sharon, to little Colin, our mums and dads, brothers and sisters would… just sod off and give me a few days' peace.'

It was at Christmas that I saw the differences between my parents: Mum would be trying to see as many family members as possible before the big day, as if there was some sort of cut-off date and she was planning a huge cull come January, while Dad sat in the background moaning about 'the bloody doorbell going every five bloody minutes' and complaining about every unnecessary indulgence.

'Why have you bought two hundred satsumas, love?'

'Because it's Christmas, it's festive.'

'Who's gonna eat bloody oranges when there's a massive tin of Quality Street to get through?'

He had a point. One year I asked him if he was going to tip the bin men, and his head nearly exploded.

'Tip? Bleeding tip? I'll tell you what I will bloody do, I'll leave them a tip in the garden and see if they'll come past the gate for that, the cheeky bastards.'

But in spite of all the moaning and the disgust at the excesses and dramas of the festive season, I knew he secretly enjoyed having so much time at home with his wife and kids, and every so often he'd do something that made me think, this guy is the best dad in the world; he really deserved that mug.

12.01am, Christmas Day, 1990

My eyes are dropping with the weight of the night and my brothers' rhythmical snoring is finally tempting me to sleep. But just as I'm descending into that world somewhere between awake and asleep, I hear a noise, a light airy familiar noise coming from outside. It's the sound of sleigh bells, the unmistakable sound of silver bells. Jingle bells and Christmas bells, hundreds of them, all jangling in the night sky.

I reach for my brother's shoulder. 'Stephen, Stephen, wake up, mate, Father Christmas is here.'

'What you on about?' he says sleepily, but then he also hears the noise.

'Father Christmas is here, in Manchester, listen.'

We both wake Colin up and we're up on our beds, leaning out of the window, craning our necks trying to see the big man on our roof.

'Santa!' We're shouting out of our window, hoping he'll stop at our house after all. The street is asleep, save for the occasional light on where a mum or dad is putting the last few ribbons on a Meccano set or a Barbie doll.

Obviously disturbed by all our commotion, my dad, sleepy and rubbing his eyes, walks into the bedroom.

'What's that bloody noise, lads?'

In unison we answer, 'It's Santa, Dad, he's here!'

'You what?' He pushes by us, stretches out the window, looks up to the roof and shouts, 'Oh aye, I can see him from here.'

Me and my brothers nearly pass out with excitement and try to scramble past him to get a view, but we can't stretch out as far as him. But who cares – our dad can see Santa! Then with his trademark timing he leans further out of his window and shouts, 'Oi, I don't care who you are – get those bloody reindeer off my roof, you fat bastard.'

He must have been planning this all day. Right down to the sleigh bells. We all fall back onto the bed, me and Stephen shell-shocked but laughing our heads off. Colin's confused – he's younger than us and doesn't understand. He turns to me and asks, 'What just happened?'

I look at him, stop laughing for a few seconds and say, 'I think Dad just bollocked Santa.'

THAT MORNING, the year we postponed Christmas, we still excitedly ran downstairs in the vain hope that it was all a big ruse and that really there would be loads of presents. But there weren't.

Where our piles of catalogue-bought presents usually sat, there was one small wrapped present each. Colin opened his and it was a small Transformer toy, which he immediately cracked open and started playing with. Stephen opened his and it was a cookbook my mum had made him herself. He loved cooking and his eyes lit up as he hugged Mum to say thank you.

I picked mine up; it was the smallest of the three, and with hardly any weight to it. I couldn't help feeling a little down but I knew it wasn't right to sulk about it, especially after my brothers had acted so well in the face of disappointment. I unwrapped it, slowly. It was a C90 cassette tape. I looked on the front and it had a list of names: Billy Connolly, Les Dawson, Dave Allen, Ben Elton, Lenny Bruce, Victoria Wood, Alexei Sayle, Tommy Cooper, Bill Cosby, Eddie Murphy.

I looked at Dad and he smiled. I opened it up and inside was a small note.

'To Jason, sorry I didn't have much to give you this year but I hope this brings you plenty of laughs. Love always, Father Christmas (and Dad) xxx'

Chapter 2

Meet the Manfords

ON PAPER my mum and dad shouldn't really work, let alone have five kids and still be happily married after thirty years.

My mum Sharon is second-generation Irish (a 'plastic paddy' according to Dad) and she's the fourth youngest of eleven brothers and sisters; a Roman Catholic who loves country and western music and going to the bingo and within minutes of meeting someone knows their life story.

My dad, on the other hand, is English (a 'tan bastard' according to my mum's brothers), the eldest of two, a card-carrying atheist who loves the Sex Pistols and the Ramones. He hates any kind of gambling and has to have known someone a couple of years before he'd even say 'all right' to them. Although he's called Ian, the only person who calls him that is his mum. Everyone else, including my mum, calls him Manny.

I'll tell you how they met in a moment but to really put you in the picture about them *and*, well, me I suppose, I'd better introduce you to their parents and their parents beyond that. The thing is, we have certain traditions on both sides of the family. You'll see. Think of this next bit as our own short episode of *Who Do You Think You Are?*

Let's start with the 'daddy' of them all, my dad's granddad, my great-granddad. Charles Manford – soldier, tram driver, City fan and all round headcase.

Charles was a sergeant in the Royal Signals before and during the First World War. He witnessed all the true horrors of that conflict and after it was all over he left the army very much disillusioned, not so much with the army itself but with those who ran it, the politicians and generals. It was understandable, really; he'd lost three brothers in that conflict as had his wife, Great-Nana Martha.

Back in civilian life, he worked tirelessly as a tram driver to support Martha and their ever-growing family of five, including Charles, the second youngest, who later found fame as my granddad. Although my dad and his cousins only remember him as a loving and supportive granddad, Great-Granddad Charles was, by most accounts, at heart a hard-drinking, street-fighting ne'er-do-well. In fact, my dad tells me his granddad actually invented football hooliganism (that might be an exaggeration on his part) and legendarily fought a bare-knuckle fight with a bloke named Owen Regan, who at the time was the acknowledged 'cock' of Rusholme. It wasn't especially about football – just two grown men kicking several shades of 1920s shit out of each other. It was just lucky (or unlucky I suppose) that it took place behind the Kippax outside the home of Manchester City, Maine Road. On derby day. Oh, and that Regan was a Manchester United fan while Great-Granddad supported City.

Indeed, his fists could seemingly be put to almost any use. Another proud family story that's been told for years was the time a PE teacher was so annoyed by my granddad's constant chewing of his fingernails he decided to teach him a lesson. He grabbed his hands and painted every single fingernail red (nobody seems to know why a male PE teacher in 1924 had red nail polish handy). Well, that's embarrassing now, but this was working-class Manchester in the 1920s so it's hard to imagine the amount of ridicule the poor lad went through that day.

When Charles heard what had happened, he went down to the school and knocked the PE teacher out cold in the playground. Ah, PE teachers: being bastards to kids for nearly a hundred years.

When I started writing this book I went to visit Nana Manford to see what else she could tell me about the good old days. It's always lovely to have a cuppa and watch an episode of *Midsomer Murders* with her but if I'm honest it was looking like a bit of a barren trip – as far as juicy stories from the past were concerned anyway. She talked warmly of the old days but it was mainly little everyday details: tin bath in front of the fire, bread and dripping, you know the kind of stuff. Lovely in its own way but not the kind of high drama I was hoping for Then, just as I was rinsing the mugs in the sink and looking for my car keys, she shouted from the living room, 'I suppose there was that time he got one over on Sir Oswald Mosley.'

I sat back down.

How on earth had she left this at the back of the queue? Finally, the Manfords involved in proper history.

My granddad, who would have been about fourteen at the time, had a part-time job at a greengrocer's in Rusholme. The son of the greengrocer, a lad in his twenties, was a 'blackshirt', a member of Mosley's British Union of Fascists. (Mosley was a man who, if Hitler had won, would have become the führer of Britain.) This lad asked my granddad to go out and post some propaganda leaflets around the local area in return for five Woodbines. Well, the promise of Woodbines to a fourteen-year-old back then would be like if you offered an iPod and some Haribo to a fourteen-year-old now. My granddad had no idea about fascism and figuratively snapped the lad's hand off.

Before he started his delivery of the leaflets, he decided to pop home and grab some late breakfast. His dad was at the table, smoking and finishing his breakfast, when he spotted the leaflets.

'What the bloody hell are these doing here?' he bellowed.

My granddad explained the situation to his outraged father, who had begun throwing them on the fire. Until, that is, he had another, better idea.

'Don't worry, son, I'll deliver them for you,' he fumed.

According to the leaflet, that afternoon Mosley himself was holding a rally in Platt Fields Park, where he would show his support to the German Nazi Party in front of thousands of supporters. It was only a five-minute walk from the family home on Hancock Street.

As he arrived at Platt Fields, Charles saw Mosley on a raised platform in the middle of thousands of black-shirted supporters. Surrounding them were hundreds of policemen and surrounding them were numerous anti-fascist groups, communists, socialists, trade unionists and Manchester Jews.

Charles, dressed in a dark shirt, made his way into the rally, through the throng of protesters, past the police line and finally amid the devotees. As Oswald Mosley made his way to his armour-plated car, my granddad approached him quietly.

'Excuse me, Mr Mosley, sir, could you sign this for my boy?'

As he handed him one of his leaflets and a pen, Oswald Mosley looked up. 'Of course. Who's it to?'

'Charlie Manford, you racist bastard,' he replied and punched him hard in the face.

Of course he was seized upon and beaten up by Mosley blackshirts before the police intervened, but he made it home alive, bruised yet proud.

Like I said, a law unto himself.

Charles's wife, Martha, on the other hand, was by all accounts a kind and gentle angel. As well as bringing up five kids and looking after her volatile husband, she was a sort of district nurse-cum-midwife for the whole street. Oh, she wasn't trained or qualified, of course (in fact she was a cleaner in the local pub), but this was in the depression and long before the NHS, so most women gave birth at home and when anyone local went into labour they would send for 'Auntie' Martha. She may have been a kindly soul but she didn't suffer my great-granddad gladly; on more than one occasion old Charles Manford heard the door of the pub open and saw his tea flying towards him after he'd stopped off for a 'quick' pint on his way home on payday.

My granddad, Charlie, you'll be pleased to hear, took after his mum. He was a gentleman in every sense of the word. He always dressed well and had immaculate Brylcreemed hair. He would comment on anyone who didn't look after their clothes or appearance (I've no idea what he'd say about some of the shirts I wear these days). It was a pride which probably came from his childhood in the depression; the family were poor but they were honest, to paraphrase the old song.

He once told me that for church on a Sunday the family would go to the local pawn shop on a Friday evening and get the smartest clothes they had on offer. But on Monday morning, he and his sister would have to take them back. He was so embarrassed by this he used to make his way to the pawn shop via the back entries and ginnels of Rusholme, although he later realised most of his mates' families were doing the same.

He was moderate in most things; he liked to socialise but no one ever remembers him being drunk, he never swore except for the occasional 'bloody' in extreme circumstances, he was in the trade union and a member of the Labour Party but never a radical. It must have amused him to see how much my dad, his son, was like his dad.

Where my granddad wasn't moderate was in his love for his family: he was passionate and would do anything for his wife, kids and eventually grandkids. Me and Stephen would take turns to stay with Nana and Granddad on alternate weekends. On Sundays we would spend the afternoon listening to cassettes he had made for my nana: Mario Lanza, Nat King Cole, Frank Sinatra and Glenn Miller. They were happy times. In fact, I'm more influenced by my granddad's music than my parents', and because I prefer 'Unforgettable' to 'Anarchy In The UK', my dad finds it amusing how much I, his son, am like his dad.

My other paternal great-grandfather has the most northern name you've ever heard: Alf Cocker. He and my great-nana, Kate, spent their married life in Withington, Manchester, but were originally from Irlams o' th' Height (so that's the most northern-named man living in the most northern-named town). They raised three kids: two sons and their youngest, a daughter, my Nana Leah. Alf Cocker was also utterly unique among my ancestors in that he was a Tory – much to the chagrin of everyone before and since. He spent most of his working life as a policeman and is remembered as a strict, bloody-minded disciplinarian. My two great-grandfathers couldn't have been more different.

His bloody-mindedness can be illustrated by the fact that during the Manchester blitz in 1940 he refused to go to the air-raid shelter when the sirens sounded because 'I'm not bloody well running away from any bloody Jerrys' and he had to be wrestled into the shelter by my great-uncles. That was the first night of the bombings. By the second night, although retired, he volunteered as a fire watcher and was on duty on top of Lewis's in the city centre, armed with a stirrup pump.

His daughter, my Nana Manford, is, thank God, the complete opposite. She's eighty-eight now and my last-surviving grandparent. If you could draw a 'nana', it would no doubt be her. As I was growing up my friends would say, 'I wish she was my nana, mine's a right moody bitch. This one gives you cakes and dandelion and burdock.'

She's probably my biggest fan. I've been making her laugh since I was about two years old and she still comes to my gigs when I'm in Manchester. To be fair she makes me laugh too, although not always on purpose. She just has that wonderful innocence about her. One year she got me a copy of Richard Dawkins's *The God Delusion* and inside wrote, without a hint of irony, 'Happy Xmas, Jason, hope you enjoy the book, God bless.'

A few years ago, to help her out, I arranged for a cleaner to start going to her house a few times a week. I went over on the first day to make sure she was happy with a stranger in her house.

The girl was called Mel and she was from Germany. After half an hour or so of cleaning, this was the conversation I overheard:

'Excuse me, dear, I can't place your accent – where are you from?' Nana enquired.

'I'm from Germany, Mrs Manford.'

'Oh, that's nice.' There was a long pause before my nana added, 'I used to make Lancaster bombers during the war, you know.'

She didn't mean anything by it; she's the friendliest person in the world. She's just startlingly honest sometimes, it's quite refreshing really. I remember I once sat playing with some toy cars under her dining-room table the day a family friend had died. He'd died only a month after his wife had passed away. Although they were very old it was still a shock to lose a couple so quickly. People were romanticising it a little 'Oh it's sweet really,' one relative said, 'he died of a broken heart, he couldn't bear to live without her.'

To which my nana said (bearing in mind this was essentially the guy's wake), 'He couldn't bear to do the washing-up more like!'

I had to stifle my laughter under the tablecloth.

In fact, I went round the other week while a man from the council fixed the drains in her bathroom. I walked in as she was shouting out of the lounge, 'Twelve down, eight letters, Michael J. Fox film about a werewolf.'

A gruff bloke's voice fired down the stairs a moment later: '*Teenwolf*, Mrs Manford.'

Anyway, that's enough about my dad's lot, for now at least.

My mum's side of the family, as I said, are from Ireland. My great-grandfather Thomas Peate was in the post office on O'Connell Street in Dublin during the 1916 Easter uprising. In fact, when I think about it, it's a good job Charley Manford was in France at the time otherwise they could have been shooting at each other; one stray bullet and I wouldn't be writing this book now.

One of Thomas's daughters, Nora, was my Nana Ryan. Nora was very fond of her father but didn't get on well with her mother. Sick of the family feuding, she left Ireland and came to England as a teenager, first to Blackpool where she worked as a chambermaid, and then to Manchester where she trained as a printer. She met my granddad, Dennis Ryan, with whom she had eleven children, my mum being the second youngest daughter of six. How on earth she managed to have eleven kids, I don't know. She must've been permanently pregnant for thirty years. Can't have been easy as a poor immigrant family in post-war Manchester.

My mum grew up in a shared bedroom with my Auntie Fiona and uncles Stephen and Brendan. A large family obviously has its negative side, certainly when it comes to space and parental attention, but a large family also comes with benefits. For one thing, there's always someone to play with. My mum and her brothers and sisters would play rounders, football, table tennis, snakes and ladders, cards, you name it – which sort of accounts for my mum's ridiculously competitive nature. All her family are the same.

You know that thing where parents let their kids win at games because, well, they're kids? Well, Mum didn't know about that. In Monopoly she was as dodgy a banker as you could know; compared to my mum Sir Fred Goodwin was a saint. Even *The Weakest Link* board game turned nasty one Christmas. With Mum in control of the Anne Robinson mask – she made my 83-year-old Nana Manford do the walk of shame to the front door and back as she hummed *The Weakest Link* theme tune.

My nana and granddad divorced when I was young so I didn't see a lot of Granddad Dennis, but I remember him as a good-looking bloke. My dad says he could charm the birds from the trees. He was a talented musician who played the mandolin and had a great singing voice.

Nana Ryan was the matriarch of the family. She was always there to help people out but could be just as quick to give out a severe tongue-lashing when it was needed. Growing up, whenever we were really naughty, the final threat my parents would make was, 'I can't wait to tell your Nana Ryan about this.' At that point we'd start being good. She really could be quite terrifying.

During the 1960s, with money being tight and a large family to support, Nana Ryan formed The Ryan Family Show Band, which consisted of her, my granddad and all her kids on various instruments bought from the Denmark Road market. They performed in Irish pubs and clubs all over the country and were well known on the circuit. They were even approached by Hughie Green and asked to perform on *Opportunity Knocks* but my granddad forbade it as they had a paid booking on the night of their unpaid scheduled TV performance.

As members left the band over the years, by marriage, divorce or to take up solo careers, they were replaced by younger siblings, nephews or nieces. The one constant was my nana, singing classic songs like

'Spinning Wheel' and 'Que Sera, Sera'. She loved to entertain people and she had groupies of old Irish men following her the length and breadth of the country. I think a lot of my confidence on stage is thanks to her. She used to make sure I got up every Sunday in the Little Western pub in Moss Side and had a sing-song with the band. I did that from the age of five and only stopped when the group finally disbanded due to her deteriorating health when I was about fifteen.

The need to perform on the Ryan side of the family continues to this day. My Uncle Dennis is an Evangelical pastor on a Sunday but on a Saturday night he's quite a passable Michael Bublé tribute act. 'We shall now be upstanding to sing hymn number 43 "Haven't met you yet".' My Uncle Brendan is by day a salesman but by night dons a sparkly blue shirt and wig and is a tribute to Neil Diamond, Neil Diamante. My Auntie Kathleen is a great country and western singer who used to take me line-dancing as a kid (and that's the last you'll be hearing of that!). Many of my other aunties, uncles and cousins earn their living playing in the pubs and clubs of the north-west and family parties often feel like our own private episode of *Britain's Got Talent* but without Ant and Dec, oh, and nobody dances with a dog. Everyone has their own party piece, whether it's my cousin Aiden doing his Lady Gaga tribute, 'Aidy GaGa', or friend of the family 'One-Eyed' Tom playing a fifteen-minute drum solo while everyone raids the buffet.

In all, Nana had forty grandchildren and twelve great-grandchildren, yet she was always ready with a present for birthdays or Christmas. Her secret was simple: she became addicted to *Bid Up TV*. Often my nana won the auctions as there was only her watching the thing. The smallest bedroom in her Longsight terrace, which she shared with her 'boyfriend' Patsy (how many seventy-odd-year-olds have a boyfriend?), was an Aladdin's cave of TV-auction-based crap, every gift you could imagine from toasters to neck chains. One year I got given Jordan's autobiography.

'I thought you might like it because she's on the telly as well.' Thank God that was the only reason.

She had a great sense of humour and wasn't afraid to say what she thought of anyone, even in the unlikeliest of scenarios. I remember we were at my Uncle Michael's funeral, a really sad day especially for her, his mother. My uncle's coffin was in a shiny black cart being pulled by one of those huge black shire horses. It was quite a spectacular sight as this imposing beast trotted slowly through the streets of Hulme, in south Manchester. My nana looked up to see a few of the extended family taking photos of the animal and its load.

'Look at these eejits. When are they ever going to get these photos out again?'

She had a point. I don't think I've ever been round at anyone's house and they've gone, 'Ooh, wait there, I'll just get the photos of our John's funeral – it was a terrible day.'

Towards the end of her life, when she was really ill, we moved her bed to the living room. The family visited her constantly and there would always be four of five of us around her bedside, looking on anxiously, our hearts breaking, seeing this once strong, proud woman helpless and slowly slipping from life.

One evening, as I stood watching her in her bed, surrounded by aunties and uncles, her eyes closed for the final time. Her lips mumbled something none of us could make out and everyone feared the very worst. No one could bring themselves to lean in and listen to what she was saying apart from me.

I thought about what a momentous moment this must be for anyone, your last words on this world. She had lived such an eventful life, so much wisdom and knowledge gathered up in that mind, so much creativity in her body. She'd touched thousands of people's hearts, borne eleven children and those forty grandchildren. She'd had terrible, terrible times in her life, worse times than anyone could ever imagine, and here she was on her death bed about to leave the stage for the last time.

I leant in close and kissed her goodbye; a small kiss on her forehead. As I moved my head to hear what she was saying I heard her faint Irish voice.

'Don't let those fecking eejits take pictures of my funeral.'

MUM AND DAD met when Dad was working as a barman at The Bridge pub in Salford. My mum used to babysit the landlord's kids and my dad was a friend of the family, as The Ryan Family Show Band played there regularly.

The night they met, Dad had been left in charge of the bar as it was the landlord's night off and like any good babysitter, my mum got the kids settled and went down to the pub for a drink. She was sixteen and my dad was twenty-five – although she looked older (so my dad says) and she didn't tell him her age.

Although they were very different, they had one thing in common: they loved each other from the moment they met. Their courtship was fast and passionate and, though I don't like to think about it, with nowhere to go, they made love all over Manchester. Even now I can be driving along with mum and she'll say, 'Hey, see that park? Well, one night me and your dad...'

'Mum, please don't... Urgh, no, not on the slide.'

I recently asked my dad how he proposed to my mum. I presumed it'd be something amazingly romantic: Blackpool at sunset or on one knee in her favourite restaurant.

'It was midnight on Salford fish market behind the Flat Iron pub,' he announced, every inch the Manc Don Juan.

As they walked through the market, my dad had the ring burning a hole in his pocket and couldn't wait any longer.

'Sharon, I've got something to tell you,' he blurted.

'Well, I've got something to tell you too,' she replied solemnly.

My dad panicked. Oh shit, he thought, I knew she was out of my league. What young woman wants to settle down and get married after only a few months of dating?' He could feel himself filling up.

'You first,' she said.

Well, what did he have to lose now? She was going to leave him anyway so he may as well finalise his embarrassment. He dropped to one knee. 'Sharon, I love you, will you marry me?'

There was a pause that lasted what seemed like forever, as the smell of the day's fish wafted by. She looked down at him, with tears in her eyes and said, 'I love you too... and I'm pregnant.'

I asked him recently what he would do if my sister Danielle came home one day at the age of sixteen and said, 'This twenty-five-year-old barman has got me pregnant and I'm going to marry him.'

And even though it stank of hypocrisy he replied, 'I'd chop his dirty little bollocks off.'

SO THAT WAS the start of me.

Everything was going swimmingly with the pregnancy until a routine doctor's appointment just over a month before I was due. The doctor couldn't find my heartbeat so my mum was rushed into Hope Hospital.

I was six weeks premature but still weighed in at 7lb 14oz. I know what you're thinking. Thank God I didn't go to term. I was also a breech birth – as in I came out backwards. Make your own joke there if you like.

My parents sat there that night, the only people in an otherwise empty ward, a young couple who'd only been with each other just a little over nine months. Here they were with a child. Most couples in this situation don't fare well; the odds are not in their favour. But hey presto, they're still together now. I'm incredibly proud of my mum. OK, she does say daft things and she does occasionally embarrass me, like the time a schoolteacher asked if she'd be up for playing in the annual parent-teacher rounders match and she replied, 'I'd love to but my tits are too big for all that running,' or a few years ago on her first flight when she tried to get all the passengers to do a whip-round for the pilot like we used to do on a coach. But she's done all right for herself. I mean, after years of playground bullying she left school at sixteen with nothing, and a year later she was pregnant and living at her parents, with an older barman as a boyfriend. It's not the starting scene of a happy ending, is it? She looked after us, collecting whatever benefits she could, while Dad held down two and sometimes three jobs to make the other ends meet. Then one day, she got the urge for more. She went back to college and got the qualifications she needed to start training to become a nurse. Three years later, Dad became a full-time house husband and Mum left for work in her spanking new uniform. You couldn't wipe the smile from her face.

But back to the night I was born. As my dad held me to his chest, and my mum slept after a long, tiring and painful day, someone walked through the corridors and started to sing.

'Born free, as free as the wind blows

As free as the grass grows

Born free, to follow your heart.'

My dad looked over at my mum and smiled. She smiled back. What a lovely moment for this new family: me asleep on my new dad, Mum quietly resting, and then this angelic voice rises from nowhere singing words which summed up how my parents were feeling at that precise moment. To them, all was right with the universe.

Turns out, from talking to one of the ward sisters in the morning, that it was some nutter who'd escaped from the psychiatric ward.

MY NANA RYAN decided she should have some input in the naming of me.

Now, recently, when we came to naming my own three daughters, I came to realise that Dad doesn't get a great deal of say in the matter. His main job is to buy three or four different baby name books for his wife to read through (which is ridiculous – I've never found a name in one book that wasn't in another: 'Hey, love, there's no Keith in this one'). Oh, he can mention names he's fond of and tell his wife which names he really doesn't like but at the end of the day, your last real involvement in all this was nine months ago (aside from the occasional foot-rub and midnight mercy errand to Tesco to buy some Jaffa Cakes and Philadelphia spread). Actually, there is a little trick you can do to push the decision in your favour. For example, any name you really don't like, just say:

'Sally? Hmmm, I think I had an ex-girlfriend called Sally.'

This immediately makes every Sally a slag. Your daughter will not be named after one of your exes.

But still, even knowing all this, surely my dad was going to have more of a say in the naming of his first son than my nana.

She had decided that my name should be 'Jonjo' after the champion jockey Jonjo O'Neill who'd won her some money at Cheltenham a few months earlier. My parents wanted Jason but my nana wanted Jonjo. What were they to do? Well, exactly what they did do: they called me Jason. They gave me the middle name of John which sort of appeased Nana. I suppose I should count myself lucky really: her favourite horse was called Sea Pigeon. I don't think Jason Sea Pigeon Manford would have made it out of school alive.

When the three of us were discharged from hospital, we went back to live in one room of my Nana Ryan's house in Irlams o' th' Height in Salford. Irlams o' th' Height. The fact that the letters are missing and replaced with apostrophes means that no matter where you are in the country now, or wherever you're from in the world, if you try and say it you will immediately sound like you're sat in a bath of coal, drinking bitter, wearing a flat cap and stroking a whippet. Sadly those missing letters were the most interesting thing about Irlams o' th' Height or 'The Heights' as my family referred to it. In fact even Wikipedia only has this to say: 'One of the main features of Irlams o' th' Height is the A6 dual carriageway running through it.'

It was no place to bring up a baby and the only incidents of any note that occurred there don't, I'm afraid, reflect well on my parents. To be fair to them, they were learning on the job, but everything my mum has told me brings me to the conclusion that Social Services should have opened a file.

Apparently, as a carefree one-year-old my favourite hobby was that old classic – bouncing. Bouncing on the bed, the couch, anywhere really. If it had springs, it had me. One afternoon I was bouncing on a bed near an open window (yeah, I think you can roughly see where this is going, like at the start of an episode of *Casualty*). Anyway, as I was bouncing, getting higher and higher, my mum turned to see me laughing at my own bouncing ability and then watched me bounce straight out of the window. Luckily we were on the ground floor so I didn't break anything – just ended up with a huge egg-shaped lump on my little head.

Then there was another time I took a nap on my nana's bed (probably tired out following a session of intense bouncing). After a couple of hours my mum came to wake me and spotted an empty pill bottle next to me. She immediately grabbed me and took me to the hospital, where they rushed me in and pumped my stomach. You hear about stomachs getting pumped but it's a horrible thing. They basically put a tube down your throat, pour in a liquid that your stomach will immediately reject, then pull the tube out quickly as everyone in the room stands back. I looked like someone had put a Mento mint in a bottle of Coke. Not a way anyone wants to be woken up.

Turns out my stomach was empty as I'd not eaten any pills at all. It was just an empty pill bottle which had been left next to a sleeping child by a still unnamed 'responsible' adult.

So I've bounced out of a window and had my stomach pumped and I'm not even two yet. The last incident, which I do sort of remember, was just after my second birthday. We'd just moved into our new house on Nettleford Road and obviously hadn't got our basic drills sorted. One night someone forgot to lock the front door so the next morning, a young me, still high on birthday cake and orange squash, managed to waddle downstairs, open the door and head off in search of adventure.

Off I went up the road, past neighbours' houses, past people walking dogs, past joggers, yet no one thought to stop a two-year-old child dressed only in a terry-towelling nappy! I managed to make it as far as the main road where luckily a police car was driving past. They pulled up, got out, scratched their heads and bundled me into the squad car.

When we arrived at the police station, I helped myself to a lovely big breakfast.

Meanwhile a house-to-house search was conducted. Finally they knocked on number 28 where a tired-looking father of one answered. The policewoman asked if he'd lost a two-year-old boy, to which my dad obviously said, 'Er, we've got one, but I think he's in bed. Oh, hang on a minute, I'll check.' I wasn't there. I was eating a mashed-up Full English.

Obviously I've picked three stories that don't show my mum and dad in a great light when they were in fact brilliant parents. For that one time they left the door unlocked I can think of hundreds where they actually locked it.

When you're the first kid out, you're basically the test subject, the prototype for all succeeding children. I take it as a compliment that I didn't put my parents off having a few more. It really is a case of you all learning together. I was learning to walk and talk and bounce while my parents were learning to lock a door from time to time or close a window.

There were actually two other short stop-offs after leaving Nana Ryan's and finally landing on Nettleford Road. Our first home as a family unit when we'd outstayed our welcome at Nana's was a council flat on St Stephen's Street in Salford. Just me, Mum and Dad and a load of second-hand furniture which had largely been donated to us by members of the family. It was always freezing cold as we couldn't afford to put the central heating on, living on just my dad's £66 per week wages. If anyone wanted a bath we'd put the immersion heater on for a couple of hours and all three of us would get in together. Poor but clean.

Dad was working in the sterile supply unit at Withington Hospital and so we endeavoured to find a house closer to his place of work, which brought us to our second solo home – a flat above a hardware store on Princess Road in Withington. The only access to it, other than through the shop, was a rickety old iron fire escape that went up two floors and was, as my dad said, 'a right pain in the arse'. He had to carry me, my buggy and the shopping every time we went home. Not ideal.

So finally we moved to our little house on Nettleford Road – a Housing Association mid-terrace in Whalley Range with three bedrooms, separate toilet and bathroom, a living room, a small kitchen/dining room and garden. We were in-between Chorlton (quite posh) and Moss Side (not that posh). At the top of the road was a spooky-looking convent and the bottom of the road was made a dead-end by a disused railway. A disused railway and an old convent, basically, I lived on the set of a Scooby-Doo cartoon. But to us it was a dream home and, boy, did we need all that new-found space because, unbeknown to me, my mum was already pregnant with my brother. Stephen came bounding out of her on 29 October 1983 at a whopping 12lb 14oz. Thank God she was a smoker or we'd have had to grease the door frames to get him in the house. Another brother Colin was born in April 1985 and that was us done for a good while. A family of five in a three-bedroom terraced house, my mum, now aged twenty-one, with three kids under four and my dad working two jobs to keep us in Chewits and Curly Wurlys.

Chapter 3
Manford and Sons

MEET, FALL IN LOVE, get engaged, marry, get pregnant, have baby. That's the generally accepted, logical way to do things. Well, not my folks. With them it was meet, fall in love, get pregnant, give birth, get pregnant again, get married, give birth, give birth, give birth, give birth.

Both sets of parents thought it would be good if my mum and dad got married. My mum's dad, Dennis, actually thought that because my dad went by his nickname 'Manny' he was from a Jewish family and therefore, in his brain anyway, his daughter must be marrying into money (for any Jewish readers, I'm sorry for my granddad's stereotyping of a whole race but he was Irish, and you know what that lot are like).

My parents weren't that bothered about getting married but they had been living together for two years with me and now had another one on the way, so they came to the smart conclusion that a wedding equalled stuff for the house, like kettles and pans. It was a marriage of convenience: kitchen convenience.

My mum probably needed less convincing. Mum has always loved a party. My dad on the other hand hates being made the centre of attention, and at any party will find a corner to sit in or will stand outside smoking all night with my uncles. So a wedding, especially his own, was his worst nightmare.

I'd like to say it was magical fairytale wedding like William and Kate's, but it wasn't; it was essentially a mixture of practicalities, superstition and a pub crawl.

The night before the wedding Mum went to stay at her parents' house in Salford. I stayed with Dad and my Uncle Brendan, who was about twelve at the time. His job was to look after me so Dad could get himself ready on time but he also had other responsibilities.

'Right, Bren, we're up early tomorrow so I'm relying on you to get us all up.'

'No problem, Manny, I'll take the alarm clock to bed with me.'

That night Brendan slept in my bed, and I was in with Dad. We slept right through and didn't hear the alarm go off at 7am. What we did hear was an almighty scream from Brendan two rooms away. The alarm clock we had back then was one of those old-fashioned wind-up ones with the metal winder on the back; when the alarm went off the winder would turn anti-clockwise till the tiny hammer stopped ricocheting off the two silver bells. Brendan, in his infinite wisdom, had put the clock on his pillow so as to hear it better, inches away from his long curly black hair. At exactly 7am the alarm went off and the winder curled round his hair until it was so tight he had woken up screaming. He came running into our room with a huge blue alarm clock hanging from his head, still banging out its wake-up noise at full pelt.

'Fuuuuuuuck!' Over and over again like the opening scene of *Four Weddings and a Funeral.* 'It's stuck in my bastard hair, Manny!' Brendan cried as my dad jumped out of bed.

So my dad's first job on the day of his own wedding was cutting an alarm clock out of a knobhead's hair.

Dad's best man, Stuart, came to pick us up in a lovely brand-new dark blue Mercedes.

'Do you like it?' he said proudly. 'Got it last night.'

'Yeah,' said Dad doubtfully, 'but is it legal?'

'Course it is.' He winked. 'Well, virtually.'

You never knew with Stuart; he was a great character but he operated in his own world to his own rules.

We drove to the Jackson's Row Register Office in the city centre in what was quite possibly a stolen car, and arrived at about ten to nine. Mum wasn't due till half past so me, my dad, both granddads and a load of uncles went and sat in the Nag's Head and had a pint of Boddies while we waited. Obviously I didn't have a pint of Boddies, I was only two. I had a half and some smoky bacon crisps.

Mum arrived, only slightly late, in my Uncle Mick's beige BMW (not one of their biggest sellers). She looked brilliant in her bright maroon maternity dress, now seven months pregnant with the giant lump that was Stephen.

The brief civil ceremony was over by 10am. The sensible half of the wedding party (the women) went back to my nana and granddad's for some tea and sandwiches. The other half (the men) went back to the Nag's Head for the rest of the day. So the day was essentially a pub crawl with a wedding sandwiched in the middle. I'm sure it was lovely, but anytime I see my parents' wedding pictures I can just taste smoky bacon crisps in my mouth.

MY DAD WAS a shop steward for many years, your average angry working-class hero of the time. There was lots to be angry about. He was anti-Thatcher and anti-monarchy and for most of the mid-eighties could be found somewhere on a picket line protesting. He wasn't a miner but he stood with them; he wasn't a nurse but he stood with them as well. After reading a copy of Marx's *Communist Manifesto* someone had left on the bus, he joined the Young Communist League (I suppose it's lucky he didn't find a copy of *Mein Kampf*).I came to the conclusion he just liked making signs and shouting rude things at the police. Don't get me wrong, as hobbies go it was great fun. I used to go with him on the odd march. I remember an anti-racism one we did through Manchester where I felt like my legs were going to break off. We walked the five miles into the city centre, it was freezing, my nose was running and I didn't even know what racism was.

When the leader of the group shouted through his megaphone 'What do we want?' thousands of people answered at the same time with the same answer, apart from my lone young voice shouting, 'Some chips, please.'

On the marches we would see the same familiar faces and hear the same voices. There was one old fella who took a shine to my dad – we called him Red Tom. He was an old-school communist and called everyone 'comrade'. As most of the communists he knew were too old to march, he'd spotted my dad's hammer and sickle lapel badge and latched onto him. Once we got chatting it turned out he was actually a cleaner at my school. He had the best voice I'd ever heard. It reminded me of Sean Connery; very deep and very Scottish. Every other word rolled off his tongue and he had a turn of phrase like pure velvet.

'They that lie down for love should rise for hunger,' he said one afternoon to a fellow marcher.

The other man nodded in agreement. 'Aye, aye.'

I had no idea what it meant but it sounded great. It sounded important and heroic.

The older I got the less interest I had in my dad on his marches. Every kid eventually rebels against his parents, but what do you do when your dad is a rebel? My dad was the one wearing ripped jeans and shouting at coppers, he listened to punk and smoked marijuana. The fact I call it marijuana tells you just how straight-laced I was. The only way I could rebel against him was to be good – it's the ultimate parent trap. I was the only eleven-year-old in the world happy to wear chinos and listen to Burt Bacharach.

During the marches we used to shout and chant at the police and at council officials and anyone vaguely in authority. That's just what you did. I remember quite clearly the few times we saw the Lord Mayor of Manchester's car driving around the city centre, every man, woman and child screaming abuse and giving him the 'Vs'. I was never sure what the fella had done wrong, other than drive round in a shiny Oxford blue Rolls-Royce Silver Shadow; the little flags waving furiously in the wind were nothing compared to the fury of the crowd. It was the first time I'd ever been part of a mob. And I liked it.

I was on my dad's shoulders, flicking the Vs at the poshest car I'd ever seen, the reflection of the angry crowd sparkling off the front grille as it roared past us with the growl of a thousand lions. It was very exciting. I think I saw the Lord Mayor's car three other times, and on all occasions, in unison with my dad, we happily flicked our fingers at this pompous fat man in his car smoking cigars. Well, I say that, I never actually saw him, that was just my image. Turns out it wasn't even always him: there were two female Lord Mayors of Manchester when I was a kid, so chances are I swore at an old lady. I feel a bit bad now but my dad's still not bothered.

I don't feel as bad as the time I was walking to school with my mum and her friend when the Lord Mayor's fancy pants car drove past. I immediately took both hands, folded down the inactive fingers and gave him my best two-fingered salute. My mum and her friend froze in horror as not only one Lord Mayor's car drove past, but three of them, all full of crying people and, in one, a coffin. I was confused. But the quick slap of a woman's hand on the back of my head quickly made me realise what I'd done. I stood there with a bemused look on my face, my fingers still swearing at the funeral procession, as twenty or so crying, blubbering faces looked back at me, just as confused. It was an odd moment. Man, was my dad in trouble that night.

SWEARING. It's not big and it's not clever, but let's be honest, it can be well funny. As a young lad growing up, swearing was both forbidden and yet familiar. Most of the adults I knew swore like wounded pirates, but of course us kids were never allowed. But where do we get the swear words from? Our fucking parents, that's where.

When we moved in to Nettleford Road, we were starting with a blank canvas. Most of our furniture was still the stuff donated by other family members, plus bits and bobs rifled out of charity shops or nicked from a skip. Mum had managed to get a credit account with a now defunct furniture store in Stretford and had splashed out on fitted carpets and a brand-new wall unit – flat pack, of course, every man's favourite! My dad, by his own admission, is not terribly good at DIY, but he was even worse at asking for another man's help. So I spent the morning idly playing with my toys and watching Dad struggling manfully to erect this wall unit. It had big brown smoked glass doors and faux mahogany wood that wouldn't look out of place panelled on the walls of a working men's club. After a couple of hours of semi-muted swearing and muttered curses, the unit was near completion. It just needed the top half to be put on the bottom half and it would be ready (ready for what, I'll never know, we only ever put glasses we never used in there). The manoeuvring of it was clearly a two-man job but Dad, so near the finish line, decided he could manage it by himself. As he lowered the top half into position, carefully dropping it onto the bottom, he trapped his fingers.

'Arghh, you twat!' he screamed, hopping around, shaking his damaged hand.

Minutes later, there was a knock at the door which my mum answered. My dad was still running the cold water over his gnarled fingers.

'Good morning, Sharon, and how are you?' asked Father Austin, beaming, his voice friendly and reassuring in equal measures.

Our house was owned by a Catholic Housing Association – St Vincent's. 'The Patron Saint of Knobheads' as my dad used to call them when they collected the rent. When we first moved in we used to get regular visits from Father Austin, the parish priest. He was a kindly old fella who always had wet eyes, as if he was just so happy with the world that he was always on the verge of tears of joy. He was like the whole road's granddad.

'Fine, thank you, Father, come in,' said Mum in her posh voice (that would later become her phone voice when we got one). 'Would you like a cup of tea?' She ushered him into our newly decorated living room.

'Lovely, two sugars, please. You've certainly got the house looking nice,' said Father Austin, looking around at our new wall unit.

'Manny's just put that up,' said Mum proudly.

'Did you, Manny? Well done.'

No answer came from the kitchen. Just the sound of running water.

'And did you help your daddy, Jason?' he asked me, gesturing at the wall unit.

I nodded, beaming and pointing. 'It's our new twat.'

For my parents, time must have frozen for a couple of seconds. The liquid withdrew from Father Austin's eyes and his smile seemed stuck to his face. The blood drained from Mum's.

'JASON!' She snatched me off my feet and carried me up the stairs and into my room. I was told in no uncertain terms to stay put and think about what I just said, as she went back down to apologise to the priest.

I stayed in my room a short while, had a quick think about what I'd done (I wasn't entirely sure) and went to explore the other rooms upstairs.

I was soon bouncing on beds (God, I loved bouncing on beds, me), trying on huge shoes and drawing on the mirror with some lipstick I'd just found. Then I struck gold. I was rooting through my mum's bedside table when I found a robot. I couldn't believe my luck! What the hell was my mum doing with a toy all of her own? It had a switch and it made the funniest noise, and twirled and moved like a Transformer. I started playing with it, making aeroplane noises as it flew all around the room. It sounded just like the huge jets that flew over our roof occasionally on the way to Ringway airport.

'Buuuuuzzzzzzzzz' went the metallic robot. I flew it out of my parents' bedroom and down the stairs. I was thinking, if anything will cheer up the grown-ups, it's this bad boy.

'Look, Father Austin, look at my mum's robot!' I flew it close and dropped it in his lap where it buzzed and whirred.

It wasn't a robot. It wasn't a toy. Well, it was, but you wouldn't find it at Toys R Us. The blood had come back to Mum's face. If anything, too much blood had come back to her face, and we never saw Father Austin again.

LIKE A LOT of kids, football became a big part of my life. And like most, my chosen team was passed down from my dad – the sins of our fathers and all that. Maybe because Dad is an atheist, City filled the spiritual void he had, and like a religious fanatic he managed to brainwash me into becoming a disciple.

As a really young kid you don't quite understand the importance that football holds over the adult male. As my dad always said, 'Your mum has the church, I have City, she has Jesus, I have Colin Bell.' To be honest, I'm not sure he was right. I think it was more like 'I have City, your mum has *Corrie*.' I mean, what is football if not a big male soap opera full of heroes, villains and last-minute heart-racing script changes?

I soon loved football but to my dad City fans were like God's chosen people, the Jews. And like the Jews we had to spend our time in the wilderness before rising in triumph over our enemies; I suppose in a way, our strict upbringing in the Blue faith made us Hasidic blues.

My dad's granddad first took him to see City, then later his dad, then when he was old enough it was home and away with his mates. In fact he quite often bores us with the unprovable claim that he didn't miss a single home match between 1966 and 1981. The end of this dedicated run strangely coincided with my birth, when I suppose match-day ticket money was diverted into terry-towelling nappies and rusks.

During much of the 1970s, Dad was technically a football hooligan, carrying on Charles's legacy, if you can count getting beaten up at every major ground in the country as football hooliganism. He was a rubbish hooligan. He basically enjoyed the adrenaline rush of being part of a huge chanting football mob and then being chased, safe in the knowledge that because he was so fast he'd never actually have to fight. But even now when we head down to Craven Cottage or Molineux, he'll suddenly nudge us and say something like, 'You see that tree over there? Some home fans hung me by my scarf once and whipped me bollocks with a stick. Ah, happy days.'

I think that's why Dad enjoyed political demonstrations so much. He liked being part of a crowd of working-class men united in a single cause in voice and mind.

It's funny that my dad was so involved in these huge social issues because these days he barely lifts his head to protest about my youngest brother Niall playing football in the house or the dog drinking water from the toilet. I suppose with age comes a sort of resigned 'ah well, nowt I can do' attitude. My dad just doesn't get involved in any sort of family disputes with relatives, whereas Mum is the fixer and peace-maker at the centre of many a family storm. Even more so since Kofi An-Nana Ryan passed away. Mum will get people back together, help parents see their children, ring in sick for you, you name it. She will bend over backwards to help you reach a solution – like Salford's answer to Oprah Winfrey.

Actually, my dad got involved in a family dispute quite recently.

One of my uncles had split up with his girlfriend and they had two boys, both brought up as City fans but only four and five, so still easily swayable. One afternoon my uncle popped round to my mum and dad's when we were all round there, and he was clearly upset. He sat at the kitchen table and Dad put the kettle on and shouted Mum from upstairs, making his exit so Mum could sort my uncle's problems out.

Dad must have walked past the door a few minutes later because the next moment he was in the kitchen, sitting down.

'What did you just say had happened?' my dad asked in an unprece-dented enquiry.

My uncle retold the story of his girlfriend's new boyfriend, a United fan no less, buying the two boys United shirts and having them wear them when my uncle came round to pick them up. A huge argument followed and he ended up not getting his lads for the weekend and suffering the upset of the kids telling him that they were going to support United from now on like their 'stepdad'.

Well, my dad's face was almost as red as the team he hated. 'She did what?' he fumed, and then he said something no man has ever said to his wife. 'Sweetheart, pass me the phone.'

'Hello, Claire, it's Manny. Yeah, I'm fine, yeah, he's here now, he's in bits. Listen, I'm not bothered about who did what and what someone said to someone else, I just want to talk about those two boys. I know you're angry, but in a few months or years, when this anger has subsided, you're going to want those boys to have a strong and healthy relationship with their dad, and nothing bonds a son and his dad together more than football... No, Claire, it's not just a game, it's more than that. Me and my boys have got a great relationship, but they're married and some of them have kids and jobs and other responsibilities, but you know what, we find time together, and that time is every Saturday afternoon at 3pm watching City... Yeah, I know some games are in the evening but that's bloody Sky TV for you. Listen, that's not the point. What I'm saying is this – don't put your boys in United shirts again. You broke a man's heart today, you nearly ruined a dad's relationship with his two sons and no matter what you think of him, if you think he's the world's biggest knobhead, those boys don't, they think he's the world's best dad, and that's how it should always be.'

He hung up the phone and me and Stephen felt like giving him a standing ovation. His words had resonated with all of us, but more importantly they'd sunk in with Claire. The next time my uncle went round to pick up his lads, they came running out with their arms open wide, both dressed head to toe in sky blue.

HAVE YOU EVER said something to your parents that seemed like the most reasonable, well-thought-out thing in the world, only for them to completely overreact? Course you have. One afternoon we were driving home from my Nana Ryan's; it was the late eighties, not a particularly good decade for City. Piccadilly Radio was on and James H. Reeves was going through the afternoon's football results. Eventually it came out: Some Other Team 3, Manchester City nil. My dad slumped forward, head in his hands.

'Bastards.'

'Never mind,' said Mum.

'Don't,' he said, without looking up from his palms.

Poor Dad, I thought, this seems to happen every week. Then I had an idea.

'Dad,' I said. 'United won again.'

'I bloody know, son.'

'Well, maybe we could support them as well. I mean, both teams are from Manchester.'

Now if you're not that into football that might seem a harmless sentence. But it's the equivalent of a devout Christian's kid deciding that maybe Satan was just misunderstood, or a fundamentalist Muslim cleric's daughter deciding to become a stripper.

Dad spun around to face me, his eyes ablaze, foam appearing in the corner of his mouth.

'Jason, don't you ever, EVER say anything like that again.'

'But, but, Nana Ryan said…'

'Nana Ryan is an old lady, not a football fan, and she is talking absolute bollocks.'

'Manny!' Mum interjected. 'That's my mum.'

'Yeah, I know, but this is bigger than that love. We are City fans. My dad was, so was his dad, we always have been, always will be.'

He turned to me again.

'No matter how shit we are or how shit we become, promise me, son, you'll never say anything as horrible as that again.'

'OK, Dad.'

'Cross your heart and hope to die?'

'He's only six,' hissed Mum.

'I know, love, but it would break my heart if any of my kids ever went to them. They can be gay, unemployed, alcoholics, even Tories and I'd still love them but if they went Red, I wouldn't have them in the bloody house.'

I WAS EIGHT years old, Stephen would have been six, when we went on our first ever visit to our family's traditional place of worship. City versus Brighton and Hove Albion in the old Second Division where we stood together in the Kippax stand. Ah, standing up at the football, those were the days eh? Yeah, those were the days when it was crap. I much prefer sitting down. I was four foot nothing, half the size of everyone else in the ground, and with everyone standing up I couldn't see a bloody thing. Oh, you can hear the football fine – every crunching tackle and kick of the ball reverberates round the ground – and you may even get the occasional glimpse of green turf through the legs of the fella in front, but being crushed by hundreds of legs as everyone moves forward in expectation of a goal while beer and Bovril spills on your head is no one's idea of fun.

The chants would start up:

'We never win at home,

And we never win away,

We lost last week and we lost today,

But we don't give a fuck,

Cos we're all pissed up,

MCFC OK ...'

The power of it was incredible. The whole stand shook; you could feel the noise as it bounced off every wall. You were carried by it. You could feel it through your whole body, never mind your ears. I looked at Stephen and he looked at me.

It was magical; I'd never heard language like it. I felt a frisson every time these words were exclaimed with joy and anger by the massed ranks of City's army of fans. So naughty, so wrong, but to a nine-year-old boy utterly wonderful. Then the unthinkable happened. Dad turned to me and Stephen.

'Look, lads, the match is a place where a working man can come once a week to let off steam. I can't be policing you two so if you want to join in the chants, you can – when in Rome and all that. But, er, don't tell your mam.'

Awkwardly at first, then in full voice, Stephen and I joined in our first chorus of 'The Referee's A Wanker' in full earshot of my dad. Well, it doesn't get better than that. We walked home like real men.

OF COURSE, years later it all backfired.

Occasionally, City would offer local schools free tickets for the lesser games. My brother Stephen managed to get a couple of tickets from our RE teacher, Mr Pendleton, and that evening, he and my dad went along to Maine Road.

My dad, Mr Pendleton, Stephen and another twenty or so parents and kids sat in the family stand to watch the game. It was City versus Birmingham, not a classic game, but one which featured Steve Bruce, an ex-Manchester United captain and now playing out his days for Birmingham. He was already getting a lot of stick from the City fans but when he tackled and fouled Gio Kinkladze, City's only hero in those dark days and mine and my brother's idol, the ground erupted. Among the chorus of boos and cat calls that greeted old Brucey, a high voice sounded out above all others, a shrill Mancunian young voice in a sea of deeper, more experienced men.

'Fuck off, Bruce, you dirty red twat.'

Mr Pendleton and a good section of the family stand turned around to look at my dad. His face pale, he offered a weak, 'Kids, eh?'

We didn't get many free tickets from school after that.

WE COULDN'T ALWAYS afford to go to the game so as we got a little older sometimes me and Stephen would walk to Maine Road on a Saturday afternoon anyway, listening to the match on Dad's tranny radio. Sometimes they wouldn't even have full match commentary, they'd just play songs as normal then, in the middle of Billy Joel banging out 'Uptown Girl', a voiceover would interrupt with a pre-recorded 'It's a goal!' or 'Oh no!', depending on who had scored. Put it this way, we heard a lot more 'Oh no!'s than 'It's a goal!'

We'd arrive halfway through the second half and beg a turnstile attendant to let us in, often bribing him with a melted KitKat or a packet of Quavers. There was one old bloke in particular on the Kippax who would let us duck underneath and watch the last twenty minutes from the back of the stand.

Then after the final whistle we'd wait outside for one of our heroes to come out. All these other kids would have posters and marker pens for the players to sign but we just stood there so we could shout their name at them as they made their way to their cars, all suited and booted.

'Rösler! Rösler! Goater! Goater! Kinkladze!'

I don't know what we'd have done if one of them had turned and said, 'Yeah, what do you want?' We were just happy to be so close to greatness. One year, Mum managed to get three of the previous season's Manchester City shirts from a bloke on the market. They were two quid each and apart from saying 'MFCC' on the badge they were pretty bang on. My dad took us to the shop to get a player's name on the back, and we spent the whole four-mile walk there excitedly discussing who we were going to get.

I was fourteen and we'd just signed the greatest player I'd ever seen, Georgiou Kinkladze. The bloke Steve Bruce had been kicking. The guy was a magician on the ball, dancing his way through defences and scoring the most unbelievable goals. Legend has it that back in Georgia his mum sent him to ballet classes while his dad sent him to a soccer school and that's why he was so nimble on his toes.

We arrived at the City shop and my dad looked at the prices on the wall: 80p per letter, £3 per number.

'OK, lads, what name you going with on your shirt?'

In unison we replied, 'Gio Kinkladze, number ten, Dad.'

I could see him counting up the 80 pences as he went into the shop with our shirts. We sat on a wall outside eating orange Calypso Jubblys and enjoying the sunshine.

Moments later, Dad appeared and handed us our shirts.

'I couldn't afford to get you Kinkladze, number ten, so I got you both Vonk, number five.'

We were gutted, especially when Vonk got sold to Oldham about two weeks later. It took me days to peel his name off my shirt. I mean, who gets a defender on their back anyway?

NOW I KNOW City fans make a big deal about there being only one football club to truly come from Manchester. And that is, of course, a fact. The other fact is that most United fans don't live in Manchester, but the myth we like to spin is that there are no United fans in Manchester at all and that they all live in Surrey and the M6 is clogged every Saturday afternoon with fans travelling home. This is only partly true. Sometimes they play on a Sunday.

To my pain, while growing up there were United fans everywhere you went in Manchester. As a Blue growing up in the eighties and nineties I was made all too aware of this. Every cup and league title the red side of Manchester accumulated was like another hammer blow to my blue heart.

Maybe that's why my dad and uncles would do anything, however petty, to keep the City flag flying high. Nothing would stop a grown man, usually my dad, from popping into Asda, visiting the magazine section and hiding any publications that featured United. Same with videos and DVDs. Songs by artists known to be Reds were switched off as soon as they came on the radio. We weren't even allowed to wear anything red. Anything that had to be in the house that was red was immediately christened crimson or cherry. Certain products and brands were banned too. One year my mum got the whole family a music system for Christmas out of the catalogue. It was the first CD player we'd ever had, with twin cassette decks (oh yeah, that's right, twin, not that crappy single one). It had more lights and switches than the flight deck of the Starship *Enterprise*. The whole family were mightily impressed, including Dad, that was until he saw five silver letters on the bottom corner: SHARP. At the time Sharp were Manchester United's shirt sponsor.

'Get rid of it,' he said.

'You're joking!' argued Mum. 'I got it half price.'

'I don't give a toss, it's not staying in this house.'

Now on almost every issue Mum was the boss and got her own way, but not this time. It was packed and out within the hour.

Chapter 4
St Margaret's

ST MARGARET'S PRIMARY sat on the borders of Whalley Range and Moss Side. It was painted a nice bright blue, had a welcoming sign and a deranged lollipop man standing guard out the front. He was lovely to us kids, but woe betide the motorist who crossed this overzealous fellow. This was in the days before lollipop men were annoyingly positioned at pelican crossings like they are now: it was just him and his lollipop. If any car didn't slow down to what this roadside professional deemed an acceptable speed he would use his lollipop stick as a weapon and bash the car on the roof. He was simultaneously loved by pedestrians and hated by motorists. Once, when he'd just hit a brand-new BMW, the huge motorist got out and threatened to batter him. Immediately, my dad and a dozen other parents surrounded the guy and scared him back into his car. To threaten a lollipop man is a new low in anyone's book – even an over-enthusiastic lollipop man.

The school itself was a real mixed bag. Kids from all different walks of life went there. The Whalley Range–Moss Side area had African and Caribbean, Indian, Pakistani, Irish and Bangladeshi influences: every class was like a Benetton advert. It was great. We celebrated every major religious holiday, Divali to Easter, Eid to Yom Kippur. Every few weeks I'd get into class and half of the kids were missing, off celebrating one thing or another. My best mate from the age of six was a kid called Rashid. He looked exactly like me, apart from being Asian. Jasian Manford, if you will. He lived near us so occasionally he'd come to Nettleford Road for an after-school kickabout.

Our dads started chatting at the school gates one afternoon while waiting for the home-time bell. Now invariably when men chat for an indeterminate amount of time, their brains go in this order: football, cars, then back to football. Rashid's dad didn't like football and my dad didn't drive a car but by chance they started talking about food. My dad loves his curry. So did Rashid's. They'd found a common ground. One born and raised in south Manchester, the other from Karachi in Pakistan, they stood at the school gates discussing the nation's favourite dish. By the time we came out, Rashid's dad had agreed to send some of his wife's curry to my dad, which my dad was over the moon about.

The next day Rashid gave me a Tupperware box of curry during class with a confused look on his face.

'This is for your dad, mate.'

I took it off him.

'Erm, thanks,' I replied and got back to my colouring-in.

That night my dad warmed up his curry and tucked in, as we watched on, eating alphabetti spaghetti on toast. He was in heaven.

When it came to food at home we didn't get much of a choice, apart from the Sunday roast; most other things were 'insert tinned food item' on toast. A curry was way out of the question. But my dad was determined to return the favour.

I can't tell you how I felt as I handed over to Rashid a Tupperware box of corned beef hash and a Findus Crispy pancake as I think my brain has deleted the embarrassment from my memory.

MY FIRST DAY at school was the only time I'd ever seen anyone shout at my mum, and I didn't like it. My mum was already upset: her first-born son was starting school and we'd never been away from each other for longer than a couple of hours. It was a freezing, unforgiving September morning and the mile-long walk to school seemed endless. For a four-year-old, a mile is a long way. It's far enough for an adult but when your legs are half the size, you're essentially walking double that in child miles, aren't you? As she dragged me by my hand, we were both quietly apprehensive. She tried to hide the fact she'd already had a good cry. But I knew. I already had a lump in my throat myself, half from not wanting to be separated from my mum and half from not knowing what was waiting for me at school. As we arrived at the gates, I suddenly became scared. It was huge. Six floors of terror, full of loud, unfamiliar, bigger kids.

As we reached the nursery, we were 'greeted' by an imposing woman hovering at the door. She looked like a bull who had mated with a tank and had quite the scowl on her face.

'I'm Mrs McKenna and you're late.' She glared at us.

It was 9.02. My mum apologised.

'Yes, sorry, I have another baby at home so it…'

Her voice trailed off as this ice queen of a woman stared her down.

'Go and hang his coat up, then he can join the rest of the children on the yellow carpet.'

How on earth you can stay mad when you've just said the words 'yellow carpet' to a stranger is beyond me. But she managed it. We went to the cloakroom, where all the hooks had been assigned a cute little picture – a rabbit or a balloon or a star. You get the general idea.

There was only one hook left, with an odd-looking picture, like a banana with a smile. 'Shall I hang it here, Mummy?' I asked.

'Yeah, pop it on the banana hook and go and make some friends,' she replied, still upset but putting on a cheery voice and brave face for her little soldier. I went to find the yellow carpet. My mum gave me a last kiss and reluctantly headed off.

After a few minutes of playing I was aware of some raised voices and I looked over. Round the corner, my mum and Mrs McKenna were in each other's faces, shouting the school down. Mrs McKenna's voice was booming and my mum's was cracking. I couldn't work out what they were saying. Me and a couple of other kids crept forward to listen.

'It's clearly a half moon, Mrs Manford!' Mrs McKenna exclaimed.

'It's not the bloody moon, it's a bloody banana!' my mum screamed.

They were the most surreal two sentences I or any other child in the classroom had ever heard. Adults argued about politics and football and well, you know, grown-up stuff. How on earth had this teaching professional and my mum come to such a disagreement? I eventually couldn't stand it and ran over, anxious that my mum and the woman she was leaving me with were close to coming to blows.

I wrapped myself round her leg. 'What's wrong, Mummy?'

'Where did you hang your coat before?' she asked.

'On the hook in that room,' I said, still confused.

'And what was on the picture?' Mrs McKenna growled.

They both stared at the other. I still didn't understand why they were so angry. The picture did look like a banana but I suppose it could, at a push, in a certain light, also look like a half-moon. The way these two were going at it, you'd think they were in the final days of the Northern Ireland peace process.

They were clearly two adults who had got out of the wrong side of the bed – one unhappy with work maybe, the other upset that their child was starting school – and they were just looking to pick a fight with the first person who disagreed with them. The fact that my mum was so young maybe made Mrs McKenna think she could treat her like one of her pupils. In hindsight, it probably was a half-moon.

Whichever way you looked at it, Mrs McKenna was pretty ferocious, and there was really no need to be. I mean, seriously, we were in nursery: we spent most of the day either asleep or playing in the sandpit. Who needs to give a kid a bollocking because he didn't use enough dried pasta in his art work.

It wasn't just Mrs McKenna I got on the wrong side of. All the way through school I had run-ins. I tried to stay out of trouble but failed. It wasn't that I was bad; I just grew bored really quickly. I partly blame my mum and dad for that. Back at home, my dad didn't have that old-fashioned 'be seen and not heard' rule of parenthood. He was happy to talk things out and come to some sort of agreement. We very rarely got smacked, just the occasional telling off. I had mates who used to get slaps and slippers; it looked brutal. My dad would often use that famous parenting phrase, 'I'm not angry, just disappointed', which when you get older hurts you at the very centre of your being but as a kid makes you think, nice one – no one ever got slapped by a disappointed guy.

Just my dad's voice was enough to make us tremble in our pumps. It was deep and mean when he wanted it to be. Imagine trying to sneak a custard cream out of the biscuit barrel in the dead of night, when suddenly the lights come on and a Brian Blessed sound-a-like is bellowing at you from behind; I felt like a criminal caught in a cop car's floodlights and loudhailer: 'Put that custard cream back, son, and back away from the tin.'

His most inventive punishment was 'the wall'. It turned out to be a stroke of genius. Whatever had happened – a backchat here, a fight with my brothers there – my dad would make me stand in the corner of the room, facing 'the wall'. Now the punishment wasn't for ten or fifteen minutes – you would be facing that wall for well over an hour depending on what you were being punished for. Giving a Chinese burn to your sleeping brother = 25 minutes. Putting the cat in the washing machine = two hours etc.

Only it wasn't just a wall, it was a bookshelf. And my dad had the most eclectic mix of books you've ever seen – from books on the Second World War to Charles Dickens. I faced that bookshelf so often that by the age of six I'd read *Lord of the Rings* cover to cover and made a start on *The Hobbit*.

The problem was, back at school we were still wading through *Spot the Dog*. I had nowt against young Spot but it didn't keep my attention. The rest of the kids in class were struggling with the complex story arc of *Where's Spot?* when I was pondering how much Tolkien's Catholicism affected his characters' world view. Suffice to say I was bored.

I'm sure the teachers were fine but I felt like my whole school life up till eleven was me being told to shut up. I spent three years in Mrs Stepney's class and we just didn't get on. I took an instant dislike to her and I'm sure the feeling was mutual. In fact, on a self-evaluation on a school report one year I actually put 'I don't really like Mrs Stepney, and I'm pretty sure she doesn't like me either'. That's a weird thing to write when you're eight but that's how I felt. It was Mrs Stepney who once locked me in a cupboard. Not that there was any malice involved, before you ring Childline. It was a Wednesday morning and the night before on *Blue Peter* Yvette Fielding had made the Teenage Mutant Hero Turtles' sewer from an old crisp box. It was wondrous. I had made notes and got into class early to ask Mrs Stepney if I could have an old crisp box from the tuck shop so I could make my own version of the Turtles' home. I had it all planned out; I'd even made a space for it on a shelf in my room and got the figures out ready to play in it.

'No,' came the terse reply. She obviously had more pressing matters, like stinking of stale coffee.

I didn't kick up a fuss. I stayed calm. But as I moved slowly away from her desk, I spotted what I needed. Her keys.

If memory serves, my chance came when I was in the middle of drawing an astronaut. Mr Carroll, the headmaster, knocked on the classroom door to speak to Mrs Stepney about something or other. I don't know why teachers did this. Just knock on each other's doors at random intervals throughout the day, maybe they were bored with their own kids and wanted to see what was going on in the rest of the school. Mr Carroll was a very old, very kind-eyed man, but as head teacher I imagine he didn't have a lot to do apart from potter about and take teachers out of lessons to have a quick chat about nothing. On this occasion, I was thankful for his timely visit. I approached the desk; some of the class looked up but I made out I was looking for a sharpener. I was like a child Bond. I got to the desk and swiped the key, looked round and the class were none the wiser. I sat down just as she came back in the room.

That break time I sat and waited for the tuck shop to close up and everyone went back to class. I nipped to the toilet to avoid the other kids and teachers. I could feel my heart beating in my throat as I popped my head into the empty corridor. I got to the cupboard, opened the door first time and slipped inside.

Once inside, I was surrounded by mountains of confectionery. Caramacs and candy whistles, Flying Saucers and Freddos: I felt like

Charlie in the Chocolate Factory. But as hungry as I was, and as much as I loved all of the sweets on offer, I wasn't a common thief: I was there on a mission. An important mission, a mission I was prepared to be suspended for. I needed an empty Space Raiders box.

I found my prize on a high-up shelf, which I quickly mounted. Just as I was emptying out all the crisps so I could steal the box, the crack of light from the door disappeared. I was suddenly plunged into darkness and then my worst fears were confirmed – the door had locked, with the key, stupidly left in the other side of the door. I was trapped.

I didn't know which was the worst prospect – being caught or being trapped – but fear kicked in and I ran to the door and banged on it. But it was no use, my fate was sealed. Panic set in; there wasn't another tuck-shop break till the following day. Would Mrs Stepney miss me? Would the rest of the class realise I'd gone? I imagined my parents might notice when I didn't come to meet them at the gates. The police would be involved, hundreds of neighbours searching nearby woods, lakes would be drained and bushes explored. Then what? A parents' press conference; my mum crying to Tony Wilson on *Granada Reports*, my family's night of sleepless tears all for a Turtle home. I sat on my empty box of crisps and started to cry.

I'm sure this happens to other criminal masterminds: the moment you think all hope is lost and your world is about to end, what else is there to do except open several packets of Pickled Onion Monster Munch and tuck in? I sat there crying and eating as what seemed like hours crawled by. Then without warning the key turned in the lock. This was it, the double-edged sword of freedom. Yes, I would be free of this dark hole, but then what? Suspended from school, grounded for the rest of my childhood, a criminal record. I didn't deserve this.

The key turned and the artificial light from the corridor flooded the room. I couldn't see anyone but heard a familiar deep baritone Scottish voice.

'Afternoon, Comrade, what brings you to this cave of confectionery?'

Bond had rescued Bond Junior. It was Red Tom, the cleaner who had made friends with my dad on the march. Turned out he popped in every afternoon for a sly Mars Bar to get him through till he went home for his tea.

I WASN'T A very serious child, you'll be surprised to hear, and any excuse to say something that I thought was funny I'd take. One afternoon in Year 4 the teacher had written a single word on the board in big letters: 'Ambition'. Then she went round the class and asked us all what we wanted to be when we were older. It was the usual mix of nurse, fireman, astronaut and footballer. Although Clifford Frame, another of my best mates at school, said, 'I want to be a substitute, miss.'

'A substitute what, Clifford?'

'Footballer, miss.'

'Well, just say footballer then like the other boys.'

'I don't want to actually play, miss. I just like watching and they get the best seats.'

I thought he was an actual genius. And now the question was coming to me, but I only had one answer, something I knew I wanted to be for as long as I could remember.

'When I grow up, miss, I'd like to be a dog.'

'You mean a vet, Jason?' She frowned quizzically at me.

'No, I'll hate vets, won't I, cos I'll be a dog, miss.'

The class giggled but I was deadly serious. I'd seen our dog and how she lived her life: it was absolute bliss. I'd like a slice of that life, thank you very much.

IT WAS ALWAYS freezing in St Margaret's. It got so cold that there was even a school directive that said teachers were no longer allowed to send us into the hallway for bad behaviour during winter. This was after one lad, Wayne Campbell, had been in the corridor for over an hour and got chilblains. Unlike other schools, when the boiler broke we still had to come in, and were just made to wear our coats in class – I don't know if you've tried colouring in wearing mittens but it's pretty hard. In most things the modern world has moved on but even today schools still get closed due to broken boilers. Who's selling schools boilers that only work when it's warm? This is surely a boiler's main job? What else are they selling? Umbrellas that disintegrate in the rain? Someone wants to get *Rogue Traders* on these school boiler installers.

It was one such cold winter's afternoon during a Religious Education class that Mrs Stepney, because she wasn't allowed to send me outside, ordered me instead to stand in the corner of the room. She'd finally tired of me using her biblical stories to work in the kind of cheap gags that appealed to the underdeveloped minds of me and my fellow seven-year-olds. I complied and stropped over to the designated spot. As I stood there, bored without the luxury of my dad's bookcase, my eye eventually wandered to a huge cobweb on the ceiling. I had soon become entirely transfixed by the ebb and flow of the eight-legged creature's handiwork when out of the corner of her eye Mrs Stepney noticed me with my eyes looking heavenward and barked over, 'I don't know why you're looking up there, Jason. It's a bit late for that – even He won't help you now.'

I turned round, aggrieved, and said, 'Yeah, well, that's obvious, he's a spider, miss.'

That was my first detention right there. I always counted myself lucky that my parents were understanding. They knew I wasn't a bad kid. That's not to say they always took my word that the teacher was picking on me, but they were supportive enough without mollycoddling. It's a difficult balance. When my mum was a kid, if a teacher had smacked her at school, she'd get home and tell her mum and her mum would give her another crack because she 'must have done something wrong'. It's not like today when parents go marching into school to bollock a teacher because they had the audacity to take their kid's knife off them.

Clifford Frame and I were bad, I suppose. Not really bad. We never bullied anyone and we never swore but we did seem to spend most of our primary school life being separated. We heard the phrase 'I'll split you two up' more than the school bell. One afternoon things came to a head for Clifford when his mum turned up at school unexpectedly. I say unexpectedly but there was a reason – we'd wound up a dinner lady so much she had gone home crying. I know, I'm not proud of it. But she must have overdosed on HRT because what we did wasn't even that bad. We had decided that during lunch we would follow her single file for the whole of the hour-long break. We'd recruited Rashid, Black Darren, White Darren and Ginger Darren to complete the team. Five of us followed her round like the Pied Piper. Everywhere she went, we went, in silent single file. She managed to take it for forty minutes before turning to us all and saying, 'Right, that's it, I'm sending you lot to the head teacher's office.'

To which Clifford replied, 'Well, just walk there and we'll follow you, miss.' That was it. She went home a psychologically scarred and broken woman. We felt it had all been a great success, until we saw Clifford's mum.

Clifford's mum was a lovely woman but she was hard. She had four kids and she was as tough on her own as she was with the rest of the street. Her husband Ralph was a bit of a star round our way. He was the local fix-it man. He'd sort our bikes out when the chain or tyres broke. He wouldn't take any money so our parents would pay him with a bag of his favourite Old Holborn from the Texaco garage round the corner.

We instinctively knew something was up when Clifford's mum walked into class and sat on one of our tiny chairs at Mrs Stepney's desk. Normally I loved it when adults came into school and had to use all our tiny things. My dad at a parents' evening once went to use our loos, and then tried to wash his hand in the little low sinks. He came out with water all over his jeans, saying, 'I feel like bloody Gulliver in this place.'

Clifford was pale with worry as he watched his teacher tell his mum exactly what he'd been up to. Not just the dinner lady episode, but everything – a whole list. The class was pretending to work but we all had one eye on proceedings. After ten minutes or so, Mrs Frame beckoned Clifford over and gave him a silent telling off. He replied sullenly and then she did something which I'll remember for the rest of my life. In fact I can still see it when I blink.

In front of a class of thirty kids, she pulled Clifford's trousers down and slapped his bare arse; one big 'thwack' across the cheeks. There was an audible gasp from the classroom, including Mrs Stepney, who hurriedly got her out and sent her home.

Clifford was stunned into silence. Mrs Stepney shoo-ed him back to his seat. He sat down gingerly next to me as I pretended not to have seen it, carrying on sticking lentils with PVA glue onto a blank sheet of paper. I said nothing. He said nothing. Nobody said nothing.

You would think that something like that would end a boy's school career, that he would be teased and bullied within an inch of his life for ever more. But no. Every kid in that class thought about their own behaviour, and what their parents are like at the end of their tether, and we all thought the same thing: that could've been me – there but for the grace of God. It was never ever mentioned again.

Chapter 5
Cup of Sugar, Cup of Dirt

MOST FRIDAYS from the age of four till I was about ten, my granddad would come and pick me up. As far as I was concerned, he was the nicest human being that had ever lived and I loved him with every bit of my tiny being. He was my dad's dad. He only ever smelt fresh, a mix of Brylcreem and Old Spice, he was always clean-shaven, and he always dressed in a shirt and tie as if every day deserved his respect. He would walk every Friday, even in his seventies, the four miles to my school to pick me up and when I saw him at the gates I would run as fast as I could and jump into his arms. We would walk hand in hand along the main road, past the lollipop man towards his and my nana's house. The same house my dad had grown up in, where his old room was now mine whenever I needed it. I'd grip his hand tightly as we'd walk through Alexandra Park in Moss Side, the scariest park I've ever been in, the ground always full of used needles and used condoms (in fact when I was about thirteen I once saw a porn film being made in the park against one of the trees – that's four hours of my life I'll never get back).

Me and Granddad would pick our way through the ne'er-do-wells to the lake to feed the ducks. He would have a bag of stale bread a few days past its sell-by date and we'd stand for ages throwing big chunks of whitey goodness to the mallards and geese of south

Manchester. I'd tell him all about what I'd done in school and he was the most interested and interesting person in my life. He always had time to listen. I can't ever think of a time that, when I was with him, I wasn't smiling.

We'd spend long summer weekends in his garden – he'd be beet-root red in the sunshine and I'd pass him tools from the shed, and we'd drink dandelion and burdock and eat ham butties at dinner time, then in the evening I'd sit on his knee and watch telly till I fell asleep and he'd carry me upstairs in his arms, before tucking me so tightly into bed that I was essentially shrink-wrapped. That was almost every other weekend of my childhood.

I used to get upset at the *Bullseye* opening credits because it meant that my weekend bliss with my granddad was almost over. He'd spend Sunday afternoon holding me up at his front window as we watched the big lorries drive past on Princess Parkway, looking for my favourite vehicle of all, the transporter. I loved transporters, which was lucky as one Christmas my dad bought me and my brothers some toy ones. We looked confused: we didn't need seven of them in our lives. It was a simple mistake. Mum had written a list and requested he 'get a couple of Transformer toys for each of the boys'. He'd misread her handwriting and we ended up with miniature versions of the car-carrying vehicle. Even his version of the cartoon's theme tune didn't make the present any better.

'Transporters, trucks that carry cars.'

One Friday, I was in the line waiting for the bell, excited that the weekend was finally here. I got to the gates and couldn't see Granddad anywhere. My mum's friend Cheryl, a lovely woman from Barbados whose son Robert was in my class, came over and said I was going to her house for tea. Brilliant, I thought. They had the biggest house I'd ever been inside and a bloody great big treehouse in the garden. So off we went to their house and we played all evening.

It got to bedtime and Cheryl said I could stay if I wanted to. I snapped her hand off; I loved staying at their house. Robert had the biggest collection of *Beano* comics I'd ever seen and we'd lie on his bunkbed with a little torch, reading Roger the Dodger and Minnie the Minx into the early hours. It wasn't my normal Friday night – I usually spent it with a pair of pensioners – but I was too engrossed in comics, to mind.

The next morning we were back in the huge garden, playing football and climbing in and out of the legendary treehouse. It was a real oasis of fun in an otherwise weird neighbourhood: Whalley Range was and maybe still is Manchester's premium red-light area. I don't know why I've called it 'premium', it's nothing to be proud of, but I suppose if you're going to be good at something, you may as well be the best.

I never really encountered any of it, apart from the time I was on Robert's swing. They had a proper swing cemented into the ground so that you could get almost horizontal without it tipping over. I remember once trying to get it above the eight-foot brick wall that surrounded their garden. I glanced into the disused garden of next door and saw a prostitute on her knees in front of some guy. I was only ten and had no idea what was happening, but they looked over and didn't seem to stop. I kept on swinging and every time I went up, she went down. Thinking back, that's a bit weird; the prostitute even looked at me and put her fingers to her lips as if to say, 'Shhhh, don't tell anyone.' Even at the time I remember thinking, who the hell am I gonna tell?

That Saturday afternoon, it suddenly dawned on me that I hadn't seen or heard from my parents since Friday morning. I found Cheryl, who was making tea. She said my folks were on their way and off I went out to play again.

A few hours later, my mum's bright yellow Triumph Dolomite pulled up in the driveway, exhaust coughing and spluttering like a vicar who's just been asked where babies come from (my dad called it the 'Triumph Dollopofshite'). Mum got out and headed into the house. I shouted at her from the swing.

'Mum, Mum, look how high I am!'

But she ignored me and went into the house. I found her a few minutes later having a cup of tea with Cheryl. I went over for a hug and she held me for what felt like five or ten minutes. I began to notice she was shaking. She whispered in my ear to go out to the car and see Dad.

I was wondering what on earth was going on. Were they splitting up? Had they tricked me by letting me play in a wicked treehouse all day and then, blam, 'We're getting a divorce'? 'Cup of sugar, cup of dirt,' as my granddad used to say.

I went out to the car and Dad was sat in the back by himself. I opened the door, expecting the worst.

'Dad?'

My dad looked up at me and I saw something on his face I'd never seen before. Tears.

'What's up, Dad?'

He pulled me into the car and held me tightly; this was my second massive hug in as many minutes and I still didn't know what was happening. He was shuddering. It felt like the force of his crying was rocking the car. I held him back but my ten-year-old arms weren't as comforting as his.

Eventually he looked up and wiped his eyes. He got his voice under control.

'Your granddad's not been very well, son,' he said, his voice quivering.

I stared at him, his chest trying to hold in a surge of pain. 'I'm sorry, son, he died this morning.' With that he let out a cry that can only be made by a bereft child. I held him and he held me. I hadn't started crying yet but my face was wet from my dad's tears, falling from his onto mine.

I pictured me and my granddad at the park feeding the ducks, stood at his window looking at cars, in the garden drinking pop, and it wasn't long before my face was wet from my own tears. To see my dad crying was almost more upsetting than the realisation that I was never going to see my granddad again. Dad was the rock of the family; sure, Mum cried, she was a girl, we cried, we were kids, but Dad? It just wasn't right. He was my Superman, he was the guy who made my pain go away, who protected me, who held me when I was upset. Now here I was holding him, a ten-year-old boy realising that my dad wasn't infallible.

His cry was deep and guttural. It was a cry that comes from the pit of your soul; a darkness I've only felt twice in my life, and this was the first. Every child will come to experience death at some point; it's the point when childhood ends and eventually you come out of the other side an adult. It's an important moment, a sad, terrible moment, but a moment we all need. It's the first time you acknowledge your grandparents' mortality, your parents' mortality and then, maybe most shocking, your own. It's a moment that first makes you realise that these fun times you're having in treehouses, or reading the *Beano* or watching a prostitute sucking off a stranger will eventually end. And there are two roads from that realisation: you can give up and think, what's the point?, or you can make sure you live every moment like the next one could be your last. Most of us eventually go with the latter, and that is probably the greatest thing our grandparents give us.

Chapter 6
Away Days

IN JUST OVER eight years of life, I had never spent longer than a weekend out of our house but that was about to change – all five of us were going away. Our first proper holiday.

Of course we had had the odd trip to Blackpool but that wasn't really a holiday – we only ever went to see the Christmas lights. These were part of the famous Blackpool Illuminations which, even though they were Christmas themed, were turned off mid-November; strange lot up that way. I'm sure we only ever went so Dad had something to compare our house to when all the lights had been left on.

'Bloody hell, it's like Blackpool Illuminations in this house.'

I remember thinking then, Blackpool Illuminations sound well shit. And why've we got Rick Astley turning them on?

But they weren't, they were magical. It might not have been the actual lights that I remember as being brilliant but just the fact that all five of us were together. Dad was working hard at this point, especially around Christmas time. He worked all day in a nursing home in Stretford, then would come and pick us up from school in his uniform, get home, have a quick kip and head out to the Bull's Head in Stockport to work behind the bar till well past midnight.

But for this one evening, we'd all be together. Every year I would always forget that we would be going up to Blackpool at some point.

Then on a random day at the start of November, it wouldn't be just Dad's face waiting for me outside school, it'd be Mum's too. I'd walk to the gates, freezing under an overcast sky, dreading the prospect of a walk home in the grey drizzle, and I'd catch sight of them both sat in her bright yellow Triumph Dolomite. Smoke would be billowing out of the back of it as she tried to get my attention with a quick toot of the horn, which was broken long before we owned it – every time she pressed it, it sounded like someone had stood on a duck.

My brothers would come out of the infants and all five of us would head off to Blackpool, the 'Vegas of the North', as people called it. I'm not sure which people called it that: people who've never made it to Vegas I imagine.

Up the M6 through the peak-time traffic, off at junction 32 and then along the M55 towards the sea, waiting with bated breath to see who could spot the famous Blackpool Tower first. We'd drive to the South Pier and get out, parking up alongside hundreds of other excited northern families, waiting for it to get really dark so we could enjoy a million lights in all their 60-watt glory.

We'd eat fish and chips swimming in vinegar for tea, and we'd swig down a can of shandy; yeah, we were allowed shandy, because we were on holiday. One of the joys of having shandy as a ten-year-old is that after a can you'd imagine you were a bit drunk, even though clearly they contained less alcohol than Osama Bin Laden's drinks cabinet. We'd force ourselves onto the beach even though it was minus three and the wind slapped our faces and the rain soaked us through. We couldn't afford the Pleasure Beach where all the rides were, but we could see the tops of some of them as they hurled and swirled and rumbled round their tracks and we'd listen to the screams of people enjoying themselves on the Revolution or the Cat and

Mouse. The smell of candy floss and popcorn merged with the freezing sea breeze, intoxicating your nostrils and tricking your parents into buying you some flashing Fanta Yo-Yos or a pair of glow-in-the-dark Deeley Boppers.

We'd get back in the car, fingers still wet with grease and salt from our chips, drive down the promenade with our heads sticking out of the window, looking at those wondrous lights. I'd have Colin or Stephen's head next to mine as our eyes tried to take in as much of the majesty as possible, worried that at any moment our parents would turn off the seafront road and head for home. Of course they always did at some point, but we never complained; we sat back, exhausted, worrying our teeth by chewing on a ridiculously hard stick of rock.

Before we'd even made it back onto the M6 heading south, Enya's 'Orinoco Flow' playing quietly on the one speaker that worked, drowning out the struggling engine, I'd have each of my brothers' heads fast asleep on my lap. My neck would be craned backwards as I tried to keep the Blackpool Tower in vision, my eyelids heavy but valiantly trying not to let go of our magical Manford night, this beguiling Blackpool of my childhood.

Years later I did the same thing for my youngest brother and sister, Danielle and Niall. I picked them up from school in my Skoda Octavia (still the best car I've ever owned) and we drove straight to Blackpool to see the lights. I told them how wonderful they were and how enchanted they would be. They were the same age as I was when my parents used to take me and I wanted to experience the feeling again, but this time from the front seat with my innocent, wide-eyed siblings in the back.

We drove down the promenade and not a thing had changed. The tower looked magnificent and the Christmas lights were out in full. I turned to ask what they both thought. Danielle was playing on her

Nintendo DS and Niall reliably informed me he thought they were 'a bit shit'. Kids, eh?

THE FIRST EVER time we attempted a few days away we all nearly died, when my Uncle Michael suggested a trip to sunny Southport. Southport is about halfway between Liverpool and Blackpool and a bit of a letdown once you've tasted the bright lights. I've had a few weekends back there since and had a great time, but as a kid it always felt like there wasn't anything to do. You would go to Southport because you wanted to go to 'the seaside', yet every time I've been there, I've never seen even a hint of salty water. A mate of mine, Brendan Riley, who's from over that way, says, 'It's so shit, even the tide's fucked off.'

We headed off in Uncle Michael's car, seven of us crammed into his Vauxhall Cavalier estate. Now as you may know, the Vauxhall Cavalier wasn't a seven-seater car; this wasn't like driving up the motorway in a Nissan Qashqai, this was hell on wheels. It was off-white; well, it was white, but after my uncle had had it for a few years it was now a permanent shade of grey. It had a broken window at the back which gave you all the coldness of a convertible but none of the fun, and the window wipers didn't work, which for a Mancunian driver would be almost laughable if it wasn't so dangerous. Not that we needed window wipers this day, to be fair: it was glorious. We might not get much sun up north but when we get it, by God it's beautiful.

Michael drove and his wife Denise was in the passenger seat. Michael looked like Elvis would've looked if he'd not got all fat and died on the loo. He used to do Elvis songs when he sang in the band with Nana. He had the lip, the voice, the look and he was funny. He was the only one of my nana's children who had an Irish accent and it seemed that everyone in Manchester not only knew him but loved him. Even years after he died tragically early from a stroke, I'd be in pubs and old Irish fellas with bright red faces would tell me, 'I knew your Uncle Michael, great man – one day you'll be as funny as him.'

Michael told me once that Elvis was still alive and working in the chip shop in Burnage. I was only a kid and couldn't wait to tell my friends, but luckily Dad intervened with his own theory on the King of Rock and Roll. 'Son, do you think if someone was going to fake their own death, they'd tell the world they died having a shit?' He was right to be fair, and more to the point, if Elvis was going to fake his death, would he choose to live out his remaining years in Burnage?

Auntie Denise had a beehive hairdo, sang like Tammy Wynette, was the most house-proud person I've ever known and, boy, could she put a spread on. When any family party happened, Denise would be the first one you called. She had a discount card at Costco and had done a picnic for our trip to Southport that was so big it could have rendered Live Aid redundant.

Mum, Dad, Colin and Stephen were crammed in the back. Was I in the back with my family? No. Was I in the boot with the two crates of own brand lager and a picnic that would feed a small christening? Nope. I was rolled up in a ball under Denise's soft-soled shoes, in the passenger footwell. For an hour. On a motorway. I will never know what possessed four adults to think this was a better idea than a) finding a second car to take or b) at least letting me lie among the egg butties and sausage rolls in the boot. I wouldn't mind but Denise was a very nervous passenger, every time Michael went over sixty she was frantically trying to press her imaginary brake. I ended up with a back like a welcome mat.

As I remember it, I didn't seem to mind. In fact, me and my brothers had argued over who got to partake in this assisted suicide. And I won. Or lost, depending on how you look at it. I had a book I'd nicked off Dad's shelf (*The Jabberwocky*, I think) and was happily reading that and sipping on a Panda Pop, occasionally looking under the foot mat where the rust had eaten into the car and I could see the road underneath. Yeah, the actual road, inches from my face. Next time you get in your car, just have a look at the passenger footwell and imagine a gangly eight-year-old curled up in there like some sort of refugee escaping to a new life in a free country; I was just after a trip to the beach.

We drove for half an hour and were hitting full speed. Jokes were being told and songs were being sung. Michael was in full flow:

'And the second nun said, "Neither have I, it must be the cob..."'

Suddenly there was an almighty bang inches from my head that shook me from my comfy cocoon. The whole car started screaming as we jerked and worked our way across the motorway towards the hard shoulder. Not only was Michael driving a Cavalier, he'd adopted the whole lifestyle. It lasted about thirty seconds. I looked up but couldn't see a thing. We stopped. There was crying and a few 'Is everyone all right?'s being asked. Everyone got out into the blazing sun.

The left tyre, the one nearest to me, had blown out while we were pushing eighty in the fast lane. It was a busy Saturday morning and Michael had managed to control the car across to the relative safety of the grass verge, where we were all stood now watching the speeding juggernauts pass us by.

A plan was formed between the adults that we would split up and one group would head to the services and the others would mind the car.

Michael, Denise, Mum and Stephen set off up the hard shoulder to find a phone box to call my Auntie Bridie, who was the only person any of us knew who was a member of the AA. I don't know what the AA policy is like now but during the eighties my family found that as long as you could memorise your sister's date of birth and postcode, only one of you needed to be a real member of the fourth emergency service. Me, Colin and Dad opened the boot of the Cavalier and sat in the sunshine watching our family disappear towards Bolton North Services. After a few games of I Spy (C for Cars, R is for Road, S for Sun, well that was it really, after you've all looked directly at the sun the game's over) we started on the sandwiches and Dad opened a can of dirty water that Safeway's cheekily called lager.

It was exciting being so near to all this speeding traffic. Stood on the hard shoulder, dangerously close to the action, it felt like the cars were travelling at a million miles an hour. The slow lane is where all the really dangerous vehicles are too – the huge lorries being driven by a bloke who's been up for forty-two hours straight – and the drag from a passing truck occasionally pulled the butty or drink clean out of our mouths. It didn't occur to us that we weren't supposed to sit in or on the car on the hard shoulder.

That was until a traffic copper pulled up in his Sierra Cosworth, lights flashing and using the loudhailer.

'Step away from the vehicle.'

We froze, wondering which way he meant. Realising he couldn't mean into the motorway, we walked up the grass verge.

'Put down the can of lager.' Dad placed the can down gently like a surrounded bank robber placing down his weapon.

The policeman walked over and paused in front of us, collected himself before he began.

'Are you the driver, sir?' he said to my dad.

He'd just seen him drinking a can of lager and obviously thought this was going to be the easiest arrest he'd ever made.

He looked at the clapped-out car, the scruffy kids and the dad drinking lager and obviously assumed the worst. The thing was, he was right.

'Are you related to those idiots skipping up the hard shoulder?' he said, as he shook his head.

'How many of you were actually in the vehicle at the time of the incident?' the policeman asked Dad.

'Erm, seven,' he replied, for once thankfully not showing his usual cheek to coppers.

'Well, if I see you again with that many people in this car, then unless one of them is Roy Castle you're all gonna get nicked.'

We eventually got into a tow truck with a big smelly driver covered in oil. There's no need for that, is there? I know it was a hot day but I was eight and even I knew about spray-on deodorant. But at least we were off, on our way to Southport at last. That's the beauty of having someone who knows someone who's a member of the AA: they take you to your destination. I couldn't have been any more excited, not just because I now had a seat rather than crouching by someone's feet but because we were finally going on holiday for a full weekend.

But of course we weren't off to Southport. We were off to join the rest of our family at the services. Turns out my auntie didn't have full membership so we only got a lift to safety, then the big smelly oily man drove off in his big smelly oily truck to pick up some other unfortunates.

I could see people eating at the Wimpy inside and all of a sudden the ham and cheese spread sandwiches left a bitter taste in my mouth.

It dawned on me that we were turning back. My Uncle Michael rang his mate to come and tow us home. Which he did. Six hours later.

In the meantime we spent the afternoon playing football on a patch of grass no bigger than our living room. Mum and Denise laid out a blanket and set up the picnic and we ate and drank, laughed and played all afternoon until our knight came to tow home our Cavalier.

Finally he showed up in a car scruffier than ours, a little worse for wear, looking like he'd finished a crate of cheap lager himself. The tow rope he had brought wasn't nearly long enough so we ended up just over a metre from his bumper. The Manford five got into the battered Cavalier complete with a new non-blown-out tyre, while Michael and Denise climbed in with our drunk friend to tow us all the way home. I say 'all the way home', we actually got to a roundabout about a mile away from our house when the rope snapped.

Up until getting in this car, me and my brothers were still disappointed that we'd not managed to go to the Southport fair and go on the rides. After half an hour of being dragged along the inside lane like an errant dog, we decided that we'd had enough excitement for one day.

My mum's knuckles were white, gripping onto the steering wheel as we approached the end of the motorway and the last stretch of tarmac that would take us home. We started to slow down and the drunk driver sped off, leaving us stranded. Now this was before mobile phones so there was no way of him knowing that he'd shed his load, other than his car was half a ton lighter to drive or possibly looking in his rear-view mirror and noticing we were no longer there.

Half an hour later (yeah, half an hour) he arrived back, chuckling away as if to say, 'What am I like, eh?' We got to Nettleford Road at nearly midnight and went straight to bed, bilious with ham and pop that had been shaken all the way home.

So when people ask me where my first holiday was I tell them the truth 'the car park at Bolton North Services'.

At LAST, in the summer of 1988, my mum and dad had scraped together enough money for all five of us to spend a week, a whole week at Butlin's Pwllheli in west Wales. We were beside ourselves with excitement.

When I say my parents had scraped enough money together for a holiday, they had in fact, it transpired, been given some of the money from a local charity –'The Lord Mayor of Manchester's Fund for Family Holidays'. And no, the irony was not lost on me and my dad.

It was a fund set up for poor families like us who couldn't afford holidays. My parents received some money from the fund and the rest they 'borrowed' from our friendly neighbourhood loan shark.

Now when you hear the words 'loan shark', you think of some perma-tanned East End geezer who lends you £600 but wants £6000 the week after otherwise he'll kneecap your gran. Well, this guy was different. He didn't have a tan. And to be fair, he never kneecapped anyone's gran. He did, however, charge an extortionate amount of interest and would come round every week to collect his £20. My mum paid it dutifully apart from those few times she didn't have it, in which case all five of us would hide behind the settee in the living room as he banged at the front door. I remember once cowering there as his fist rained down on the door. I had hold of Colin, who would have been about two at the time. My parents were holding Stephen and we were all crouched on the floor behind the couch for what seemed like hours.

It wasn't hours, it was about ten minutes, with this guy shouting through the letter box, 'I know you're in there, I can smell you.'

I was scared enough as it was but when he said that I was actually shaking. Could he smell us? Like an actual shark smelling his prey from several hundred miles away? Of course what he was referring to was the smell of our dinner cooking on the stove, but at the time, at the age of eight, I was terrified of this man with fists like loaves of bread and a voice like cracking thunder.

'Sharon, Manny, come on now, it's only twenty fuckin' quid.'

I coughed and my dad put his hand over my mouth to stifle it.

'All right, have it your way. I'll be back next Tuesday.' His voice trailed off.

I let go of my brother as my dad silently mouthed, 'Nooooo.'

As I leant out to grab him, I looked round at the window where the loan shark's mean face was peering in. That feeling of losing my grip on Colin as the shark's eyes scoured the room for signs of life made me tremble to my core. I managed to hold him still as the dark sunken eyes darted one way and then another, until he fixed them on me and smiled. I could see his dirty teeth even from ten feet away. He shook his head and left.

I'm sure he came back the following week for his forty quid, but it was too late, we were already on our way to Butlin's to spend it.

LOAN SHARKS and charity funds, I know, they're such clichés of the hard luck story, but we really were poor. I mean it wasn't quite *Angela's Ashes* but we had our moments. Take our telly, for instance. Nobody believes me when I tell them about it. There were some crazy inventions for poor people back then. We had a telly that had a 50p meter on the top. It was well annoying. You'd be in the middle of watching *The A-Team* and then, 'bink', the telly would go off. Invariably nobody would have a firty-pence piece and it didn't take any other coins. Embarrassingly one of us would be sent round to a neighbour's with a handful of change to get a 50p so we could find out how they were going to get Mr T on a plane this time. One afternoon the telly went off while Mum and Dad were at Safeway doing the big shop. Can you imagine the panic in three young boys' faces as the telly turns off? We might even have to go outside and play! Then our Colin had a brainwave. He got a plastic 50p from a toy till we'd had for years and put it in the slot. 'Click.' At first I thought he'd broken the TV, but no, it actually worked! We told Mum what Colin had done and later that afternoon she arrived home with a big bag of plastic 50ps from a toy shop and from that day we had uninterrupted viewing. Well, until the end of the month, anyway, when a bloke from Rumbelows came to empty the meter.

'Mrs Manford,' he said, 'the box appears to be full of plastic coins.'

'Plastic, you say? It must be the young 'uns. How much do we owe? £5? There you go, love.'

Then the next month.

'Mrs Manford, it's full of plastic coins again.'

'Colin, what have I told you? How much do we owe? £5?'

By the third month the feller stopped asking. Mum would silently give him £5 without the pretence of a back story and she'd get her bag of plastic coins back.

AH, LOVELY PWLLHELI. The camp we stayed on was built by Billy Butlin in 1947 and by the look of our chalet that was the last time it had been cleaned as well. We were crammed into two bedrooms. Mum and Dad took the twin room and me, Stephen and Colin all shared a rock-hard double bed. Checking-in time was 12pm and we arrived at

11.50, keen not to miss out on a single second of our borrowed holiday. Me and my brothers changed into our shorts and asked Mum if we could have some money so we could go on the rides at the small funfair in the centre of the camp.

'You don't need money here – it's all-inclusive,' said Mum.

'You mean it's all free?' I said.

She nodded. I left in a daze and went to the fair, still trying to work out how this luxury haven was making money. I couldn't understand it. I quickly found out.

There were only about three rides. A small rollercoaster, the teacups and the bumper cars. It had started to rain which meant only the bumper cars were available, so we queued. We went on the bumper cars then queued up again for the bumper cars. We did this for two hours before succumbing to whiplash and heading to the indoor pool. After trying to swim in a half-closed swimming pool we trundled, bored and dejected, back to the chalet where we spent the rest of the afternoon playing football and watching Welsh Channel 4.

The next morning, the three of us got up, ate our breakfast and went out. Mum and Dad were still sleeping so rather than wake them we popped to the shop to get some sweets. At the shop was the biggest pick 'n' mix I'd ever seen, every single sweet you could think of was there. The three of us were soon filling bags with as many sweets as we could carry; climbing on each other's shoulders to get the out-of-reach Flumps like two midgets trying to get into a club. All for free! This company must have been losing money hand over fist. We left with bulging bags, more than we could possibly get through in a day. I had also got myself a He-Man, Masters of the Universe football and was kicking it across the grass while eating Flying Saucers. Heaven! This was the best holiday ever.

Come on, admit it, you're thinking 'cute' yeah? I've seen a picture of Michael Owen at this age and he looks exactly the same but a little thinner.

My and my brother Stephen's school photo. I didn't always pose like Stan Laurel, it was just a one-time thing.

I was always bouncing back then, occasionally out of windows, but this time safe on my Nana Manford's knee.

I always know where the camera is, me. My Nana Ryan and brother Colin are not quite so professional.

I can almost
smell the
Brylcreem
coming off
this photo.
Nana and
Granddad
Manford with
my dad and his
sister, Batgirl.

Me all in red for the only time in my
life, with two of the greatest
grandparents a kid could wish for.

No, honestly, they're still happily married. I know they don't look it here but they're a right laugh. Really, I swear!

Dad proposed to mum on Salford fish market when she was just sixteen and already pregnant. Then she found out he liked wearing braces, but it was too late to back out of the deal.

Me and Colin with my mum, and Stephen trying to find a ball bearing to put in his cock (read page 93, you'll understand).

Manford and sons. My dad, Manny, looks a bit John Lennon in this photo. Who would have thought twelve years later I'd be going out with his daughter (John Lennon's, not my dad's, urgh!).

Preparing for a lifetime of heartache as a Man City fan. My face is almost asking 'Why Dad? Why?'

Before we had a PlayStation. Our boxer dog Ghost wearing City colours and some sunglasses. Don't tell the RSPCA, yeah?

Me and Stephen holding a football while wearing the Manford winter away kit, circa 1987.

At Wembley for the 1999 play-off final against Gillingham where we finally answered the question, 'Who ate all the pies?' It was me.

Me, Stephen and Colin.
I think you can see
the flash reflecting
off that ball bearing.

For some reason, my
youngest brother Colin had a
bigger head than both his
older brothers put together.

Ok, so it wasn't the
only photo where
I looked a bit Stan
Laurel. This is me,
Ste and Col in our
annual 'who can wear
the worst top'
competition. Stephen
obviously won in his
Brown Tron jumper.

After a couple of hours in the chalet eating our own weight in sugary goodness, there was a knock at the door. I peered out of the window and saw a man in uniform. My dad answered it.

'Hello.'

'Good morning, sir, three boys were spotted this morning stealing sweets and toys from the shop and then heading this way. We're trying to find out which chalet they're staying in.'

My dad gulped. Not even a day into our first family holiday and he was harbouring three known fugitives. His eyes darted to the left to get a quick look at us while his head stayed forward, facing the stern security guard.

Cherry Fizz Wizz popped guiltily on my tongue, Stephen was halfway through a cherry gummi worm and Colin, unaware of our trouble, was polishing off a Sherbet Dip Dab. We were out of sight of the guard, and Dad closed the door a little to further obscure his view.

'Do you have kids in here, sir?'

'Erm, I erm…' stumbled my dad, not sure whether to lie or not. His kids were right there listening. What sort of example would this set, lying to an official simply because he didn't want to be thrown out of Butlin's? I sat there frozen, terrified that if my dad decided to make an example of us we'd all be on our way home to Whalley Range and our first family holiday would be over and we'd never get one again. He, of course, made the right decision – the decision that any good dad would make.

'No, I don't have any kids,' he lied.

What a legend. Even though he was denying my very existence I couldn't have loved him any more at that point. I turned to smile at my brothers but accidentally knocked my He-Man football off my knee. It rolled along the floor to Dad's foot. The security guard looked down at it, as did my dad.

'Big fan, are you?'

My dad blushed. 'Yeah, well kind of.'

After a long hard look, the security guard gave Dad the benefit of the doubt and wandered off. I think he must have known but he wasn't up for a full-on confrontation. It was our lucky day. But Dad would be another matter once the door closed.

His face still red from his humiliation, Dad turned to us. I knew we were in for it: even though Mum had said everything was free, a part of me knew that the shop didn't count. I'd led my brothers into a life of crime and I was about to be grounded on my first holiday. While others queued for three rides and swam in half a pool, I'd be stuck in here trying to work out what the presenters were saying on S4C.

Dad looked stern, the smiles fell from all our faces, my mouth went quiet – even the Fizz Whizz was scared. Dad looked all three of us in the eye, saw our fear and sorrow, and smiled.

'Give us some cola bottles then,' he laughed. 'And for the rest of the holiday, if anybody asks, you're all diabetic.'

Chapter 7
First Kiss

HERE'S SOMETHING you don't know about me. I'm circumcised. I know this might fall in the 'too much information' category, but hey, it's my story and this, as you can imagine, was a huge moment in my life. It wasn't for any religious reasons obviously, it's not like I've got to chapter seven of the book and neglected to tell you my family are all Orthodox Jewish. It was for medical purposes.

It's hard when you're a kid to know if everything is in the right place and you've got the right number of them and that. I mean, when do you get to compare what you've got with what everyone else has got? OK, so you'll occasionally see your dad in the bath but he's a grown-up so things are bound to be a bit different. You might get changed at school but apart from the occasional accidental glimpse, you pretty much keep your head down and put your PE kit on. Luckily I had brothers only a few years younger than me who I could compare and contrast with to make sure that everything was right and proper.

Me and my brothers would get up at the same time in the morning and all go for a wee at the same time. The three of us stood round the loo all trying to wee the Toilet Duck off the sides of the ceramic white bowl. (For any foreign readers, Toilet Duck is a product used to clean the toilet, not an odd place to keep a pet duck and a serious case of animal cruelty.) I remember one day, at the age of eight or nine, looking down and seeing my brothers pull back their foreskin and then looking at my own tightly fitted hood and wondering why I couldn't do the same (I told you this was in the 'too much information' category). But it wasn't till a few months later when my brother Stephen pulled a practical joke on my mum that I summoned up the courage to mention it to my parents.

Colin and I were in Mum's room as Dad was working nights. We would all read a book in Mum's bed before getting tucked up in our own. At the time my mum was training to be a nurse, which makes the fact that she was fooled by what my seven-year-old brother did even more unbelievable.

'Mum!' A shout came from the other room.

'What?' she replied, never one for getting up and finding out what was happening.

'I've lost a ball,' Stephen said.

'Well, have a look in the garden in the morning for it.'

'No, not that type of ball, one of mine.'

He came in, clutching his willy. Me and Colin looked over, concerned. Mum quickly sat up straight. 'What are you doing?'

'Look, one of my balls is coming out.'

We all looked down in horror as a spherical object, which my nine-year-old self presumed was one of my brother's balls, slid out the end of his penis and fell on the floor. My face went white, my mum retched a little and I jumped up and frantically scoured the floor, believing that one of my brother's testicles had just slipped under the bed.

Then I saw it properly: a shiny silver ball-bearing nestled on the floor. For some reason Stephen, who was now – along with Colin – laughing himself daft, had thought it'd be hilarious to get a ball from one of our board games, wrap his foreskin around it and then pretend one of his testicles was falling out of his willy. What seven-year-old would do that? He'd ruined a perfectly lovely evening and we never played Mouse Trap again.

The only good to come of it was it started me thinking about my own tackle. I mentioned to my dad that unlike Stephen's elasticated foreskin, mine was as tight as a swimmer's cap.

We went to see Dr Michael (his real name was Dr Michael Unwin but for some reason we always called him Dr Michael, like we were learning English as a second language). He had a look, a pull, a shake, a squeeze – I can't remember exactly but I was just glad it was him doing it and not Dr Sally. There really is no place to look when a doctor has hold of your genitals. It feels wrong to look him in the eye and chat but to look away seems awkward too. I was flushed with young embarrassment but not as much as when my dad tried to fill the silence. 'So how will this fix his sore throat, doctor?' he chuckled. By himself.

Each time I've been in that situation (which, to be fair, is only twice) there always seems to be an awkward moment, even with a professional medical practitioner in the driving seat. I recently went to see the doctor about a lump I'd found in one of my balls and we found ourselves in a similar situation, with me lying on the bed and him having a shufti around to check all was well with my boys. Again, I didn't know where to look but after what felt like a lifetime I clumsily caught his eye. And then to make things worse, I smiled. And because it's the socially accepted thing to do when someone smiles at you, he smiled back. Now that's OK when you're in the pub or the park, but it makes it a little bit weirder when one has the other one's bollocks in his hand. Just as I thought things couldn't get any more embarrassing, the doctor decided to fill the silence with, 'So, erm, what's Jimmy Carr like?'

'Yeah, he's lovely, really nice fella.'

I don't think I've ever told Jimmy that a man feeling my testicles asked me what he was like. There's just never seemed a good time to mention it.

Anyway, Dr Michael sent me home with this piece of advice: 'Practise pulling it back four or five times a day.' If only he'd have give me that advice when I was fifteen.

It didn't make a difference and a couple of years later I was booked into the Duchess of York Hospital for an operation. I don't have good memories of this place. A few years earlier I'd had my tonsils out there and was lied to by more than one healthcare professional. I remember being nervous going in for that operation but they all jollied me along, saying, 'Don't worry, little fella, all you can eat after the operation is jelly, ice cream and blancmange.' I didn't even know what blancmange was but if it was alongside jelly and ice cream, I was sold. It was as if the surgeon was Willy Wonka and I'd won the golden ticket.

But when I came to, the rules had suddenly changed. The hospital had altered its post-tonsil operation policy, and rather than soft food, another nurse was telling me the cruel news that toast and dry cornflakes were the best thing to eat as it helped 'scrape off any blood from the throat'. I felt cheated and vowed I would never have my tonsils taken out again.

But back to my penis. My dad took me into hospital on the Monday morning but soon had to leave me to go to work. I was alone and terrified, worried that at any moment, as I lay in that pale blue ward, a strange man was going to come in, put me to sleep and chop my willy off – which in a roundabout way was actually going to happen. Anyway, I tried, as my dad had suggested, to be a big brave boy. I settled down, read my *Beano* and began to relax. I had everything a twelve-year-old boy could need: some comics, a bag of Jelly Babies and a two-litre bottle of Lucozade (of course at this point in time, Lucozade was still seen as medicinal and only sold in chemists).

'What are you in for?' It was a young voice.

I looked over at the other side of the ward and the most beautiful girl I'd ever seen was sat up in her bed, a Judy Blume book on the bedside table resting against a mountain of grapes. She was blonde, had huge blue eyes and as she smiled the liquid in my mouth dried up.

I pondered her question and wondered what the hell I was going to say, I couldn't tell her the truth, could I? But I had to say something. Something subtle. Something that wouldn't get too many questions, but would keep her talking to me.

I took a swig of Lucozade and just went for it.

'I'm having brain surgery,' I told her with my best straight face.

She was suitably impressed and luckily knew less about brain surgery than I did, which wasn't much. I'm not sure what she was in for but I presume it wasn't the same thing as me. Well, at least, I hoped not. I think it was for tonsils so I made sure she knew that she'd be getting dry Kellogg's for breakfast and not a Solero.

We chatted and laughed all afternoon. I may have told her I could die on the operating table, you know, that sort of thing. I don't know why I was making things up but she seemed to like me and I definitely liked her. There was a bond. Later on the doctor came for a look and drew the curtain so the girl couldn't see he was actually having a look at my penis and not my brain.

My parents arrived for visiting hours and the girl, whose name I can't remember, was busy with her folks, too. I couldn't wait for everyone to leave so that I could talk to her for the rest of the night, have her back to myself. I think that, even though I was only twelve, I was falling in love.

That evening, my last evening with a full penis, we got told off by the nurses, and told to be quiet by other kids in the ward who were trying to sleep. I went over to her bed and shared her grapes and let her have a few swigs of my Lucozade. She told me all about her school and her family and I told her all about mine. At gone one o'clock, a nurse came in and told us that we had to go to bed or she was going to ring our parents. I stood up, the nurse left, and in the darkness, with the quiet background hum of a Coke machine and the gentle beep of some poor kid's heart monitor, I leant over and kissed her. And she kissed me back. I was twelve, she was fourteen, and it was my first kiss.

Well, I want it to be my first kiss. It was sweet, it was with a lovely older girl, it was all lips. I remember my heart bouncing around my chest like Tigger on Red Bull.

My real 'first' kiss, if you can call it that (I prefer to call it assault), was actually a year earlier with a Revel kid. I probably should tell you why she was called a Revel kid. Back on Nettleford Road, there was a house a few doors down which often had foster kids staying. The couple who lived there had different kids every few weeks, so we'd knock on to see if the current kid wanted to play out but you never knew who you were going to get. Sometimes you'd get a fun lad who wanted a game of footie, other times you'd get a bully who battered everyone and took your sweets. You'd stand at the door never knowing what you were going to get, hoping it wasn't coffee flavour this time.

One time a girl was staying there. I can't remember her name but I do remember we called her Bulldog. I know, I know, it's not very nice, but we certainly didn't call it to her face; her jowly, low-jawed, Bulldog-type face. She didn't really look like a bulldog but kids can be cruel and so for the few weeks she was a resident, that was her name. I'd probably feel bad about it if she hadn't been such a bully.

One night, some of the lads were playing Wembley at the front of our house. Me, Clifford Frame and Paul Demitri were kicking the ball about when we were approached by Bulldog and a couple of other girls. As you can imagine, a lot of these Revel kids were a lot more streetwise than us Nettleford kids. They'd had it hard and didn't mess about with niceties.

'Which one of yous wants a snog?' she barked. (She didn't bark, but I'm having fun.)

We looked at each other and shrugged. We all seemed pretty happy playing Wembley. She wasn't taking this as an answer.

'Come on, let's go down the ginnel and you can feel me tits.'

The fact she didn't have any didn't seem to worry her. More kids came over to see what the commotion was, but I was pretty adamant that I wasn't going to be snogging anyone that night, even with the growing peer pressure. Then the dreaded 'f' word came out. No one wants to be called this, not at any age, but as a kid, it's worse than being poor.

'Why not, you frigid?'

Now the Oxford English Dictionary describes the word 'frigid' as 'persistently averse to sexual intercourse'. And as the whole group of kids that were shouting it were no more than thirteen, I think we could all be described as 'frigid'. But I doubt if I'd have gone to fetch the dictionary from the house that any of the kids would have listened to reason. And anyway, being called 'frigid' had the same effect on me as being called 'chicken' did on Marty McFly.

So I agreed, alongside Clifford Frame, that we'd snog Bulldog. Clifford went first, brave, brave Clifford. He disappeared into the abyss of the ginnel, rigidly holding hands with our potential suitress, and I'll be honest with you, I didn't think he was going to come back.

When he did eventually return, he was never the same. He was wide-eyed, staring into the distance, his jacket was half pulled off and his cheeks were wet. His cheeks. Wet. Why? Why were his cheeks wet? I wasn't looking forward to this. I asked him how it was. He said it was 'fine' but couldn't seem to look me in the eye. I could tell he didn't mean it. I can imagine him even now, nearly twenty years later, waking up in a cold sweat screaming, 'No, Bulldog, no,' as his now wife gently calms him down.

It was me next. I did some stretches and smelt my breath, which as you remember is a quick test of licking your hand and then smelling the result or breathing into your hand and quickly sniffing up before the smell gets away. Both tests are as pointless and as useless as the other.

Off we went, me and Bulldog. It was dark in the ginnel. I couldn't see a thing, but Bulldog's eyes had adjusted to the light like a rat and she guided me behind a couple of bins (why I'd bothered to see if my breath smelt when we were in such romantic surroundings I'll never know). She stood up, towering over me. I pursed my lips together, readying myself for this kiss. I opened my eyes and she opened her mouth. I looked inside. I felt like Sigourney Weaver in *Alien*. This darkness with teeth came at me and I couldn't move. I was frozen to the spot. My dry lips met her open mouth and she clamped on.

I'd never seen a kiss with a mouth open. I wondered whether to open my mouth as well, but before I could make a decision a huge slimy tongue pierced my lips and wriggled inside like it was alive. Round and round it went, my tongue valiantly fighting back like Lancelot fighting a dragon. But it was no use, I just had to take it. As I tried to quietly think of anything other than what was actually going on, a thought entered my head. If she'd done this to Clifford as well, and if some of his spit was still in her cave-like mouth, and now in mine, does that make me gay? Upping the ante, she grabbed my hand and pulled it onto her 'breast'. It felt very much like feeling my own flat chest and I quickly pulled it back down to my side. Eventually she released me and we came up for air.

'That was top, shall we do it again?' she asked.

'Erm, I'm all right with just that, to be honest,' I said, as nicely as I could, wiping spittle from my chin.

'Why, you frigid, are ya?' she stormed.

'I think I'd rather be, yeah.'

And with that she marched off and told the group of kids that not only was I frigid but I was gay, and also kissed like a washing machine. I just stood there frozen to the spot with my head down in shame.

Then Clifford, to his eternal credit, came to my defence and exclaimed, 'No, Bulldog, it's you who snogs like a washing machine.' Not the wittiest answer, I know, and it cost him an instant leathering in front of all our friends, but at that moment I knew he was a true friend. Even if we did technically snog each other.

So you see why I'd rather keep the hospital kiss as my first kiss. Of course, the relationship with the mysterious girl in the hospital bed could never last, certainly not once my penis/brain operation happened the next morning. But that night as I lay in my hospital bed, sheets wrapped round me so tight I could barely feel my toes, I thought about my 'first' kiss. I went to sleep with the biggest, most blissful smile on my face.

When I woke, the girl had gone for her operation and I was being prepped for mine. I said my goodbyes, not to her, to my foreskin, and off I went. I counted back from ten and when I came to, I was hood-less. And in pain. Why on earth you'd be part of a religion that practised this I'll never know. I'd be gone after the first meeting.

'So, Mr Manford, you get to be born into the world not tainted with original sin, but blessed with original purity.'

'Cool, sounds good.'

'Oh, you do have to have a bit of your knob sliced off though.'

'Oh, OK, I'll, erm, ring you back, yeah?'

Of course for religious reasons it's done at birth where everything is a bit crazy anyway. You've just spent nine months in a warm protective womb, then you're out in the cold, people are staring at you and manhandling you, putting you in clothes, 'Oh, and now someone wants to slice a bit of my willy off – sure, yeah, why not, go for it.'

I got wheeled back into the ward and the love of my twelve-year-old life was sat up in bed, fully dressed, eating jelly and ice cream. Lying bastards. I smiled weakly. She smiled back, although obviously confused that I didn't have any sort of bandage on my head. My parents were waiting for me and I got a kiss off both of them, which, as it was in front of my potential girlfriend, left me somewhat mortified.

'Mum, pack it in!' I said quietly.

They both smiled, and then my mum did one of the most embarrassing things any mother has ever done in the history of motherdom. She had recently qualified as a nurse and she asked me, subtly and quietly so none of the other kids could hear, if she could have a look at how they did the stitching on my penis, sans foreskin. Under duress I consented. She closed the curtain and pulled back the covers. Now, even though this was the first time she'd had a good look at my penis since I was potty training, it doesn't excuse what happened next. From nowhere, the volume control on her voice disappeared and I heard her screech:

'My God, Jason, when did you get all this pubic hair?!'

My immediate thought was, why couldn't I have died on the operating table? I looked at my dad, who had clearly sided with his fellow male and told my mum to keep her 'bloody voice down'. My face was as red as my swollen cock. I had tears in my eyes. I knew that my girl was sat at her bed, as well as all the other kids on the ward. I never wanted the curtain to open again.

Eventually, after the doctor had been and told us we could go home, my dad opened the curtain. I looked over, sheepishly, at my future wife to see what she had made of my mum's outburst. But all that was there was a freshly made bed. No grapes, no Judy Blume books and no girl. I looked around for her but couldn't see her anywhere. I asked a nurse where she had gone.

'I'm afraid she left a few minutes ago with her parents.'

The stab of pain in my heart was worse than the pain in my willy.

The love of my life had gone and I'd never see her again. I had a lump in my throat. My dad could see that I was suddenly upset. In a hurried stream I told him how I'd kissed a girl and now she'd gone. He seemed a bit confused but seeing how concerned I was he put his arm round me and calmly suggested we left our phone number with the nurse in case my new friend rang to ask about me. With that done, I hobbled out of the hospital to an uncertain future. My dad tried to reassure me. 'I'm sure she'll ring the hospital and ask for you.'

'I know, Dad, but I didn't even give her my surname. How will the nurses know she means me?'

He smiled. 'I'm sure there can't have been many lads your age having a circumcision today, son. She'll mention that and they'll know it's you.'

What he didn't know was that if she ever did ring the Duchess of York Hospital to ask about me, she'd be asking for a boy who had had a brain operation.

Though I was inconsolable at that moment, there would soon be other kisses, and not always from where you might have expected them.

Chapter 8

Lead Us Not Into Temptation

I HAD THAT job every schoolboy has at some point in his life: the paper round. I'd played 'Paper Boy' on the Atari at my cousin's house and decided that for the money on offer it looked a piece of piss. Of course the game is based on the American paper round where a boy cycles up a road with no brakes and throws rolled-up newspapers through people's windows and doors whether they have a subscription or not. That game gave a real false excitement to the mundane reality of the actual job of a paper boy. Not only do you not get to throw newspapers from your ever-moving bicycle but you don't really have many obstacles in your way at 7am on a freezing October morning in Whalley Range. But thankfully, unlike the game, I was never attacked by bees, hit by a tornado or needed to dodge rogue break-dancers.

I did, however, cycle past a prostitute every day.

Now if you'd have put that in the game, people would have said it was unrealistic (or unsuitable for a game aimed at kids) but there she was on the corner of Brantingham Road every late afternoon as I delivered the *Manchester Evening News*. She was pleasant enough and I was only thirteen so it never really dawned on me what she was doing dressed in a low-cut top and short leather skirt. I was happy for a woman to say hello to me on occasion, a fellow street worker just going about our day, trying to please 'The Man'. Although my 'The

Man' was an actual man called Mr Patel, whereas hers was, well, anyone with £45. 'Hold on Jason, how did you know it was £45?' I hear you ask. Well.

After over a year of saying hello, she waved me down off my bike one afternoon. I got off and said hi.

'What's your name?' she asked me.

'Jason,' I replied.

'You're cute.' She smiled. I blushed, not sure what my response should be.

She wasn't the typical drug-addled hooker you'd see on TV cop shows. She was sort of normal-looking, maybe mid-twenties, blonde, huge boobs being pressed out of her top by an ill-fitting bra. She was as normal as I imagine you could be selling your body at 4.30 on a Tuesday afternoon.

'How much do you earn delivering papers?' I remember thinking, I can see where this is going, but I carried on, excited by the thrill of whatever she was going to say next.

'I get £5 a round per week and I do three rounds,' I said, acting innocent.

'Wow, big money for a young boy. How old are you?'

'I'm thirteen.' I presumed this would be the bit where she stopped talking to me, but it didn't seem to put her off.

'Well, Jason, why don't you save up three weeks' worth of your wages and come and see me – I'll give you an hour of my time and I'll make you feel like a man.'

I cycled home. My head was buzzing. It was the first time I'd ever had the real possibility of sex come into my thirteen-year-old paper-boy world, and it was confusing. I lay in bed that night and couldn't stop thinking about her, and what sort of things she meant. A few of the lads at school had talked about it, the telly was awash with references to it, and my parents were pretty open so I knew the basics. But it'd never even dawned on me that you didn't have to wait till you were old enough and that you could just finish your paper round and lose your virginity.

That phrase 'lose your virginity' stuck in my mind. Even at that young age, I knew that the moment was important. Obviously I was a boy, who was one day hoping to do it every second of every day (yeah right!), but right now my mind was in two places. I could pay this fairly attractive woman to take it from me, and the biggest moment in my adolescent life would be a moment I could never tell anyone about. I knew it was wrong but the proposition was exciting.

The next day I cycled to Mr Patel's, did my paper round and went to school. I did my evening round, rode past my seductress and went home. I was confused for the whole three weeks, but I saved up the money anyway, just in case. On the three-week mark, I cycled towards her, my bag weighing as heavily as my conscience and £45 burning a hole in my pocket. I was still unsure but at the very last minute I made the decision.

She smiled as I got closer and I could feel my face burning crimson. She waved and I stared straight past her. I was terrified. What the hell was I thinking? I couldn't have sex with anyone, let alone with this woman of the night, well, day. I tried to ignore her but she stood in my way.

'So, have you saved your money, Jason?' she asked, winking at me sort of sexily.

'Yes, I have.'

She smiled suggestively and pushed out her huge chest. 'So, what are you going to spend it on?'

'Erm, stickers, I think.'

'You what?' She looked confused.

'I'm gonna buy £45 worth of footie stickers to finish off my book.'

It was the perfect thing to say. What she was offering to this big-eyed teenager, or child, was wrong on so many levels. I knew I didn't want to lose my virginity that way; for some reason I knew that that moment was supposed to be special, a moment that shouldn't be bought and definitely shouldn't be between a schoolboy and a prostitute.

She gave me a kiss on the cheek and laughed. 'You're right – go and spend it on stickers. It's lucky one of us is thinking straight.'

I rode off, with a newfound excitement: forty-five quids' worth of Panini stickers were about to be mine. This is what life was truly about. I bought every single pack Mr Patel had in his shop. I filled that Panini album in no time; I was the kid to hang around with at school. No longer was I scrimping to get a Vinny Samways or a John Scales; I had the top prizes of Robbie Fowler and Jürgen Klinsmann all the way. I suddenly went from the guy doing swapsies saying 'need, need, need' to the kid who had it all: 'got, got, got'.

I carried on my paper round and cycled past her pitch for a fair few months but shortly after my rejection she had moved on. I don't know if she found another corner to patrol or if she'd decided she'd reached a new low in her life, but I hoped she'd moved on from propositioning confused paper boys on warm afternoons in south Manchester.

The rest of my paper-boy life wasn't as eventful, to be honest. Every afternoon I'd finish school and walk to Mr Patel's where I had left my bike after my morning round. I used to do two rounds in the morning of about seventy papers that would work my way towards school and then an evening round which would take me near home. Mr Patel had six paper boys and I was the youngest and, if I do say so myself, the hardest working. I'd pick up extra rounds whenever I could and some weeks could earn up to £20 (I'm not sure what that is in today's money, but I think it's roughly £20). I used to give my mum £4 of it in return for bed and board: she never asked for it but I remember my dad saying he used to pay digs when he started work but was still living at his parents. So I thought it was the right thing to do to start paying my way. She bloody took it as well.

It'd be pitch-black when I'd get up at 6.30 and head to the shop, and Mr Patel would be in the back sorting through the papers. Me and a couple of the other lads would stand in his shop waiting for him to give us our fluorescent orange bags and send us on our way. The older paper boys would have a sneaky look through the *Daily Sport* at whoever was on show but I always thought the funny headlines were the best bit: 'Woman Pregnant for 65 Years Gives Birth to Pensioner', 'Aliens Turned My Son into a Fishfinger' and the all-time classic 'Bus Found Buried at South Pole'. You may as well have got your news from the *Beano*.

Because the pay was so low, some of the older paper boys started stealing stuff from Mr Patel's shop while his back was turned sorting out the morning's deliveries. He would be working out which paper was going to which house while David, the most senior paper boy, would be filling his boots with as many chocolate bars and porn mags as possible. I never understood how Mr Patel didn't notice; he was basically like one of those WWF referees who, while telling off a wrestler in one corner of the ring, fails to notice another wrestler coming on and whacking someone over the head with a steel chair. I might have thieved from the pick 'n' mix at Butlin's – obviously my young mind rationalised that as a victimless crime – but this was different. Mr Patel was my friend and trusted employer. I could never steal from him.

I came in once and caught David loading his bag up with Mars Bars and cans of Fanta. I was thirteen and he was sixteen, a big strapping lad with broad shoulders who could carry two or three paper bags at a time (I could just about manage the one). He turned and saw me watching him and I looked away, hoping he'd think I'd not seen his light-fingering. He looked straight at me.

'Steal something.'

'What?'

'Steal something from the shop,' he whispered.

'But… but… but I don't want to,' I stammered, as I looked towards the back, praying Mr Patel or one of his family would walk through the dangling coloured beads that separated his shop from his home.

'Take something now, or I'll batter you when you get outside.'

I panicked and grabbed the nearest thing to me and shoved it into my pocket. Mr Patel eventually came out to give us our papers. My blood was pumping. I felt rotten. He smiled sweetly at me as usual, handed me my bag and sent me on my way. I got out of the shop and David came over.

'If you tell him I stole anything, I'll grass you up as well,' he threatened as he cycled off with his three bags of the morning's papers. I got on my bike and rode round the corner to take a moment and see what I had stolen.

I reached into my pocket, sweat pouring down my neck, my heart beating in my ears. As I pulled out my swag I felt so guilty. It was a Kinder Egg. The famous chocolate/toy combo that's delighted children the world over was now going to be my downfall.

I shoved my chocolate booty into my school trouser pocket and did the rest of my deliveries in a daze, worrying myself silly as I slotted the *Sun* into number 42 and left a *Guardian* on someone's porch step.

Had I seen a flicker of recognition in Mr Patel's eyes when he handed over my bag that morning? Was he biding his time? I went to school and resigned myself to being in the most trouble I'd ever been in in my life when Mr Patel rang the police. As the day tick-tocked away from me, I contemplated not going to do my evening round but then my dad would ask questions and my mum wouldn't get her four quid.

I got to Mr Patel's shop, with this slightly melted chocolate egg in my back pocket, and went straight for my bag of papers, hoping not to bump into the old man. The ringing of the opening door alerted someone in the back and they shouted, 'Coming.' As I walked past the Kinder Egg stand, I noticed there was still an empty spot where my egg had once lived. I looked round the shop and it was empty. I could hear Mr Patel in the back, making his way to the shop, so in a flash, I got the egg out and placed it back on the stand.

Mr Patel came out and stared at me hard. I felt like his dark brown eyes were boring into my very soul, as he said, 'Oh, it's you, I thought it was a paying customer.'

He looked past me and at the Kinder Egg as he went in the back room.

I thought I was done for. He must have known. Why else would he have looked at the Kinder Egg stand? He was probably going in the back to ring my parents. He shouted me from the back but I stood frozen at the door, keen to keep an escape route in clear sight in case the need arose.

He brought out two bags.

'You want extra round, Jason? Extra £5 a week?' he asked in his strong Indian accent.

'Eh?'

His stern face changed to a warm smile. 'I had to sack David today. He was stealing from me. I saw him on camera.' He pointed up to a small CCTV camera hidden behind an empty box of Coco Pops. I blushed and looked down at the floor, knowing he must have seen me swipe that egg too. But why wasn't he sacking me?

'You're a good boy, I like you. Have extra round, son, buy even more stickers.' He laughed as he put both bags over my shoulders and rubbed my hair like adults occasionally do. I turned to leave, still confused but happy that he'd forgiven my minor indiscretion that morning. I opened the door, and the bell rang as it swung back.

'Jason, catch.'

I turned just as Mr Patel was throwing something at me. As I caught it, I looked down in my hands: it was a Kinder Surprise, the same slightly melted one I'd stolen. I looked up and smiled.

'Enjoy it, boy.'

I DID THAT paper round for what felt like ages but as I hit the peak teenage years I started getting lazier. I kept sleeping in and in the end Mr Patel had to sack me. Sleep cost me many a job but I never really cared that much. While I was interested, I gave my all, I'd work every minute that they wanted me to and I always put in 100 per cent, but the second I'd had enough, I was a complete nightmare. I always felt that no matter what job I found myself in, it wasn't my long-term career.

Chapter 9
Girls and Boys

HIGH SCHOOL IS a five-year popularity contest, and kids have got long memories. You call your teacher 'Mum' by accident in your first year, it will still be remembered the day you collect your exam results. I started Oakwood High School in 1992 and as the raging hormonal madness of puberty and adolescence spread through us all, I had two wishes: firstly, let me stay popular enough to not become the habitual plaything of bigger boys, and secondly, please let me get a girlfriend.

My best friend at school was Lucy Kellaway and we first met in Year 8 (that's second year for anyone older than forty). We hated each other at first. We both thought we were really funny, although she really was. We'd both try and crack the same jokes to impress the same people. At first we clashed and competed but gradually we managed to form a kind of double act (although we were more Hale and Pace than Laurel and Hardy).

We began to enjoy each other's company and I walked Lucy home every day from school; then as we hadn't finished talking she would walk from her house to mine, then we'd walk back again. How on earth we managed to spend that couple of hours every night talking after we'd had the day in school together I'll never know. Sometimes after we'd walked each other home four or five times, we'd even phone each other to finish what we were saying.

Lucy was tall and blonde with the hugest pair of glasses you've ever seen, really thick ones like the bottom of a milk bottle. I was as tall as her, lanky and pale; we must have looked a sight. She used to make me laugh from the soles of my feet and I can honestly say she was the first person who wasn't family that I truly loved.

It's a confusing age when you first hit those teenage years. Any girl who doesn't hate you, you fancy. And even then you don't always discriminate. I think over the years of our friendship we fancied each other at different times but never in conjunction so we never got together. We remain friends to this day and luckily haven't got that awkwardness of opposite-sex friends who once had a thing and are now ignoring it.

Actually, now I think about it there was one moment when we came close to kissing. I used to stay over at hers a fair bit (those walks home from school were tiring) and we'd often share a bed. It seems odd now but at the time we were just two friends who happened to be a boy and a girl. I was in the year above Lucy and one night we were lying in bed, just dropping off to sleep. It must have been a time when I fancied her and she didn't fancy me and even though – or maybe because – she was lying next to me, I had a dream about her.

Nowt mucky, mind. I can almost hear your mind jumping to a conclusion there but, no, it was something daft and pointless. Nevertheless I woke up with a strange feeling. I looked over to her as she slept, her breathing was rhythmically in time with mine. I always thought she was really pretty even though she didn't think she was. I often think that makes someone better looking, when they don't know that they're attractive. Her glasses were on the side table and she was facing me on the pillow as I sat up. I looked at her lips and had an urge to kiss her, but it washed over me and I lay back down, smiling to myself at how weird it would've been to kiss my best mate.

She opened her eyes and smiled at me (even though she probably couldn't see a bloody thing).

'Hey, you OK?' she said, still half asleep.

'Yeah, just had a weird urge to kiss you,' I told her.

She smiled and said, 'You should have.' As I turned, confused, to see if she was joking or not, her eyes closed and she went back to sleep. The moment vanished as quickly as it came.

I think her parents thought I was poor and took pity on me. I mean, we were poor so they were right, but every time I walked to their house to knock on for Lucy I'd be invited in and fed. I had more hot dinners at the Kellaways' house than you've had hot dinners (at the Kellaways' house). Even now her dad Mike calls me 'Two-dinners Manford' as I would often walk to Lucy's from school, have my dinner at theirs, then go home and have my dinner again. I was like a cat who gets fed by a kindly neighbour before going home for its Whiskas.

They were a fun family, always laughing and joking with each other. They loved walking and would occasionally invite me along. I was an overweight schoolboy so there was no chance I was going to walk somewhere just for the sake of it. I only walked when there was a promise of a meal (or two) at the end of it. But I loved spending time with them. They were like a middle-class version of my family. (In hindsight they weren't that middle class but compared to my family they may as well have been in the monarchy. I mean, they ate hummus, for God's sake!)

Me and Lucy did the Duke of Edinburgh award scheme at school. If you don't know what this is, it doesn't mean you have to go to foreign countries and be slightly racist to people, it's just camping and stuff. At our school it was run by Miss Pritt. She had done the award when she was younger and had obviously decided other kids should suffer too.

The kids who signed up for it at Oakwood were all fairly well behaved. The problem was all the other schools in south Manchester seemed to be using it as a convenient way of getting rid of their hardest, baddest kids for a few days. So while we'd be setting up camp in Whitby or wherever, toasting marshmallows and singing 'Ging Gang Goolie', some scally from Wythenshawe would be trying to decapitate a seagull on the beach.

The scheme did seem to have a knack for attracting oddballs. Like Sandra, who barely said a word for the whole trip, but when she did speak she would say the same thing three times in three different voices. One afternoon as we walked alongside Lake Windermere, I got too close to the edge and nearly fell in. Sandra, with her super-human strength, grabbed me and pulled me back.

'Don't go near the water,' she said in a deep chesty voice.

'Don't go near the water,' she repeated in a softer, friendlier voice.

'Don't go near the water,' she said in a tiny child's voice.

It was only then I worked out what she was doing. She said things in her dad's voice, then her mum's voice and then a little girl's voice. It was absolutely terrifying. But she could be as eerie as she wanted as long as she kept saving me from drowning.

I've never been a good swimmer. I did learn at primary school like most people but the scary teacher would use a huge wooden pole to push us off from holding on to the edge as we tried to swim the length of the pool, at which point I'd panic and start to sink. So I only ever got my width certificate, never a full length. Even now I'm terrified of the lifeguard coming over and asking me, 'Excuse me, sir, can I see your licence, please?' and then when I can't provide it making me swim widthways while all the other adults swim proper lengths.

I was as terrible at camping as I was at swimming; I'm not an outdoor kinda guy. We would walk for miles through the dense woods of Sherwood Forest in June, or camp near the shore of the beautiful Coniston Water in November. What Miss Pritt lacked in outdoor knowledge she made up for in enthusiasm. We travelled in the old school minibus; the new minibus that actually worked was used by the school football team and there was no way Miss Pritt was going to go toe to toe with Mr Hamilton. This minibus was so old it had Jesus down as a previous owner, though it only had '425 miles' on the speedometer, but that was because the dial had gone right round and started again. As we drove up to the Lake District we had to take it in turns to hold the back door shut so it didn't fly off in the middle of the M6 and we had to stop a dozen times on the way to give the minibus a 'rest'.

On one trip, by the time we got to the campsite it was dark, and we began to pitch our tents in the light of the minibus's headlamps. As I was hammering a tent peg into what felt like granite, I looked up and saw a half-moon (or was it a banana?). I don't mean the classic half-moon that we've all seen, I mean I saw the top half of the moon. I thought nothing of it and carried on hammering. Me and Lucy slept in one tent, both huddled together, freezing in our sleeping bags.

The next morning I woke at first light with a sense of panic. My immediate thought was that I'd wet the bed. I've never been a bedwetter. My brother Colin was, though, weeing his bed till he was about eleven. (I've no story to tell about Colin being a bedwetter, I just really wanted to include it after the time he tried to kill me with a giant ashtray.)

As I struggled to open my eyes, I unzipped the tent to see if anyone was up. As I looked out, I saw my shoes float past, followed by several other pairs, then a duck quacked as it swam past my head. I was suddenly bolt upright and realised we'd been flooded. I woke the others and we all jumped out to assess the damage. It looked like we'd set up camp in the middle of a lake. There'd been a heavy downpour overnight and we'd camped without knowing it at the bottom of a rise. The reason I could only see the top half of the moon was because I was looking up a great big bloody hill.

That was the last I saw of the Duke of Edinburgh award. We went our separate ways and I've never slept under canvas since. Why on earth people continue to camp when there are perfectly good hotels and B&Bs knocking about I'll never know.

Nevertheless, me and Lucy had become Miss Pritt's favourites. You're probably wondering how I know that. Well, one night she was having a fancy dress party at her house in Northenden and we were the only two kids invited. Why we were invited, I'll never know. I presume it was our Duke of Edinburgh bonding. But I'm so glad we were.

I'd never been to a fancy dress party before, it wasn't something we did in our family. I suppose with one uncle dressing as Neil Diamond and another auntie occasionally doing Kate Bush it would have been a bit of a busman's holiday for our lot. I tell a lie, there had been that one at primary school, when I was about eight and Saffron Buchanan dressed as a Pringles tube. She, or probably her mum, must have been up every night for a week creating this amazing costume. It was bright green and it went from the floor to about six foot in the air. Her face came through the middle like the Pringles man and she had a big thick black 'tache on her face. It looked fantastic, and all the more so because no one else could really be arsed. I went in my uniform as a schoolboy and my mate Rashid put on a pair of ripped jeans and an old oil-soaked jumper and went as a refugee.

For Miss Pritt's do, though, I decided to make more of an effort. I'd borrowed a Stetson, boots and shirt from my Uncle Dave and went as a cowboy; I looked pretty good. Lucy went as a fairy and looked ace and we spent the night feeling a little awkward in the corner of the garden, drinking Sprite and wondering why the hell we were there. It was fun to people-watch though: Elvis was trying his best to chat up Cruella de Vil and Mr T had just stopped Colonel Sanders falling into the pond.

But there was one character we just couldn't take our eyes off – a fat guy in a nappy who was becoming increasingly loud and obnoxious by the hour. He'd used fake tan all over his body and had a white bedsheet as a sort of toga. We couldn't guess what he was at first until Lucy worked out; he'd come as the Tango Man. The advert was massive at the time with kids banned in school from slapping other kids in the face and repeating the accompanying catchphrase: 'You know when you've been Tangoed.' Apparently someone had done it to Kelly Clayton in Year 10 and popped both her eardrums.

As the night wore on, people were getting drunker and drunker until finally there was an incident involving Indiana Jones trying to feel up Xena Warrior Princess in the downstairs loo. Once the Tango Man, who had some interest himself in Xena, heard about this he was seething.

'Oi, dickhead, you trying to feel up my missus?'

Me and Lucy looked at each other. This party was about to get started.

Indiana Jones and the Tango Man locked horns, grappling each other to the floor. Two Blues Brothers and a Ghostbuster tried to separate them as the naughty Sandy from *Grease* called them all bastards. This was turning into one of the best nights of my life.

The Tango Man clocked Indiana on the chin and he went down hard, hitting the floor. The brief shocked silence that followed was swiftly filled when Batman shouted out from the upstairs bathroom window, 'You know when you've been Tangoed.'

Nobody laughed. Well, I say nobody – I pissed myself. Then the Tango Man looked up to the window and said the best sentence anyone has ever said:

'Tango Man? I'm fucking Gandhi, you daft prick.'

The man who started the huge fight at the fancy dress party had come as Mahatma Gandhi, the world's most famous pacifist. He was now three sheets to the wind with lager on his breath and blood on his knuckles.

The police arrived and asked us all for a statement. Because me and Lucy didn't know anyone's real names, we had to use their characters. I hope somewhere in Wythenshawe police station there's still a page of a notebook that starts, 'Well, of course Gandhi started it.'

THE ONLY OTHER time I'd been outward bound was when I was thirteen – with the church. My mum had long stopped taking me to church and my dad, as you know, didn't buy in to any of it, but for some reason I kept going by myself. Don't ask me why, I just really enjoyed it. I think it was the singing.

It wasn't the Catholic church I'd been brought up with either. I went to an evangelical church called St Edmund's on the border of Whalley Range. The choir and much of the congregation was black and I sometimes felt like I was an extra from *Sister Act*. I loved it. Oh and they did free biscuits so it really was win-win. I eventually stopped going after a couple of years. I believed in a god but I wasn't sure he was the same guy the church kept going on about. I feel like God is like a car, and the church is like the salesman, trying to sell us his specific model of a car, and often ripping us off in the process.

One half-term before I left, they took us to a place called Fort Rocky, which, when I describe it, you will not believe existed. It was a

Youth for Christ residential weekend run by Canadian Mounties somewhere near Kidderminster. There, told you. All the kids at St Edmund's
had been going every year. They all had T-shirts and shouted slogans
like, 'Who's Fort Rocky?' to which I would reply 'Apollo Creed?'

It was actually brilliant, with loads of sport and activities. The
church paid for it so all I had to bring was my purple shell suit. I mean,
they didn't tell me to bring it but I knew they'd want me to. The only
problem was that every activity would be linked to Christ in some way,
although that's not too bad during five-a-side.

'Hey, good save, Jason, but do you know who else saves? Jesus.'

But during rock climbing it was a different matter. I was halfway
up a rope once, terrified, sweating and bricking it while a bloke
from Coventry dressed as a Mountie pulled me up. Halfway up, he
suddenly stopped.

'You know, Jason, this rope is a lot like Jesus – you can depend on
him to pull you up any time you need him.'

I was in no mood for this. All I could think was, if I ever get to the
top of this wall I'm gonna wrap Jesus round his bleeding neck.

ALL THE WAY through school I was in love with a girl called Amanda
Rose. A pretty brunette, I followed her round that school like a
lost puppy.

I had discovered her by a quirk of fate. She was best friends with a
girl at my school called Julie, who by a strange coincidence had my
surname. Julie, it turns out, was from a family of Manfords who were
descended from my granddad's cousin. I only became aware of her
one morning in Year 8 when I was sat, bored out of my skull, in geography. I found myself gazing up at a picture on the wall of an oxbow

lake and noted that it was drawn by a 'J. Manford'. I thought to myself, I didn't draw that. I'd been at school just over a year and I would definitely remember drawing this U-shaped body of water.

After a bit of detective work, I discovered Julie and thought she would be as interested as I was to know that we were distant kin. She wasn't. But in the middle of talking to her I noticed her friend, Amanda. I was only thirteen but I was besotted with this girl for the next two years. I chose my options to suit hers and worked really hard in maths simply so I could get into the top set and sit in the same room as her three times a week. It's a great motivator to work harder in maths so you can see the pretty girl more often. I think that was the original idea behind having Carol Vorderman on *Countdown*.

It was far from the chatty relationship I had with Lucy. I was in speechless awe of her. As a boy at that age you hold girls up in such high esteem; they are like goddesses, out of reach. I was once watching her walk home from school when, because she was sapping so much of my attention, I walked into a lamppost. Still, it made her laugh. I was helpless – Amanda was the girl for me. Apart from the fact she was never the girl for me.

Though I say these girls were out of reach, that wasn't wholly because of their goddess-like beauty. It was also because as a young boy you don't have the confidence to talk to them; terrified that your voice will break halfway through asking them if they want to go and watch *Jumanji* at the Cine City in Withington.

There was one lad who didn't have the fear and led the way where others feared to tread – my old friend Clifford Frame. It's not that he was a junior, well-groomed Lothario either. In fact, he was just as odd and awkward-looking as the rest of us – a skinny little thing whose mum cut his hair with a pair of blunt scissors and a cereal bowl. But one day he just went straight up to one of the fittest girls in school, Karen Atkinson (you know the girl who has boobs before anyone else so immediately becomes a source of wonder to the school's male population), and asked her out. And she only said bloody yes.

Clifford immediately flew up several rungs of the school's social ladder. He'd gone from people not knowing his name to being discussed in the staff room. Even teachers couldn't believe it when they saw them holding hands in the playground. He became an instant hero to all us lower-runged lads.

While I certainly had the fear, the one talent I did have at school was the ability to make people laugh. It proved a useful way to keep the bullies at bay, but more importantly it was a way to get noticed by girls. I got in trouble on more than one occasion trying to make Amanda laugh in class.

We were in a lesson called PDP (Personal Development Programme) which included sex education – the moment every teacher dreaded. We were doing the classic, rolling condoms onto bananas, and the whole room was in uproar. The teacher wasn't enjoying it. When he asked, 'Are there any questions?', for the first time ever every single hand in the room went up. We all had the same question. He sighed and pointed at me. With the banana-filled condom in my hand I asked, 'Sir, who's having sex with bananas? Pervy monkeys?'

The class chuckled but it wasn't enough for me, not quite as funny as I thought it was in my head. I set about taking the inside of the banana out so all that was left inside the condom was its flaccid yellow skin. After a few more questions from the class, I put my hand up again.

'Sir, sir?' The whole class turned round as I held up my limp banana condom. 'I think my one's come already.'

As I sat in detention that night, I basked in the memory of Amanda's warm, laughing eyes.

I didn't get many detentions, to be fair, apart from a week-long one from our German teacher Mrs Muir. There was no malice involved; I wasn't trying to embarrass her. In fact, I was trying to impress. I'd walked into class and she had on a tight-fitting dress. Her belly was sticking out. Wow, I thought, she's pregnant and, sharp-eye that I was, I was the first to notice. I sat down and started to flick through my German textbook. After half an hour of making notes, I put my hand up.

'*Frau Muir, sind Sie schwanger und wenn ist ihre Baby durch?*'

I couldn't have been more proud of myself. I was beaming. The class just stared at me as Mrs Muir's face went a beautiful shade of red made up of 40 per cent embarrassment and 60 per cent anger.

I WASN'T A BAD KID. Some kids were – punching teachers and storming out of school – but for the most part we were mischievous more than violent. Most teachers knew how to deal with it. I'm sure the Physics teacher Mr Stylianou knew we called him Mr Sillyarsehole. Not terribly clever but when you're thirteen that's up there with Oscar Wilde. Miss Bullock didn't have it easy. I mean, come on, we've not even had to change that for it to be hilarious. Miss Pritt was another, although she was lovely so she managed to get kids to call her Miss Pritt-Stick rather than, well, Miss Prick, I suppose.

Mr Cockburn, of course, was doomed from the off. Yes, it may be pronounced 'Co-burn' but then you shouldn't have written it out on the blackboard, should you, sir? He ended up having a nervous breakdown primarily as a result of a lad called Nicholas leaving stickle bricks on his chair every day. When he came back he had a different air, but the kids in his class still smelt a weakness and thought they could finish him off.

It came to a head the day poor old Mr Burnt Cock was trying to show the class an episode of *Geordie Racer* on that huge black telly inside the big wooden box all schools seemed to have. During the film the telly kept turning over to *Neighbours* on BBC1, albeit a terribly fuzzy picture. Amir Shah, a lad who sat three tables down, had a Casio watch that had a remote control on it. God bless the people at Casio – they don't half make some shit. But at the time it was the most amazing piece of technology any of us had ever seen and because it was brand new, it was the last thing Mr Cockburn would guess was changing the channel. After half an hour of the telly randomly changing channels and turning its volume up and down, we were all on the floor laughing, our bellies hurting from the slapstick of Mr Cockburn turning his back and the telly switching over to Helen Daniels talking to Jim. Mr Cockburn finally realised it must have been one of us and properly lost it – just as the head teacher came by to check on what was happening.

'Why don't you all just fuck right off, you little shits!' he shouted as he grabbed his coat.

We, of course, all started working really hard, which made Mr Cockburn look even more mental.

'Mr Cockburn, can I have a word?' the head shouted sharply.

'You can fuck off as well, you bald bastard.'

With that he pushed past our bald head teacher and was never seen again.

ULTIMATELY, though, no amount of classroom comedy could help. Amanda and me never got together. I'm pretty sure she knew I was infatuated with her but she did her best to dissuade me without actually telling me to sod off. Little did I know, though, that through my devotion to her another infatuation was developing. In all the time I was running up a dead end, someone was chasing me – Amanda's younger sister, Hannah.

Hannah was in the year below and I had truly never noticed her. She'd tried to speak to me on several occasions but I had ignored her, oblivious to anything else when in the presence of Amanda. I had basically treated her the same way her sister had treated me, which, as you know yourself, doesn't put you off but makes you work harder for what you want.

Finally the penny dropped. I went out with Hannah for over six months and she was the first girl to break my heart.

Six months doesn't seem so long now, does it? I'll tell my family that we're going on holiday in six months or there's six months' tax left on the car: as an adult it's just a short passage of time where you do roughly the same things each day: work, rest and watch *Loose Women*. But when you're fifteen, six months is a massive amount of time, especially to spend in a relationship. It was the equivalent of nearly eight per cent of my life at that time (I told you I'd worked hard in maths; cheers, Amanda).

It was a typical teenage relationship where we spent most evenings after school in her parents' front lounge snogging – occasionally coming up for breath and Jaffa Cakes. It's a time of exploration and working out which things do what. 'Ah, if I press that she makes that noise, if I rub that her leg quivers, if I put this in there, I get a slap in my face.' I soon forgot about her older sister.

I don't know why she broke up with me. I was a nice lad, I never touched anything I wasn't supposed to and I was always respectful to her parents. In fact, all my life I've often got on better with girls' mums than I did with my girlfriends. At any kid's birthday party, while my pals were in the lounge and bedrooms trying to finger someone, I'd be in the kitchen helping their mum load the dishwasher and chatting about *Corrie*.

One sunny summer afternoon, post exams, I walked to Hannah's house to see if she wanted to go to the cinema. She lived nearly two miles from mine but I was young and in love. Her mum answered the door and we had a good old gossip about nothing and then Hannah came out and we walked to McDonald's in Chorlton. I thought it was odd that she hadn't held my hand but I put it down to the warm weather.

As we sat down with our Big Mac meals, I asked her what was wrong.

'I don't want to go out with you any more.'

Bloody hell. Don't beat around the bush, love. She wasn't messing about. None of this 'It's not you it's me' bollocks – just straight in for the kill.

'Why?' I pleaded, still punch drunk from her revelation.

'It's just not working any more. We don't do anything or go anywhere,' she said.

'What do you mean, we're in McDonald's!' I exclaimed.

'Exactly, this is the only place we ever come!'

'Well, I'm fifteen, I've got no money to take you anywhere else. I just bought this meal with the last of my paper-round money,' I said.

'Well, my friend Charlene's boyfriend takes her out all the time.'

'He's nineteen and works at Kwik-Fit. He can afford to take her out.' I couldn't understand what was going on but I felt tears in my eyes and heard my voice break halfway through saying the word Kwik-Fit.

I soon worked out that the money and going out was just an excuse and the real reason was because she just didn't love me like I loved her.

I was crying in McDonald's, using their rough serviettes to wipe away my tears. Hannah got up and left as I chased after her, and for the first time in my life I left a McDonald's meal uneaten on the table.

I walked her most of the way home as the weather changed to match my heart, from baking hot sun to wind and rain. She turned left at the Four Banks in the centre of Chorlton and said goodbye. I sat on the kerb outside the Abbey National and sobbed, shoppers passing by ignoring this rain-sodden little boy who'd just had his heart ripped from his chest for the first time in his life.

At home I sat in the garden, still feeling the rain pouring down on my head. The dog came out and licked my hand and my dad came out with a towel. He didn't ask why I was crying or why I was so upset, he just brought me into the house and dried my hair and face. He gave me the biggest hug I'd ever had and just held me while I sobbed.

My brother Stephen came in.

'What's up with him, broke up with his boyfriend?' He laughed, but he suddenly realised no one was laughing with him.

It must be hard for adults when kids talk about heartbreak and relationships to not just think, what do you know? You're only a kid. But of course it's all relative. When you have nothing to compare it to it's the worst thing in the world. My dad knew that; he'd been fifteen, he'd had his heart broken, and as I rested my sobbing head against his shoulder in the kitchen he told me it was all going to be fine.

He even dropped in the classic line: 'There's plenty more fish in the sea, son.'

To which I distinctly remember replying, 'Yeah, but there's not many dolphins.' I don't exactly know what I meant. I think I might have been trying to say that although there may be millions and billions of fish out there, the truly special ones, the most sought-after ones, are often the most difficult to come by and even harder to keep hold of. Or that she had a brilliant blow hole, I can't remember now.

That night I was babysitting at my Auntie Kathleen's house in Clayton for her eight-year-old daughter, Kirsty. By the time I'd got there on the bus she was fast asleep and Auntie Kathleen and Uncle Dave were on their way out for a gig. They were playing at a country and western convention in Wigan and would be out till the early hours.

I sat on their big blue comfy sofa and wept until I fell asleep. While asleep I had one of those annoying dreams, you know the ones where everything is fine? I dreamt that Hannah hadn't dumped me and that my life was the same as it was that morning. I don't know if it's the brain's way of helping you through upsetting moments in your life but it's no bloody help at all. Like after loved ones die, you sometimes dream that they're alive and you spend some time with them, and then you wake up to the reality and you have to go through another mini-grieving period again.

I woke up feeling great and actually rang Hannah's house. She answered and was very short with me. I made up some excuse that I was just checking to see if she got back all right but really I was hoping she'd had a change of heart and we could go back to McDonald's and finish our meal, even though it'd be well cold by now.

That night, as I slept on my auntie's couch, my face stuck to the cushions with tears and snot, what I didn't know was that in a couple of years I would lose my virginity on that very same couch. So, you know, swings and roundabouts and all that.

Chapter 10

Best Day
of My Life

RECENTLY A JOURNALIST doorstepped my dad at his home and asked him about me. Now, my dad hardly talks to his friends and family so what on earth he was doing talking to a stranger, I'll never know. The reporter must have gone for his Achilles heel: the pride he has for his kids. I don't know if the journalist tickled up the story to make my childhood sound more desperate, or if my dad was trying to impress with his own exaggerated storytelling ability, but what transpired has since embarrassed my dad at several family dos.

The article started: 'Growing up in Manchester's notorious gang-land territory, dubbed "The Triangle of Death", the chubby comedian grew up in poverty.'

Now, I'll admit it wasn't a 'leave your doors open' kind of place but it certainly wasn't 'The Triangle of Death'. In fact, until I read the phrase 'Triangle of Death' in the paper, I'd never even heard of it! Actually when I put 'Triangle of Death' into Google, it told me it was a violent area south of Baghdad during the second Gulf War.

My favourite bit of the piece was undoubtedly: 'Jason was keen on sport; he once did a trial for Stockport County.' I had to ring my dad when I read that, and was amazed to hear he'd completely rewritten history, not just in the newspaper, but in his own mind.

'Dad, why did you tell the paper I did a trial for Stockport County?'

'Well, you did, remember? You and your brothers went down and did a trial at Edgely Park.'

'No, Dad, that was an open day. A Stockport County open day. It cost us a fiver and we spent the day playing on a bouncy castle, running round traffic cones on a soggy field and taking penalties against Eddie Large.'

'Oh, right.'

This led me to thinking back to the time my Uncle Brendan rang me and asked me to play for his Sunday League football team, the Throstle's Nest FC; and how disappointed he was when I eventually donned a pair of shinpads and a tatty green top, three sizes too big. I was rubbish. I mean, in my head I was brilliant. I have a great footballing brain. I can see the pass, the shot, the tackle, but there's a wire missing between brain and foot, and it's an important one.

Every man has the feeling as he's growing up that one day he'll play for England. Then you downgrade it: maybe I'll just play for Manchester City. Then you think, hey, as long as I can play occasionally in the lower leagues, I'll be happy. OK, Sunday League it is then. Ah, forget it, it's freezing, I'd rather stay here in bed and watch last night's *Match of the Day*. The moment in your life when you realise you'll never be a footballer is a momentous one. It's the moment you grow up. The moment you think, right, I'd better get thinking of a trade to fall back on. But the moment a footballer who's younger than you breaks into the England squad, that's a real heartbreaker. I said to my dad recently, 'Cor, I can't believe Paul Dickov [hilariously named ex-Manchester City striker who was a hero of mine as a teenager] is a manager now. You know you're getting old when players who were once your boyhood heroes are now managers and pundits.'

'Count yourself lucky,' Dad said, 'most of mine are statues.'
Touché old man, touché.

The player that broke my young dreams was Michael Owen.
Although a little older than me, Owen burst onto the international
scene at the age of eighteen years and fifty-nine days. At the time I was
sixteen years and 257 days and wasn't even close to playing for the
school team, never mind making my England debut. Actually, come to
think of it, that's not strictly true. I played for the school team once,
but only once.

I was never the first to be picked for teams in games lessons, but
not last either – just comfortably in the middle. We used to play with
a tennis ball at break time, no managers, no coaches, and certainly no
tactics. Just sixty-eight kids running after a tiny sphere of soggy green
fur as the rest of the school found their pocket of the playground to
inhabit, some smoking in the bushes, some catching up on homework
in the library and others getting felt up by the school gates. You never
saw that on *Grange Hill*.

But not us: we played football every chance we got. They call it
grass-roots-level football, but we didn't even have grass. Just concrete
with stones on it. Not many sliding tackles I can tell you about but
plenty of magical moments, goals scored, shots saved. No worries over
goal-line technology or female referees; our only concern was whether
we should we have 'fly goalkeeper' or 'last man back'. They were the
real footballing issues.

I played three times a day yet I could never get in the school team.
I'd been for the annual try-outs but was never good enough. You'd
think that playing every day would somehow improve your skills but
alas, no, not even a nightly game of Three-and-In or Wembley was
enough to get me in that hallowed shirt of Oakwood High School.

Imagine playing so often yet never improving. I was like a young Emile Heskey.

But then, one cold November afternoon, it changed. It was the greatest moment of my school life but it was also the last time I played football at school.

I was making my way across the playground after school when I heard my name being shouted. Of course, I didn't turn round as I presumed it was one of the resident detention kids coming out at the same time and I didn't fancy getting my shoes stood on or my bag thrown into the river Mersey.

'Manford, Manford.'

Eventually I turned round, as the voice was old and Scottish rather than young and Manc. It was my PE teacher Mr Hamilton.

'Yes, sir?' I replied.

'Have you got your kit with you?' he asked in his raspy Scottish voice, more Rab C. Nesbitt than Sean Connery.

'Yes, sir, I had PE earlier on.'

'Good, come with me.'

I knew I had to get home for tea but was also intrigued as to what he wanted. The PE teacher talking to me, that was unheard of. The drama teacher, yes, maybe the English teacher at a push, but the PE teacher, he only spoke to the kids who were of some use to him.

I followed his brisk pace to the school football pitch where I saw a rival school team warming up. There were a few parents knocking about the edges, and the odd member of staff, but where were our boys?

I caught up with Mr Hamilton and followed him into the changing rooms, where ten of the lads were sat fully dressed in their kits, all with stony looks on their faces. 'Get into your kit, son, you're playing for the school today.'

There had been a flu outbreak at school and the team was missing several of its usual players. They were down to ten men and Mr Hamilton had gone on a search of the school to see if there were any other boys who he could rope into playing. I guess my extra hour and a half in the library reading up on photosynthesis had paid off. As they say, sometimes you make your own luck, but sometimes loads of kids just get flu.

The smile on my face could not be wiped off even by ten of my peers looking so dejected you'd have thought their new eleventh man was Stephen Hawking. Although my beaming smile soon dropped from my face when I noticed who was sat in the number eight shirt, staring at me with what I can only describe as rage in his eyes. Eric Obasi was the school bully. He was regularly suspended or in detention. The only thing that stopped him getting expelled was his starring role up front for the school team.

He was a bruiser of a man. And yes, I'm using the word man. Even though I was fourteen years old, he looked like a man to me. He was well over six foot, with dark hair, dark skin, dark eyes and a dark soul. He terrified me from the age of eleven. I'd mainly been able to stay out of his way as there were much more easy to bully kids than me, but that didn't mean he was pleased to see me pull on the number ten shirt beside him. He leant over.

'Every time you get the ball just give it straight to me,' he said menacingly. I just carried on putting on my shinpads, as another lad, David Lyndsey, was complaining to Mr Hamilton.

'Sir, these shinpads you gave me are odd.'

'What you on about, lad?'

'One's a large and one's a regular.'

'That's left and right, you daft wee sod.'

It wasn't the brightest team in the world.

I could not contain my excitement that I was part of the team. The game kicked off and I was running around like an excited kid who'd just made the school football team, if you can imagine such a thing. You know when you hear a commentator say, 'That's good to see, he really plays with a smile on his face,' well, I was so excited I had a smile on my face and a semi in my shorts. It was fantastic. Although none of the players would pass to me and I didn't get a touch of the ball for the first forty-five minutes, it was still the greatest game of football I'd ever played.

It got to half time and we were one–nil down. Mr Hamilton got us to gather round and shouted at us. Everyone was looking serious apart from me, who was still smiling like a simpleton, sweating like hell.

I couldn't believe I was getting told off alongside ten of my team mates. My team mates. It was the best telling off I'd ever got. Mr Hamilton told us to go and score a goal or something; I can't remember his exact words of encouragement but I felt suitably inspired.

We ran back out onto the pitch. I managed two touches of the ball, both of which I passed straight to Eric, and things were going OK. Then the most momentous moment of my life thus far happened. Thirty yards away from goal the ball came bouncing to me from a cleared corner. I managed to control it on my chest, and then onto my knee as I looked up. The keeper was off his line. I could hear Eric screaming in my direction 'to me, pass to me' but my brain, my foot-balling brain, told me not to. The wire that connected my brain to my foot, which was ordinarily defunct, had managed to attach itself for a split second. And in that split second, I volleyed the ball thirty yards. The keeper stumbled back, Mr Hamilton was shouting something excitedly in Scottish, the ball dipped down, Eric was still telling me to pass it even though the ball was no longer in my control, and my eyes followed the ball as it fell over the keeper's head and into the net. I'd scored on my debut. Take that, Michael Owen.

All the times I'd scuffed the ball, passed it to the opposition, kicked the floor instead of the ball, or the time that Casey hit me clean in the face on a freezing December morning and my nose swelled up to Elephant Man proportions couldn't take this moment away from me. Mr Hamilton was having some sort of seizure because his master-stroke of picking a random kid in a desolate playground had paid off; he must have felt like Sir Alf Ramsey for a few moments over there on that touchline.

I turned to my fellow players, who were celebrating as well. Football is a great leveller; all men are equal; race, religion, popularity, money, status go out of the window when they're on a football pitch. They are a team, a team of men – of brothers, connected by a single desire, the desire to win. Just as these feelings ran through my body, I turned and saw Eric Obasi. He punched me full in the face with the words, 'I told you to pass it to me, you little shit.'

I'd like to tell you we won the game and I became a regular player for the school team before injuring myself in a cup final in front of some scouts who signed me up for Manchester City. But no. We got beat 4–1 and I had a very bloody nose and a terrible headache. I got home, smiling through the blood-soaked cotton wool protruding from my nose. My mum came to the door almost in tears, as I was over three hours late and looked a sight. 'What the hell happened to you?'

'Mum,' I said, 'I just had the best moment of my whole life. What's for tea?'

Chapter 11

Extended Family

'ASHES TO ASHES, dust to dust...'

Mum hugged her two closest children as she sobbed and the rain fell relentlessly.

There's no sadder sight than a family huddled together in the cold winter rain, mourning the passing of a loved one ripped from the bosom of his home too young and too soon.

Families are a great source of security and the only way to get through some of the saddest times in our lives. It's important to have someone who loves us unconditionally no matter how stupid we've been. Of course every so often families fall out and you need to find your love source somewhere else. That's where pets come in. Pets, I'm proud to say, have always been a part of the Manford family ethos. We love our animals. Some we've loved more than others, some have left us when they found a better offer but most have been downright strange.

Our first love was a dog called Rene. She was a stray border collie cross who followed us home one day and was happy to stay with us for the next eleven years. She was everything you could ask for in a dog: cute, loyal, protective and brave. Scared of nothing, she was. A family up the road had a Dobermann but Rene used to chase it off if it came near me and my brothers.

The only questionable thing about her was her morals. Quite frankly, she was a bit of a slag.

Whenever she was on heat our house would be besieged by every randy male dog for miles and she'd do anything to get out of the house, and we'd only realise when a random kid would knock on the door and tell us that 'there's a dog stuck inside your dog up the ginnel'.

Walking to school became a nightmare as we were followed by packs of sex-starved dogs. They would rush up and hump your leg if you dared to stop. It was bad enough for me, Stephen and Dad – it was only our legs they tried to rut against – but Colin, being a lot smaller, would sometimes be sent sprawling under the weight of these canine Casanovas. To be honest, me and Stephen found this piss funny but Dad didn't, cursing at them in the street, with threats of castration 'get off the lad's face you dirty bastards'.

Despite Dad's best efforts at protecting Rene's honour, and believe me he tried, running all over the estate with buckets of water and a broom, the inevitable happened and Rene fell pregnant. Being an optimistic family, we made the best of it. Dad thought the father of the impending pups was an Alsatian called Bodie, and if your dog was going to get pregnant then Bodie was the one you'd want. He was a good-looking, intelligent dog, from a posh house on Withington Road, so at least the pups would be middle class, we reasoned. Rene had the pups. Twelve of them in total and no two looked the same. Like I said, low morals.

Around the same time that Rene followed us home we got two budgies, both light blue, so naturally we called them Manchester and City. Every evening we would open the cage and let them fly around the living room for an hour. City would have a little fly around then go back to the comfort and safety of her cage; Manchester on the other hand was a bit of a rebel and wouldn't go back to the cage until he was absolutely knackered and had to be picked up and placed back in by hand, which ultimately lead to his downfall. One evening after his lengthy exercise period, he landed on the carpet. Rene, being somewhat curious, wandered over to him and gave him a friendly pat with her paw. Manchester went down heavy. You could tell it was serious and he wasn't faking it, like when a footballer does his hamstring.

We shouted to Mum and Dad, and soon Manchester was in a shoebox on the way to the vet's. An hour or so later Mum and Dad were back, with Manchester, his little leg in a plaster cast. He was expected to make a full recovery.

It was a couple of days later when me, Dad and my brothers had been to the match. On entering the house, we could see Mum bent over the kitchen table sobbing.

'What's wrong, Mum?' we asked.

Our tearful mother looked up from what she was doing, which was giving a CPR to a rather sodden Manchester.

'Give up, love, he's gone,' Dad said, touching her shoulder, which brought more wails from our heartbroken mother.

With Manchester in a plaster cast and no longer able to sit on his perch Mum was worried he wouldn't be able to drink so she'd put a bowl of water on the bottom of the cage where, to quote my dad, 'The poor little bastard must have fell in and drowned.'

So Manchester the drowned budgie became the first inhabitant of our very own pet cemetery in the back garden. We got rid of City soon after: Mum couldn't stand the feeling of guilt whenever she looked at her, one morning she swears the surviving budgie tweeted 'Murderer' at her as she hoovered the living room. I think it was Manchester's fate which prompted my mum to begin training to be a nurse, so his watery death wasn't in vain although she still can't have Trill in the house.

The first pets which were actually mine, as opposed to the family's, were two hamsters. I christened them Thelma and Louise. They were adorable little things, the very picture of innocence. Except after a week I woke up, went to the cage and found them both dead. A friend of the family told my dad they'd probably shagged themselves to death; apparently this is quite common in the hamster population. Turns out it wasn't Thelma and Louise but Thelma and Louis.

To lose my two hamsters was bad enough but what made it worse was my brother's hamster, Taz, which had been bought at the same time, lived for bloody years. It was a huge, like a hamster version of Charles Bronson, the infamous convict. It was constantly working out in its cell. Sorry, I mean cage. Using its wheel as a treadmill, doing pull-ups on the roof of the cage and weight-lifting with slices of apple – it never stopped. We never handled him much, not after he took a chunk out of Dad's finger. Dad was convinced it was in fact not a hamster at all but some form of tailless rat.

It was after my mum qualified as a nurse that the pet situation escalated. You see, she took this job as matron of an old people's nursing home and if any of the newly admitted geriatric residents were having difficulty rehousing their pets, Mum would step in and offer to have them.

At this time, as well as the ever-present Taz, we got a new dog, Ghost, a white boxer, so called because my dad said there wasn't a ghost of a chance we would be getting a second dog. Mum thought otherwise. She worked overtime for months, and then one night she took me, Stephen, Colin and Dad out for a meal at the Blue Moon curry house in Withington. After the meal she said she had a surprise for us: she then produced four season tickets for Maine Road, before matter-of-factly announcing she had bought a white boxer puppy for £400.

So that was Ghost and Taz. Then Mum came home from work one night and said, 'Manny, how do you fancy getting some kittens?'

'You're joking, we're not having kittens, and that's final.'

The kittens arrived the next day – Milo and Gizmo. Ghost took to them straight away and wanted to play; unfortunately the feeling wasn't mutual and these two little bundles of fluff scratched the hell out of poor Ghost's face, as they would continue to do intermittently over the next few years.

Next was the fish tank.

When Mum raised the possibility of getting one, Dad agreed in theory, thinking it would be nice to have on a shelf of the wall unit. The fish tank arrived that afternoon. It was enormous, a good five foot long and two foot deep. It would become the dominant piece of furniture in our living room for the next couple of years. Well stocked too: there must have been thirty fish of varying species in it. A real thriving community; it was like having a city of fish in the house. Dad even took to turning his chair to face it, saying it was more interesting than most of the crap on TV.

But this idyllic situation wouldn't last. It was not long after we added a couple of our own fish to the fishy metropolis, bought from a pet shop in Chorlton. One morning as I switched on the fish tank light I noticed the first body – one of our larger fish was dead. Not just dead, savaged. There were huge chunks bitten out of it.

'I bet it was that bloody shark thing Stephen got,' said Dad.

Our Stephen had indeed bought some type of shark – he's been obsessed with the things since he was scared by *Jaws* when he was about four – but the one he bought was only four inches long and quite harmless-looking, or so we thought.

Next morning two more bodies were found in the tank, also savaged, but this time Stephen's shark was one of the victims. So it went on: some mornings there were bodies, some mornings nothing. It was as if our little city was being stalked by a serial killer, Dad called him Jack the Kipper, and like his Victorian namesake, we never found the fish responsible.

Mum never even told Dad about the arrival of our next animal refugee. She just came in from work and said, 'I've got some things in the back of the car, Manny – can you bring them in?'

Dad went out and we heard, 'What the fuck!'

Dad came in carrying a three-foot-high cage in which sat the most malevolent-looking bird you'd ever set eyes on.

'What's this?' asked Dad.

'A cockatiel,' said Mum.

'I can see that! What's it doing here?'

'Well, there was an old lady and she…'

Out of all the pets we've had, I just couldn't take to this bird. None of us could. It had no redeeming features. It would sit there sullenly all day long, looking down on you with its cold little eyes – I think it just couldn't believe it was living in a council house. Then as soon as you turned your attention to the telly, it would start this horrible screeching. Another thing it did was get on the floor of the cage and whistle the dog over. Ghost, being the gullible type, would fall for it every time. As soon as she put her nose to the cage bars, this evil little avian bastard would peck it, with its razor-sharp, oversized beak. It stayed with us for twelve long months, by which time we had all had enough of it and let one of Dad's mates take it home. Sucker.

After psychotic fish and a cantankerous cockatiel you'd have thought we'd strike lucky with our next pet. But no, we ended up with two really rough rabbits. My little sister was Mum's excuse for bringing them home.

'Wouldn't it be nice if we had a rabbit for Danielle?'

'I suppose so,' said Dad, 'but I bet it will be me that ends up looking after it.'

'Right, so when they get here...'

'They?'

'Yeah. There's two of them. So cute.'

'You can't have two of them.'

'Why not?'

'Because they'll breed like rabbits! That's why not.'

'Don't be daft, they're from the same family.'

'Rabbits don't give a toss about that, love.'

'Well, they're both girls.'

They weren't, they were both boys, and we named them Jake and Elwood, after the Blues Brothers. At first everything was hunky-dory, then one day when I was getting ready for work I heard a commotion in the back garden. I looked out to see the hutch bouncing all over the grass. At first I thought a cat or a dog had got in to the rabbits. I ran out and opened the hutch, but nothing could have prepared me for what happened next. This giant ball of fluff came flying out the hutch – it was Jake and Elwood knocking seven bells of rabbit shit out of each other, and there was blood and fluff everywhere. Ghost did a runner as soon as she saw them, closely followed by the cats. I don't know if you've ever seen rabbits scrapping but believe me they're bloody vicious.

Me and Mum eventually separated them, putting Elwood in the kitchen and Jake back in the garden to keep them apart.

'Right, Jay,' said Mum, 'you'll have to keep your eye on the rabbits for me.'

'But I've got work.'

'Look, you're late anyway now – just phone in and tell them.'

Can you imagine that? 'Sorry I can't come in today – my rabbits are fighting.'

We ended up getting one of my uncles to build us a massive run in the back garden, the only problem being we had to let the three of them out at different times. That's right, three of them, as we'd now acquired Bubbles, a charmingly stereotypically female bunny. We couldn't let Jake and Elwood out together because they'd fight like rabbit brothers who hated each other. We couldn't let Bubbles out with either of them because quite frankly they'd rape her. What was meant to be my little sister's pet corner was more like a B wing in a maximum security penitentiary.

Sure enough, one of them escaped. It was Elwood; he chewed a hole in the wooden panel fencing behind a tiny poster of Rita Hayworth. Dad reckoned he must have been planning it for months. So off we all went, searching for him. As me and Dad were looking, two little girls came up to us and said, 'You looking for a rabbit? There's a big white one out the front.' We ran around and sure enough it was Elwood sitting there on his hind legs, bold as you like. As soon as he saw us he was off, with us chasing after.

As we ran after him, Dad looked up and saw a few gangster type lads who loitered on our road from time to time.

'Lads, stop that rabbit,' he shouted. Only my dad would look at these possible criminals, all hoodied up with bright white trainers and no doubt concealing a knife, and think that they were the sort of people who would help out.

But he's obviously a better judge of character than I am because at once they spread out to stop Elwood's retreat. Elwood veered right and shot down a ginnel with me, Dad, two little girls and three teenage hoodies in hot pursuit.

Though out of breath, Dad laughed. 'Ha, it's a dead end, that knobhead.' Everybody looked up at him to see if he realised he'd just called a rabbit 'knobhead'.

So we stopped running, thinking it was just a matter of picking him up. As we approached the entrance we heard screams from the hoodies who'd run ahead of us, then Elwood darted out, straight past us and into the night.

'Why didn't you pick up the bloody rabbit?' Dad asked the pretend gangsters.

'We tried,' they apologised. 'The fucking thing went for us.'

He was on the run for a week. In fact we had given him up as lost and had already explained to a tearful Danielle that he was probably living happily with a colony of wild rabbits rather than nestling in some wily fox's belly as Uncle Gary had rather tactlessly suggested. Then one day he was back, just sat there in the garden. Whatever experience he had had out there, he was a rather more subdued Elwood after that.

Which brings me to the last hutch in the run. That's right, there were four. If Jake and Elwood were your ordinary cons, and Bubbles was in protective custody, this fourth hutch was psycho wing, for it held the most evil creature we ever had. A guinea pig called Nigel. Alongside him in the hutch was a timid thing called Colin, my sister had named him after our brother, but he may as well have been called Victim.

'Well, I'd better take care of the livestock,' my dad said one afternoon as he gathered what he needed to feed the rabbits and guinea pigs. He grabbed some carrots and apples and headed out.

Only moments later, he walked back in, his face ashen.

'Jason, come and look at this.'

We walked out to the hutches and squatted down.

'Look.' He pointed to the corner of the hutch. Colin was lying there, his throat ripped out.

'Jesus!' I said. 'What's done that? A fox?'

Dad didn't say anything, he just pointed to the other end of the hutch. We both looked. There sat Nigel, his mad red eyes staring, his face all covered in blood, and as we stared he seemed to pull his lips back and grin, making that horrible noise similar to the one Hannibal Lecter does in *Silence of the Lambs*.

'That little bastard must never get near the rabbits,' Dad said. I agreed.

'Or the kids, Dad,' I suggested.

'Oh, yeah, or the kids,' he agreed.

That night Mum phoned from work.

'How's everything there, Manny?' she asked, wanting her nightly update.

My dad replied matter-of-factly. 'All right mainly – tea was OK, we had beans and sausages on toast; your mum rang to see if you could take her to Bury market tomorrow; oh, and Colin's dead.'

I think Mum must've dropped the phone but when she came back on Dad quickly explained that my brother was OK.

THE CLOSING EPISODE I'll give you in the Manford pet soap opera was when Elwood died on Boxing Day night a couple of years later. Dad went out to feed him and he was dead in his hutch, frozen solid. We weren't going to bother with one, but my little sister Danielle insisted we gave him a proper funeral.

Me, Dad and Stephen dug a hole in the centre of the cemetery area using dessert spoons because we couldn't find a spade. Colin checked the CD rack for something appropriate to play, Danielle and Niall wrote a poem, 'Ode to Elwood', and Mum looked for some candles (well, she is Catholic). Elwood was wrapped in an old beach towel and lowered into his quite large grave, bearing in mind he was now as big and stiff as a bread bin. Then we stood there, all seven of us, Robbie Williams's 'Angels' playing in the kitchen, the rain pouring down on a freezing-cold Boxing Day night. Mum, Danielle and Niall sobbing and holding candles, Dad, me, Stephen and Colin saying what a great rabbit Elwood was. Now you may not think Elwood was a particularly nice rabbit, and you'd be right. But he was family.

Chapter 12
Hard Labour

PEOPLE OFTEN ASK ME, 'What do you think you'd be doing today if you weren't a comedian?' To tell you the truth, I haven't a clue. Having said that, there are some jobs I can rule out for certain. Removals for one.

It was spring 1997, and I'd just turned sixteen. My GCSEs were finally done and dusted and although it was still term time I'd unofficially left school. I woke up to the warm May sun shining through my bedroom window. The house was quiet, Dad was at work and my brothers were at school. Mum was still asleep, having a well-deserved lie-in on one of her rare days off, so to all intents and purpose I had the house to myself.

Whistling, I walked downstairs, opened the kitchen cupboard door and poured myself a bowl of cornflakes. I sat on the couch in front of *Jerry Springer*, remote to myself, school finished, pressure off, house quiet, weighing up my options on how to spend this most glorious of days.

'DING............................DONG.' The house had faulty wiring and a dodgy doorbell. There was an unnaturally long pause between the ding and the dong, where you knew the dong was coming, but still that pause always irritated me every time. But I wasn't going to let it ruin my first day out of full-time education.

I put my cornflakes down and answered the door. In flounced Barry, my mum's gay friend. I know 'flounced' seems like I'm stereotyping but, trust me, Barry 'flounced'. He was a big lad, like a mix of Dolph Lundgren and Alan Carr, if you can imagine such a thing.

'Morning, Jay, where's ya mam? Woo, love the boxers. Still in bed? Sharon, get up, you lazy mare, I'll put the kettle on. Guess who just passed his driving test?' This was all said without pausing for a breath.

'Congratulations,' I muttered, closing the door behind him and heading back to my cereal.

Barry and Mum sat drinking coffee in the kitchen while I went upstairs and got dressed. As I came down, I caught a little of Barry's soap opera of a life. It seemed two of his friends had had a row, 'a lovers' tiff' as Barry said, except this lovers' tiff had resulted in one friend stabbing the other to death. Does that sound like something you would describe as a lovers' tiff? No, me neither. Sounds more like manslaughter but, hey, semantics.

So with one friend dead and the other on remand in Strangeways, and due to be there for a considerable length of time, it had fallen to our mutual friend to sort out their affairs.

One of his jobs was clearing out their council flat before handing back the keys. It seemed he'd almost finished this somewhat macabre task as he nattered on to my mum.

'There's just some odds and sods left. Oh and a lovely cooker.'

Mum's ears pricked up. She loves anything for free – even if she was sat not two metres from our perfectly good cooker.

'A cooker? Is it working?'

'Course it is, I only ate round there last month, but if you want it, it has to be today cos I'm handing the keys in.'

'Well, what are we waiting for? Let's go.'

I turned to sneak back upstairs but there just wasn't time to save myself.

'Jason, come and help me and Barry get this cooker from Barry's dead mate's flat.'

I should've said no right there but, well, it's your mum, innit? What ya gonna do, eh? She went to get ready while Barry and I went to put some petrol in his car.

The quarter-mile drive to the garage was uneventful, barring Barry making some crude remarks about sleeping policemen. But as we approached the petrol station forecourt, I was suddenly worried. Cycling aimlessly around the forecourt were four local 'gangsters' from the Nell Lane estate. Nell Lane was so rough it was twinned with Basra. The BBC once went there to film a documentary about inner-city incest and had their entire camera and lighting equipment robbed on the first day. Obviously it's easier being light-fingered when you've got six of them on each hand.

I sort of knew these lads from school. I didn't like them and I'm pretty sure they didn't like me. And I was pretty sure sitting in a car with a gay Big Foot wasn't going to do my street cred any good – I looked like a rent boy. But I thought to myself, no, that's not fair – just because Barry is gay, I shouldn't be embarrassed to be with him in public in front of these rough types. It doesn't make me gay by association and even if they think that, that's their own small-mindedness, not mine.

Barry got out of the car in flamboyant style and flounced across the forecourt, calling back to me at the top of his voice: 'Fill her up, Jay, I'll go and pay. Ooooh, that rhymes that does.'

I put my head in my hands and waited.

The mountain-bike mobsters noticed him, and then me, and a chorus of jeers boomed across the forecourt.

'Hey, batty boy.'

'Ya big poof.'

'Do you take it up the arse?'

Well, you get the general idea. They weren't going on any Gay Pride marches any time soon.

Barry stopped and turned round dramatically.

Just ignore them, Barry, I thought, feeling a mixture of outrage at the abuse he had suffered and fear that they thought I was his boyfriend. But big Barry was not one for ignoring things. He walked up and faced his tormentors. With one hand on his hip and the other pointing up around his shoulder, he looked them straight in the eye and said in a voice that was half Russell Crowe and half Julian Clary, 'Oh fuck off, you little knobheads. I might be queer but at least I'm not fucking black.'

I wanted the ground to open up. Not only was I gay by association but now I was racist too. If ever the phrase 'two wrongs don't make a right' was called for, it was this very situation. I got out of the car. A racist he may be but he was my mum's friend. I'd have to at least try and stop them killing him. That's what friends' sons are for.

But instead of the prolonged savage attack I was expecting, there were only howls of delighted laughter and then a friendly, 'Yeah, nice one, batty boy,' from one of the bike boys.

It turned out they lived near Barry and that this was a daily ritual they went through with no serious harm meant to either side. I was confused but also relieved: a day which had started off so brightly wasn't going downhill as fast as I'd feared.

We arrived back home and Mum came out to the car. I leapt out to go and change my trainers.

'You'll be all right with those ones, Jason, it's not a big job,' Mum said.

'But these are my only good ones. I don't wanna get them messed up.'

'Messed up? How you going to mess them? We're only moving a cooker, for God's sake. Get in the car.'

We drove to a particularly ugly block of flats in Cheetham Hill in north Manchester.

'The flat's on the twelfth floor,' said Barry.

'Well, I hope the lift's working, I'm not walking up twelve flights of stairs,' I moaned.

Mum, Barry and I entered the foyer of the flats, the sudden gloomy chill of the entrance hall making me shiver after the bright spring sunshine outside. Barry was filling Mum in with some lurid details of his late friend's 'tiff' while I pressed the lift button and read the sprayed graffiti on the walls, mainly 'UTD' and 'City are Shit', which only increased the feeling of hostility. I just wanted to get in, get the cooker and get out. In fact I didn't want either of those first two, I just wanted to get out.

The lift arrived after what seemed an age, accompanied by a metallic groan you only get in horror films. With Barry, me and my mum inside the lift, there wasn't much space once the door had locked, and the smell of stale urine was overpowering, so it was with a sense of relief we disembarked onto the twelfth floor.

'This way, team,' said Barry, leading us down the hallway to his mate's flat. 'Voila!' he said, opening the door. 'Feel free to take anything. It's all gotta go.'

It seemed that quite a few people had already 'felt free' as there wasn't much left in the flat, save for a few clothes, books and videos. I entered slowly, feeling the odd sensation of being in a house where someone had been killed only weeks before. Mum wasn't bothered, she was straight in, picking stuff up, shaking it, flicking through books to see if anything fell out.

'Mum,' I hissed, 'pack it in.' I was somewhat unnerved by the flat; there was still yellow and black police tape everywhere and, I kid you not, an actual chalk outline of a body, complete with a massive blood-stain. It was like CSI Manchester.

'Right, I'm going home, this is wrong,' I said, heading for the door.

'Don't be daft, we're here now. There's the cooker,' said Barry. 'Come on, Jay, let's use those big muscles of yours.' He winked.

We went for it. 'Right: one, two, three, lift!' Barry grunted. Nothing budged. We couldn't get a decent grip on the cooker's grease-coated sides.

'Ah well, we'll just have to walk it. Right, Jay, you come round the front – that's it, now I'll just tilt it towards you.'

As Barry tilted the cooker, there was a scraping sound followed by the cooker door opening and banging me on the shin, then a chip pan fell out and emptied its contents of five-week-old, semi-congealed dead man's cooking oil all over my trainers.

'Bloody hell, Barry!'

'Well, I always say you can't have too much lube,' laughed Barry.

'Fuck you, Barry,' I muttered under my breath.

'You should be so lucky,' he replied.

It was like arguing with a *Carry On* film.

We eventually got the cooker out of the flat, leaving a trail of oily footprints, and pressed the button for the tiny lift.

'We're not all going to fit in,' Barry said as the lift door opened.

Mum got in the lift first. The thought of walking down twelve flights of stairs did not appeal to her. We got the cooker into the lift beside her.

'Enjoy your walk, boys,' she laughed as the lift started moving and I took my Adidas Crisp'n'Drys for a walk.

Out of breath, we got to the bottom of the stairs and went over to the lift. The doors were still closed. I pressed the button. Nothing. Well, nothing apart from a distant banging.

'I think the lift's stuck,' said Barry. 'It happens sometimes.'

'But my mum's in it,' I said, worried.

'Ah well, back upstairs, then.'

We walked back up the twelve flights of stairs and over to the lift doors, both of us shouting my mum.

'Sharon!'

'Mum!'

'The bloody lift's stuck!' came my mum's voice from somewhere below.

'Press the emergency button!' Barry said.

'Which one is it?'

The next instant the whole building was filled with the sound of alarm bells and doors opening as the residents of the flats evacuated the building.

'I think it's that one, Mum,' I said drily.

This ended my hopes of a low-profile exit from the building. Soon the alarm bells were joined by the sirens of a fire engine. Down twelve flights of stairs me and Barry trudged again. Well, I trudged, Barry suddenly had a spring in his step.

'Whee, firemen!' he squealed. The man was a walking stereotype.

The foyer was chaos as residents left and firemen entered.

'Cooee, it's us you want!' shouted Barry, waving at the men in uniform. 'His mam's trapped in the lift,' he added, pointing at me.

'Come on then,' said the chief fireman, and back up the twelve flights of bastard stairs we went again.

'Will you be getting your hose out?' Barry leched all the way up; that amount of double entendres was quite a skill.

'Barry!' I hissed.

'What? I'm just saying. I really love your helmet by the way.'

'Oh Jesus.'

The fireman glanced sideways, winked and smiled. 'Getting a bit jealous, are we?' He laughed.

'No, no, I'm not, he's not... I mean...' I stammered.

Barry thought this was hilarious and carried on flirting. My face was bright red, partly because of the increasingly risqué double entendres on offer and partly because I'd run up and down about a thousand steps and my trainers smelt like Friday night at Harry Ramsden's.

At the lift doors on the twelfth floor, a fireman turned to me and said, 'What's your mum's name then?'

Panting, I replied, 'Sharon.'

'Right, Sharon, don't worry, it's the fire brigade – we'll soon have you out of there,' he shouted down at her.

'Will you give me a fireman's lift when I get out?' said my mum.

Now both of them were flirting with the fire brigade, another fireman appeared. 'What's the situation?' he asked.

'This joker thought it'd be a good idea to send his mum down in a lift with a cooker.'

Eventually they released Mum and the cooker on the ground floor, and all that was left was to get the bloody thing in the car and leave. As Barry and I struggled out of the tower block with the cooker, we did so to sarcastic cheers and ironic applause from the temporarily evacuated residents. Oh, the shame.

We got the cooker back to ours and I went to get a wash and see if I could salvage my trainers.

Mum came up to the bathroom. 'They're ruined, aren't they?' she said sympathetically.

'You don't say!' I didn't even turn round.

'I've got something for you.'

She passed me a carrier bag.

'What?' I opened the bag

'They're Rockports,' she said. I couldn't believe it. Rockports. At the time, they were the must-have shoes at our school. Loads of the kids had them and I was relieved that I'd be leaving my Clarks at home when I started college.

'Thanks, Mum.' I gave her a kiss and we went downstairs to where my dad was struggling to get the cooker into its allotted space in the kitchen.

'It's too bleeding big, love,' my dad said. 'Help me get it in the garden, son.'

'You are joking?' I said. 'You're just gonna throw it away after all we went through today getting it?'

Mum was disappointed but practical. 'If it's too big it's too big. Ah well, you live and learn.'

'What a nightmare of a stupid day, Mum – a waste of bastard time!' I shouted.

Mum usually would have told me off for swearing but instead smiled and said, 'It wasn't a complete waste of time,' nodding towards my brand-new shoes.

'Where did you get them from?' I'd meant to ask earlier.

'Barry's mate,' she said, all innocent.

I had a sickly feeling as it suddenly dawned on me that I was wearing a pair of dead man's shoes my mum had taken from the murderer's flat. I couldn't get them off my feet quick enough.

LATER THAT SUMMER, when I'd failed to find a job myself, my mum got me off the sofa and into a family business. Another line of work I knew would never be for me.

At the time my Uncle Brendan ran his own building company. Cowboy builders is what you'd probably call them. With no formal training other than the gift of the gab, he'd managed, very successfully, mind you, to build up this business of blagging jobs and surprisingly getting them done; on time, but overpriced. Pushed by my mum, I asked him if he needed any help and he said he could always do with a shit-shifter.

So that's what the last twelve years had been for. All those mornings studying medieval crop rotation and algebra had been building up to this moment where my Uncle Brendan wanted me, for £3 an hour, to shift shit. And in some cases, it was literal.

To be fair, it didn't turn out all bad. He'd pick me up from home every morning in his van and off we'd go. It was the first time I'd felt like a real man. I had a dirty white T-shirt, a pair of paint-stained jeans and some old trainers that stank of chip fat. I had my butties in a Safeway's carrier bag and I'd climb into the van every morning at 7.30 and do a not-so-honest day's work. In fact, it felt good.

Brendan was fun. He's only eight years older than me so we've always been close. He even used to live with us when he was a teenager.

He'd often babysit, and as any right-minded fifteen-year-old babysitter looking after three brothers would, he'd often have us fighting each other for his own amusement in the living room. Armed with only one pair of boxing gloves, we'd wear one at a time and knock each other about the head like some sort of Baby Fight Club. Afterwards he'd tell us not to tell Mum but we wouldn't tell anyone; after all, the first rule of Baby Fight Club was not to talk about Baby Fight Club. The second was no punching each other in the bollocks.

He was also a prankster and would often hide around the house, jumping out at random intervals and scaring my mum or dad. His favourite was to wait in the bin cupboard in the kitchen. My dad would come home with the shopping, presuming the house was empty, only for Brendan to burst out, resulting in the week's groceries going all over the kitchen floor. Sometimes he'd get it wrong. Once he sneaked up behind my dad in the kitchen and grabbed him on his fleshy bits. My dad is the most ticklish person in the world, so naturally enough he jumped about two foot in the air. This would have been really funny if he'd not been cooking chips at the time. Not only did my dad jump two foot but so did the chip pan and so did a litre of boiling hot chip fat. I can still remember Dad trying to get his jumper and shirt off before the burning oil soaked through them, all the while cursing Brendan: 'You absolute little bell-end.'

Mum would always defend her brother. 'Come on, Manny, he's just a kid.'

'A kid? He's a fucking maniac is what he is. He could have killed me.'

But retribution would soon come. He had prepared another ambush for Dad, hiding at the bottom of the stairs with the intention of leaping out at him as he came through the front door. Which he did, only it wasn't Dad, it was Dad's best mate, Tony. Now Uncle Tony was the loveliest guy you could ever wish to meet but he came from a really hard street-fighting family who would punch first and ask questions later. His reactions were quick, like a northern Mr Miyagi. As Brendan jumped out shouting 'Boo!', Tony's right fist shot out, catching Brendan square on the nose and dropping him to the floor, knocked out cold with a broken nose.

THE GREAT THING about being out in Brendan's van (or any van for that matter), which I miss now I'm in a car all the time, was the height. You're above everybody else, surveying the world below. Maybe that's why White Van Men have a reputation for being rude and obnoxious – it's the elevation, it gives you a sense of power, you feel untouchable. Quite often on the way to work one of my uncles, Brendan or Gary or Stephen, would lean out of the passenger window and slap a cyclist on the back of the head, shouting, 'Wear a helmet, dickhead.' Then we'd laugh as we sped off at forty miles an hour, safe in the knowledge that we'd never get caught.

One sunny afternoon me and Brendan were making our way to Denton to price up a job, windows rolled down, Safeway's carrier bag making a deafening noise as a warm breeze blew through the van, radio on, R. Kelly's 'I Believe I Can Fly' blaring full blast. We pulled up to a zebra crossing.

As the four or five people made their way across the road, I noticed this one fella. His head was shaved, he was easily six foot six and built like the proverbial shithouse, his shoulders were the size of medicine balls and his head was like a pink watermelon with a face painted on it. He looked like he'd never smiled in his life. Then I realised he had a tattoo on his face. Yeah, his face. What sort of person has a tattoo on his face? I'll tell you who. Two types of people: Maoris and massive hard bastards who want a fight, and this guy was no Maori.

As he walked past the van, I heard a voice I recognised shout out. 'Oi, Baldy.'

It was Brendan.

The man mountain turned and looked at us, but Brendan was looking straight ahead, stifling his laughter. I was doing the same but it wasn't laughter I was stifling, it was fear. He looked at the few cars queuing up and decided to leave it and walk on.

For some reason Brendan decided that only risking your life once wasn't enough, so as he turned back round and went for it again.

'You bald bastard,' he said, without moving his head or mouth.

By now, this bloke's bald head has gone a shade of red. I think Dulux describe it as 'Angry as Fuck'.

As the last few people made their way over the busy zebra crossing, he looked round again. As he turned, for some reason Brendan decided that three times was the charm and out of the window, a little louder this time, he shouted, 'Oi, I'm talking to you, Baldy.'

Now this overconfidence was his downfall, as the extra words in the sentence meant the baldy in question had time to turn round and catch him in the act. The smile was wiped off Brendan's face and the colour drained from mine.

'Put your foot down, knobhead!' I screamed as the zebra crossing emptied.

Brendan obliged and soon we were cruising away from the danger site. Relieved, Brendan started laughing wildly.

'Oh, your face was a picture then! You thought I was gonna let him get us?'

'My face? You looked like you'd seen a ghost when he caught you.'

'Ha, ha, you shithouse. He was all meat anyway. He just looked hard – probably as soft as you.'

'I very much doubt that he was...'

I stopped. As I was expressing my doubt, I looked in the wing mirror on my side of the van. In the distance, and quite a distance, I saw movement.

'Bren?'

'What?'

'Erm, I think he's chasing us.'

Brendan looked in his mirror and saw the same thing. This white Mr T had started running after a van doing thirty on a main road.

'Well, he's not gonna catch us, is he? We're going thirty miles an hour and we're half a mile away.'

We both looked towards the traffic lights in front of us. They were on green. We both quietly sighed in relief. I looked back again and he was still running. Even from this distance I could feel the pent-up anger coming off him. This was a man who few had dared to test his reaction to being called a bald bastard.

As I turned back again, to our joint horror the lights changed to amber. Brendan sped up but it was no use: the car in front had decided to be a good citizen and stop. We screeched to a halt. I locked my door and started winding up my window. I looked in the mirror but couldn't see him. But I could sense him. Like the Velociraptors in *Jurassic Park*, he was close. Brendan was frantically winding up his window but with only an inch to go, two huge hands with eight sausage fingers gripped the top of the glass. We both looked over as a red, round-faced man with hate in his eyes and froth in his mouth pulled the window down, the handle spinning wildly clockwise as Brendan tried in vain to keep it closed.

'Which one of you called me Baldy?' growled Baldy.

I froze. Brendan decided honesty was the best policy and owned up. 'It was me,' he said in the highest voice I'd ever heard from a grown man. Turns out honesty isn't always the best policy.

Before he could offer any sort of apology, the man took one of his huge hands, folded it into a fist and punched the side of Brendan's head. He fell momentarily onto my lap until the seatbelt pulled him back up again like a slightly bloodied Weeble. As he sprung back up, the man clocked him again with his fist, and Brendan was out like a light.

I was still frozen in the passenger seat as the terrifying man looked me in the eye.

'Get out,' he said.

'Erm, no, I'd rather stay here, mate.' I stumbled over my words as my heart beat in my throat.

He walked around the van, shouting, 'Get out!' He got to the front and started punching the bonnet. His huge hammer-like fists were denting the metal, and he waded in on the headlights, smashing them both with his bare hands. Shards of glass and blood were everywhere. 'Get out!' he screamed.

I must say he was doing nothing to convince me to get out. I wasn't happy about getting out of the van before he started putting holes in the grille with his hands and by now I was fully convinced that I'd be staying put. I tried to bring Brendan round. He was groggy but coming to.

'Brendan, we've gotta go! Wake up! Put your foot down!' I was panicking as this Manc Mauler made his way round to my side of the van. He'd snapped the window wipers and pulled the wing mirror clean off. He head-butted my window. It cracked. If he did it again, he'd be through. Blood was pouring from his bald head. Not that I was gonna tell him he had one.

'Brendan, Brendan, wake up!'

I looked round and Brendan was up, dazed but putting the van into gear. As one more head-butt came crashing through my window, we took off. The relief poured through my body. As the engine roared into life, Brendan leant out of his window.

'You bald bastard!'

I looked at him with incredulity.

'WHAT are you doing?!'

'Well, he's not gonna catch us twice, is he?' he said, a lump the size of an apple forming on his temple.

I looked round but I didn't even have a wing mirror to see if he was in hot pursuit. We approached the motorway and we were off, both startled, one of us bruised, and sat in a van that looked like it'd been in a crash with a Volvo.

He actually caused over a grand's worth of damage, and if that man is reading this book now (highly doubtful, let's be honest) I'm sorry my uncle called you a bald bastard, but to be fair you were bald and, let's face it, a bit of a bastard.

Chapter 13

Stephen, Gary and Dave

MY DEATH-WISH Uncle Brendan was not the only 'characterful' influence I had from my mum's side of the family. As I mentioned, Uncle Stephen and Uncle Gary would often be in the white van along with Brendan.

In a family of black sheep it's often hard to find the darkest of the flock but I think most would agree it's Uncle Stephen, our family's answer to Howard Marks. Uncle Stephen was always a bit of a Jack the lad. When I was young he would turn up at our house in the early hours of the morning, more often than not with a carrier bag of stolen goods. He practised twenty-four-hour shopping years before anyone else, including the actual shops.

As our house was the closest family home to the city centre, most weekday mornings me and my brothers would come downstairs to find him asleep in the living room with a different 'girlfriend'. It must have been odd for her to wake up on a couch with a strange man while three boys under ten were sat in their boxers watching *Wacaday*. He settled down for a brief time, met a girl, moved in, had a baby – the usual journey of life – but then things started to go wrong, and in a big way. He became addicted to heroin. I don't know how or why, that's not the sort of conversation a nine-year-old is privy to no matter how many times he sits at the top of the stairs and tries to listen.

He would come to ours at all hours of the night. My bedroom was at the front of the house so at three or four in the morning, stones would start rattling against my window and I'd have to go and let him in. Each time he appeared he'd look even worse than the last time. Whereas before he'd been curled up on the sofa with an attractive girl, now he was lying alone, unconscious and twitching or walking round like a zombie. It really took the fun out of our weekends.

Sometimes the doorbell would go and we'd hear, 'Does Stephen Ryan live here?' Dad would sigh and let the police in to search the house. They came so often my parents were on first-name terms with the officers and Mum would make them a sausage butty while Dad chatted about the football.

Every time Uncle Stephen turned up he'd swear he was off the gear, but a few days later one of us would find burnt tin foil down the back of the couch and Dad would tell him to leave.

One night he 'borrowed' Mum's car and then disappeared. We got it back three days later, albeit with no windows or tyres, the bodywork severely battered and a bullet hole through the driver's door. Seemed he had tried to rip off some dealer in Moss Side. He'd got away but our car hadn't, although quite why Stephen thought he could keep a low profile while trying to scam drugs round Moss Side in a bright yellow Triumph Dolomite is anyone's guess.

The last time I saw him like that was when I was ten. My mum had sent Dad to speak to him. She couldn't do it herself, to her own brother.

'Stephen, you can't stay here any more.'

'Why not, Manny? I'm clean now, mate.'

'I'm scared the kids are going to come down one morning and find you dead.'

To be fair, that really *would* have put a dampener on *Going Live!*

We didn't see him for a few years. He was missing presumed dead I suppose, until one day this tall handsome man appeared on the doorstep and asked to see his sister. My parents throwing him out was the last straw. If you could get to a point where my parents had turned their back on you, then you really were in trouble. He'd cleaned up and actually trained as a drug rehabilitation professional, using his frightening experience to help others – sort of like when they get really good computer hackers to work for the government.

MY UNCLE GARY is one of the most miserable men I've ever met. He hates the fact there's more than two flavours of crisps.

'Salt and vinegar and ready salted. Why would anyone need any others?'

He thinks charity is pointless.

'Why bother? I sent £15 to Bob Geldof twenty-five years ago and there's still famine in Africa.'

At least he's not prejudiced; he detests everyone equally. You might be thinking, you can't say this about someone who's real – what if he reads this book? Well, I know for a fact he won't. The only thing he hates more than reading is people who read. On holiday one year I was reading a book on the beach and he accused me of 'showing off to impress girls'.

Now I don't know about you but I've never met a girl who looks past all the tanned musclebound bodies on a beach to a pale fat lad staying out of the sun in factor 50 reading *Bridget Jones's Diary* and thinks to herself, mmmm, he's a hotty.

Once, during an argument, I used a fact and he said without any irony, 'Yeah, you've learnt that from a bloody book.'

I thought, yeah I know, that's where all my information comes from.

He also accused me of only having bookshelves in my living room so I could show off to visitors all the books I've read. I'll give him that one. I mean, why do we keep books that we've read and are never going to read again other than for when people come to our homes and you can subconsciously say to them, 'See all those books, I've read them. All that information is in my head.'

If I ever complain about having a tough day, I will get no sympathy from Gary.

'You wanna live my life, mate.'

Which is true, to be fair: the man has had enough knocks, both emotional and physical, to finish most normal blokes off, yet he's still here. And for all his miserable tendencies, he's actually great company. The fact he can get riled at anything is just funny: from old people to babies, left to right wing, racists to all different races, he hates every one of you.

I used to babysit for him. Well, not for him – he's a grown man – but for his baby daughter. I was twelve and he had this really horrible scary house in Gorton. Everyone said it was haunted and I – and I don't mind admitting it – am a shit bag about this kind of thing. I'd never liked Gorton, it was rough as a bear's arse. But what specifically made me hate it was that I was once walking home from Gorton Tub (a crap indoor water park we would occasionally go to on a Saturday afternoon) and two scally lads pushed me into the canal. I know it seems unreasonable to hate a whole suburb of the city because of one incident but that water was really really dirty.

One night Gary and his girlfriend had gone out and I was left with this eight-month-old baby in her cot. She was a really good baby and often I'd get a fiver for watching telly all night and eating Nutella out of a jar – in many ways it was the best job I'd ever had.

It was halfway through *Gladiators* when the crying came over the baby monitor. It took me by surprise as it was the first time in all the weeks I'd babysat that I'd even heard her. If it wasn't for all the pictures around the living room I wouldn't even know what she looked like. I got off the couch and headed upstairs to find out what was wrong with her. The house was being renovated and only the living room had been done, so the dining room and the hallway still had wallpaper on from the sixties and the carpet wouldn't have looked out of place in a nursing home. Lit by a bare 40-watt bulb, I walked gently up the creaking stairs to the baby's room.

I nervously approached the cot and could see by the orange glow of the street light outside that the baby was fast asleep, arms in the air either side of her head like Shirley Bassey hitting a high note. Confused, I quietly left, tiptoeing out of the room like a cartoon burglar. As I reached the bottom of the stairs I heard the crying again, so up I went, over to the cot. She hadn't moved an inch.

I wasn't experienced in looking after babies. I touched her cheeks to see if she'd been crying in her sleep but they were bone dry. Completely dumbfounded I left, hoping to catch the last few minutes of *Gladiators* before *Cheers* started on Channel 4. Before my arse touched the cushion, the baby let out the loudest cry I'd ever heard. The baby monitor actually moved on the coffee table. As I got up to run upstairs, I heard her bedroom door open on the monitor. I froze. How the hell could she have opened the door? But then I realised it wasn't her who'd opened it; it was someone or something else.

I heard footsteps and then over the baby monitor I heard a voice, a man's voice.

'Don't worry, sweetheart. Daddy's here now. I'll keep you safe.'

Holy shit! I don't mind telling you that right there and then, for the first time in my life, I pissed my jeans. You hear people saying that someone was so scared they pissed themselves – well, I've been there, I've lived that fear.

I didn't know what to do. Who was I going to call? Ghostbusters? I knew one thing: you can't leave a baby with a ghost, that's a real babysitting faux pas. I ran upstairs with my eyes closed, swung open her door screaming Hail Marys, grabbed the baby from her slumber and hot-footed it downstairs, heading for the front door. Just as I approached it, the lock started to turn from the other side. My uncle walked in to see me holding his screaming daughter, in piss-wet-through jeans.

'What the bloody hell's going on?'

I threw words at him. 'Gladiators, Baby Monitor, Ghost, Stairs, John Fashanu, Baby, Man, Piss, Travelator…'

He took the baby and calmed me down. It turns out there was a rational explanation. If you're a parent you may have already worked it out. The baby receiver was set wrong and was picking up a neighbouring monitor. I had heard a doting dad caring for his baby, not a baby-napping poltergeist.

IT'S NOT JUST the Ryan uncles either. Even in-laws are a bit nutty in our family. Take my Uncle Dave who was married to my Auntie Kathleen. Remember, the ones with the couch. He was a small, rugged Glaswegian, the spitting image of Harvey Kietel – the kind of bloke who called a spade a spade and did not suffer fools gladly. Don't get me wrong, he had a heart of gold and would go out of his way to do you a favour. Me and my brothers thought the world of him, particularly our Stephen who he'd take fishing on the Manchester Ship Canal and then cook whatever they caught when they got back. There's no meal like roasted Nike trainer with a side of Sainsbury's shopping trolley.

Like most of my family he was an entertainer, he sang and played guitar, which is how he met my auntie. They were both on the same bill one night, met, got on and became a duo, both on and off stage.

One weekend I'd been babysitting for their daughter Kirsty and had stayed over. The next day they were having my Nana Ryan over for dinner. Nana and Dave had something of a fractured relationship. Like many sons-in-law and mothers-in-law they didn't get on with each other but every so often Dave would try and bridge the gap by offering an olive branch, and my nana, always trying to keep her daughters happy, would take it. But it just seemed no matter what he did, he would always mess it up at the last minute.

Dave was a great cook, he looked Italian and he cooked Italian. He made the best spaghetti bolognese I'd ever had in my life. We were all sat round the dinner table tucking in, my Nana Ryan, me, Dave and Kathleen. Kathleen was bigging Dave up to Nana, trying to get her to like him.

'Davy made this from scratch Mum, tell her you made it from scratch, Davy.'

So Dave told us how he made it, in minute detail, and everything sounded great. Thrifty too in the traditional Scots way.

'And you'll never believe me but this whole spread for the four of us cost me less than two quid to put together!' he continued.

Right there, my nana stopped him in disbelief. 'I'm sorry, two quid? How much did you pay for the minced meat?'

'Well it's that posh butchers round the corner, but it was 12p per pound.'

'Twelve pence a pound?'

'Aye, bargain eh?'

'Well yeah,' my nana said as she tucked into her dinner, 'seems a bit to cheap to me, it's usually about £2 per pound isn't it?'

'Aye, well, they had that one for sale as well, but they sell pet mince for 12p a pound for people's dogs and that. So I just thought, sod it, it comes from the same animal doesn't it!'

He laughed, but by himself.

'What?' we all asked in unison as our forks left our mouths for the final time.

In an incredulous Glaswegian accent he protested, 'Ah come on, when it's cooked ye cannee tell the fucking difference.'

Nana's fork hit the plate, her chin hit her chest, she got her coat on and left, muttering 'Dirty bastard,' as she stormed to the bus stop. I pushed my plate away, suddenly not very hungry, but Dave couldn't give a toss, he just scraped everybody's dinner onto his plate and tucked into his pet mince bolognese.

Chapter 14

Do You Want Cheese With That?

As THE TIME CAME to leave school, I had decided pretty swiftly that I would go to college and take my A-levels. It was either that or get a full-time proper job with no chance of parole until sixty, and why would I do that unless I had to? I planned to stay away from the treadmill of the real world as long as humanly possible. Plus I had that other classic catch-all excuse – all my mates were doing it. That's pretty much a done deal at that age. There was a local college – Loreto in Hulme – that had a connection with our school and so once again I let the path of least resistance take the strain of my fate. Loreto it would be.

Having said that, despite being in college, I still needed to earn some money. I'd had a blast working with Brendan over the summer, but my college hours meant I couldn't do that any more. I needed something part-time that could fit around my classes. So I jumped on the 85 bus into town carrying a pile of CVs in my bag, with the sole aim of getting myself a job by the end of the day.

As I got off the bus, the first place I saw was Burger King. I'd been a fan and regular customer since shunning McDonald's the previous year when Hannah dumped me, so it made perfect sense to turn my hobby into a job. I went in and queued up. As I got to the front of the queue the girl behind the counter asked, 'What can I get you, sir?'

I said, 'A job, please.' And offered my best can-do smile.

She asked, 'Would you like fries with that?'

I did. She went to get the manager and I waited, tucking into my fries and staring out of the window, doing a bit of people-watching as the worker ants rushed around the bus station in the blazing September sunshine.

Suddenly there was a total eclipse. The light completely blacked out. I looked up to face the manager; she was absolutely huge. If this was Burger King, I'd just met the Burger Queen.

She took me up to the office and sat me down, asking the usual interview-type question. The problem was I'd never been asked them before so when she asked me 'Where do you see yourself in five years?' I answered, laughing, 'Well, not here unless something's really gone wrong with my life.'

From her stony face I deciphered that she herself had been there a lot longer than five years, and my reaction to her question was not only rude but a complete insult to her entire life's work.

Despite the faux pas, she offered me the job. Training would start at nine on Saturday and work would start at ten. Real chefs train for years but at Burger King they're ready in an hour: that's fast food for you.

On the Saturday I turned up half an hour early and was given my uniform – navy trousers with elastic waist, brownish shirt and a blue visor-style hat with a firm peak and your hair on show. The training video was an American guy telling us how to wash our hands properly. There were four of us about to start work with only an hour to find out how things were done around here and this one-hour presentation just wasted five minutes on rubbing our palms together 'using soap and water'.

Now I'd always been a big fan of Burger King but a part of me died that day as I learnt how they made their famous flamed-grilled

Whoppers. I got into the kitchen with the other rookies and we were taken to the griller. Hundreds of burger patties were moving through this flaming silver monster every minute. It was hypnotic. The manager showed us where we got the beefburgers from and that's when I knew I couldn't do this job for life. Before they got put on the grill to give them that barbecued look, we had to zap them in the microwave for a minute to really cook them. The grill was mainly for show: this is where the basic cooking happened.

The manager could see my expression of surprise and disgust as I looked round at my new colleagues for support, and there and then she'd pretty much decided I was trouble.

'If you don't like it, you can mop the floor.'

'All right,' I said. For £3.80 an hour, I wasn't bothered. This was the most money I'd earned in my life.

When our break came we were told that we were allowed a Junior Whopper meal with a small Coke. That's not a very hearty meal for a ten-hour shift but it was free so I suppose it was fair enough. You had to make it yourself so I supposed you could load it with extra lettuce if you were really starving.

I made my burger, fresh from the grill/microwave, loaded it with tomatoes and lettuce and then finished it off with a slice of cheese. I wrapped it, popped it in a bag alongside my fries and went to walk over my freshly mopped floor to sit and eat my lunch.

'Excuse me.' It was Mrs Whopper, the manager. I turned. 'Can I have a look at your Junior Whopper meal, please?'

In front of the rest of the workforce and a fair amount of customers, she opened my burger, took off the top part of the bun, then peeled the slice of yellow cheese off the burger patty and dropped it into a nearby bin.

'As you were told in training, young man, you're not allowed cheese on your free burger.'

I could feel all these people staring at me and my face was beginning to burn hotter than the flame grill metres away. I took the burger and threw the rest of it in the bin too. As my lunch joined the cheese, I looked up at Whopzilla, her smug fat face looking down at me, and I asked her, 'Have you tasted that burger without cheese? It's rank.' I don't know why I said this – I love a bit of Burger King but I knew this would hurt her. This was a woman who lived and breathed Burger King.

I worked a total of six hours that day and should have been paid £22.80 for my time, but due to some clerical error at the head office I was paid £76 for a weekend shift. If that wasn't good enough stick-it-to-The-Man news, I was paid this amount every week for the next eight weeks!

How brilliant is that? Free money! Incredibly, it wasn't the only free money I received in the next few weeks.

'A bank error in your favour.' It only ever happens in Monopoly, doesn't it? And then it's not real money and your brother is the banker until your mum comes in and takes the control off him like he's Northern Rock. I'd been doing some more cash-in-hand work for my Uncle Brendan on a building site over a couple of weekends, carrying bricks and suchlike up and down ladders while I was supposed to be doing college homework. After a few weeks, he gave me £140, which I immediately took to the bank.

The cashier was a trainee. He was nervous and I was being jolly with him, chatting away as he counted my money and logged it into the system. As I stepped out into the fresh air, I looked at my slip and noticed that the new guy had given me an extra digit. Instead of typing

£140 he'd given me £1,140, an extra grand! That's right. One. Thousand. Pounds. I suddenly forgot how to walk and move normally as I tried to keep my cool, walking away from the bank slowly. I must've looked like a drunken THUNDERBIRDS puppet. Round the corner I checked the balance and there it was, out of my overdraft and into the black in some style: the perfect crime, the ultimate bank job. I didn't spend the money for months, in case they asked for it back, but they never did. I'd like to tell you I wasted it on drugs and booze, held Playboy-style parties and filled fast cars with faster women, but in truth I bought myself my very first PlayStation and gave half to my mum so she could take my Nana Ryan to the bingo.

Chapter 15

1471

DID YOU KNOW my whole stand-up career came about from someone dialing 1471?

After a few months of college work and with Christmas out of the way, I was completely out of money (even the free money from Burger King had dried up). Thankfully Mum was on hand with some wise parental advice.

'Jason, get off your arse and get a job.'

So I briefly got off my arse to grab the Yellow Pages, sat back down on it and rang round a few pubs and bars in Chorlton. I'd grown bored of having nothing and thought an evening job might be more fun than the jobs I'd tried so far, as well as fitting in with my college hours. After a full morning of unsuccessful phone calls, I'd eventually worked my way to 'S' and found myself ringing the Southern pub on the Nell Lane estate – one of the toughest, most notorious areas of south Manchester. The customers were a mix of friendly old Irish fellas and young, rock-hard knobheads. Oh, and my dad. It was his local.

A pleasant woman answered and politely declined my offer of 'collecting pots or washing up or whatever' and so I carried on with my phone calls. After a fair few hours of more ringing round with no success, the phone rang me. I answered and it was the lovely-sounding lady from the Southern pub. Someone had not turned up and she'd done a 1471 and rung me back.

I started that night. They had a wedding and were short staffed so I put on my only shirt and my dad's tie and walked round to this imposing off-white building on the edge of the hardest neighbourhood around.

I would be working in the upstairs suite of the pub and although I'd never been inside before, as I climbed the stairs it seemed all right – old-fashioned, yeah, but nice enough. I met the pleasant woman off the phone, Lorraine, and she introduced me to her mum, Anne, the landlady of the establishment. She was quite a formidable Irish woman, hard-looking and with no hint of a smile. I was polite and willing as she took me through the already-started wedding reception to the kitchen, where there was a mountain of washing-up. The sink was full, and the plates, pots and pans on the side were stacked about eight foot off the ground.

'I need you to do the washing-up,' Anne said in her deep Irish brogue.

'OK, no problem, where's the dishwasher?' I innocently enquired.

She fixed me with a look and then smiled. 'He's wearing a fecking shirt and tie.'

It was a tough job but as I got to know Anne and Lorraine I discovered they were great fun and I loved making them laugh from their bellies as we finished up after each wedding, christening or bar mitzvah (we never did a bar mitzvah, really – not that big in the Irish or rock-hard knobhead communities).

I was too young to work behind the bar but I collected glasses and stood at the little sink washing up till my hands were sore. I was being paid £4.50 an hour, cash, and I took every party I could. I even did the odd funeral but was taken off them after a series of unfortunate events. The Southern pub did well with wakes because of its close proximity to Southern Cemetery, the biggest cemetery in Manchester ('and the dead centre of town' – yes, thank you, Dad, you've told that joke every time we've passed it for my whole life. 'There's people dying to get in there, you know.' OK, stop now, Dad, you're embarrassing yourself).

It's not like I got loads wrong but odd things kept happening to me although they weren't always my fault. Well, apart from that time I got sugar and salt mixed up and made three dozen cups of tea before anyone realised (luckily when dealing with funerals it's mostly old people and they don't like to make a fuss even when their cup of tea tastes like chips). Oh, and there was the time I was accused of trying to generate business when an old guy had a heart attack halfway through a piece of quiche at his brother's wake.

The worst was probably the Monday morning after a particularly late-finishing wedding party the night before. There was so much washing-up I decided to come and do it the next day as I was knackered. Anne didn't mind – 'as long as it gets feckin' done'.

Halfway through the mammoth washing-up session, the phone went. I slipped off my Marigolds and answered.

'Hello, the Southern, how can I help?'

'Good morning, are you all ready for us?' a woman asked.

'I'm sorry, who is this?' I enquired.

'It's Mrs Gale, we've a funeral this morning and I just wanted to make sure everything was OK?'

I prickled with panic: there was nothing in the diary for a wake today. But what was I going to do? I was the only one there and had to make an executive decision – and quick. I couldn't tell her there had been a mistake on what was already one of the most difficult days of her life. Plus Anne would kill me if I turned away business and gave her a bad reputation among the dying of south Manchester.

So I improvised as best I could. I asked her for some details as I started to scan the kitchen for food. 'How many is there of you again?' I asked.

'About forty, I think, maybe fifty. That's what we agreed for seating, didn't we?'

'Oh yeah, yes, of course. I'm just checking what I've got written here is correct.'

As I was talking to her, I was ransacking the cupboards and fridges for bread, butter, ham, cheese, eggs, anything I could lay my hands on.

'Thank you. We'll be there in an hour,' she told me.

'Oh, thank God,' I said as I opened the fridge and saw about two hundred chicken drumsticks and sausage rolls. I took them over to the oven and whacked it on.

'Sorry, what?' She started to sound worried.

'No, nothing, absolutely nothing, I'm just putting the oven on now and it'll all be piping hot when you get here,' I reassured her.

'What?' she exclaimed. There was a short silence and what sounded like gentle muted sobs started, then the phone clicked dead. I had no time to worry about her, though; she was obviously upset after losing her loved one. I just cracked on like a madman, making butties and slicing flans.

After over an hour, I had the full area ready to welcome the funeral party. Tea was brewing, the sausage rolls were hot and it was definitely sugar in the sugar pot. I finally drew breath and waited for the influx… and waited, but nobody came. I headed back to the phone and did my own 1471 to call her back.

'Hello, Mrs Gale, it's Jason from the Southern pub. I spoke to you about your husband's wake and I was just checking where you all are.' I have never heard a bigger laugh from a recently bereaved woman in my whole life. 'Mrs Gale, is everything all right?'

She eventually stopped laughing. 'Oh, oh, God, that is so funny. Bernard would have appreciated that if he was here. Thank you for making me laugh on such a sad day.'

I was completely bemused. 'I don't understand.'

'Oh, I'm sorry, dear, I've wasted your time. I got your number out of the Yellow Pages earlier. I must have misread it as I was trying to call the Southern Crematorium for my husband's funeral service today, but I rang you by accident.'

This woman was clearly mental. I still couldn't see why this was the funniest thing that had ever happened to her.

'I still don't get it, love.'

'Well, I thought you were the rudest, most insensitive boy ever earlier this morning, telling me the ovens were on and it would be piping hot when we got there. I thought I was on the phone to the crem!' She laughed again and we said our goodbyes.

I suppose it was an unfortunately funny story but there weren't many laughs later on when I had to explain to Anne why there was hundreds of pounds worth of food cooked but no one eating it.

It didn't get me the sack but she left me in no doubt that event management wasn't for me.

THOUGH I ONLY ever worked upstairs, the downstairs bar at the Southern was my dad's local. He used to say, it took twelve minutes to walk to the Southern from our house and twenty-five minutes to walk back.

The upstairs and downstairs bars were like two different worlds – one a relatively safe haven, the other a no-go area, unless they knew you or you knew how to handle yourself.

One night my dad took me for a drink downstairs. As we stood at the bar waiting for our turn to be served, I couldn't help but overhear the conversation from the father and son standing next to us. You could tell they were father and son as they had matching earrings and shaved heads. The dad had a tattoo on his shoulder that said 'Becky' but it'd been crossed out and underneath it said 'Sandra' in the same font. The son was in tracksuit bottoms and shoes, as if he was ready for anything, the gym or a job interview, whichever came up first.

The son was telling his dad how he'd just been stopped and searched by the police and how they had failed to spot the five bags of cannabis hidden down his socks. The dad beamed proudly at his son and said, 'You're one lucky bastard, you lad. There's your pint, now fuck off.'

His son grunted and wandered off. The dad turned and grinned at my dad.

'Bleeding kids, eh?' he laughed. 'He was only up in court this morning for possession.'

'Aye,' my dad said bemused, 'they grow up so fast, don't they?'

Rough it may have been but what it lacked in security it made up for in entrepreneurial spirit. Every day a black-bag-toting scally would come in and try and flog you everything from freshly shoplifted meat to an industrial-size tin of Nescafé. I don't know how precious you are about what you put in your body but I'm wary of meat I buy at Tesco, never mind some bloke in a pub. Once I asked him what meat it was and he said, 'Erm, sheep, I think.' Sheep? Sheep? Not even lamb, or mutton? Nope, this guy was selling 'sheep'.

In the weeks leading up to bonfire night, you could only get into the pub through a gauntlet of mini-scallies demanding 'a penny for the guy'. I don't know if you've seen a scally guy, but often it was better dressed than the scally. Other times they wouldn't try at all. I once saw one guy demanding money for the guy, and it was just a pair of jeans with a 20p Power Rangers mask laid on top. Sometimes they didn't even bother making a guy and got the smallest scally in their gang to lie there with a mask on. I don't know how far they took it and whether they eventually chucked him on the fire or not.

The favoured technique was never to say no to these little beggars as it would only lead to a barrage of abuse and, if you'd come by car, slashed tyres. Nor could you give them a handful of coppers as that would just earn you their contempt. Your best bet was to say, 'Sorry, lads, no change' and hope the little bastards had gone before you left. But even this could backfire. On one occasion, my dad's mate Uncle Tony offered the 'Sorry, lads, no change' excuse and carried on into the pub, unaware that one of the little scroats had followed him in. As he got to the bar and pulled out a tenner, this artful dodger grabbed it and was out through the door like shit off a shovel with a cursory, 'Happy bonfire night, dickhead.'

The highlight of the week at the Southern was the Sunday night karaoke, sort of Jeremy Kyle the Musical. You'd have a pregnant teenage girl crying while singing Whitney Houston's, 'The Greatest Love Of All', and her older sister, complete with three black eyes, belting out Gloria Gaynor's 'I Will Survive' as she stares past the karaoke machine at her boyfriend sipping a pint of Stella. There were a lot of oddballs. My favourite was this six-foot-six skinhead with 'cut here' tattooed on his throat who used to sing a falsetto version of Peter Andre's 'Mysterious Girl'.

But for all its faults, it was a place where a middle-aged bloke could go for a bit of peace and refuge from the kids during the week; and on Sundays a place where a whole community could gather together, buy some sheep, murder a power ballad and then have a fist fight with their dad over a bag of weed. And at the end of the day, isn't that what community is really about?

Chapter 16

Yo, Student!

MOST DAYS I was at college from nine till five doing my A levels. I'd taken Psychology, English Language, Sociology and Theatre Studies. My choices were a bit of pot luck really. Being fluent in the English language (Manchester edition) I figured I had a head start there. I mean, how hard could that be? All you needed, as I saw it, for Psychology and Sociology was an understanding of what makes people tick. With all the sociopaths in our family I felt I'd pretty much completed the field study modules already. But Theatre Studies was different. I loved Theatre Studies. In truth it soon became clear I wasn't a four A level kind of guy. In fact by the end of the two years I was barely an any A level kind of guy. I failed them all apart from Theatre Studies.

While I wasn't over-enamoured by the work of Stanislavski and I couldn't care less why Ibsen chose to have macaroons in *A Doll's House*, what I did love was getting on the stage. I enjoyed being surrounded by like-minded people and having fun together in the theatre, sparking off each other.

The teacher was a wise old woman called Margaret Delargy. She was old and wise then and I've seen her since and she's still old and wise. She talked about Bertolt Brecht so much I think she must have known him. Her room was backstage from the college's only theatre space, where she sat most days chain-smoking and pontificating about method acting. When you opened the door and walked in the room, smoke would billow across the ceiling like a scene from *Backdraft*.

From the week I joined I just felt, for the first time in my life, I belonged somewhere. The thing about further education is you only really get people there who want to be there. At school you had no choice and lots of kids were just counting the days until they'd done their time and could get out of there. But here you had to really want it. I really wanted it. I loved it all. Anything that got offered, from sound and lighting to compering, my hand was the first to go up.

Margaret liked me and I liked her. We were very similar (other than the fact that I was a sixteen-year-old, non-smoking boy and she was a fifty-something, chain-smoking woman, of course). I made her laugh and in return she let me off when I was continually late for class or I'd not done that week's homework on *Abigail's Party*. She even gave me a part in the upper sixth production of Sheridan's *School for Scandal*. I played a smarmy Frenchman with a ridiculously huge 'tache, and I got to sing a song in French, I thought my accent was spot-on but Mum said I sounded like the policeman in *'Allo 'Allo!*.

The other thing about Theatre Studies is that the ratio of boys to girls is weighted strongly in our favour. I was surrounded by girls, older girls, girls who smoked and drank and went to clubs. I had been going out with a girl called Cheryl for six months, but she was still at school, and that's where the problem was. Suddenly, it felt like we lived in different worlds.

It was that weird age of teenage relationships where a boy turns sixteen and starts to become a man and the girl is fifteen and is still playing hockey and taking tins of beans to the school harvest festival. I was backstage during shows, getting dressed and undressed into costumes with these girls, well, women, flirting and growing up and I was growing further and further away from Cheryl.

It had been a long summer relationship; she was the best-looking girl I'd ever seen, but now I was worried that I was turning into the kind of guy I used to hate when I was at school, the guy who was dating a schoolgirl even though he was no longer at school. I suppose that's the natural order of things but in the end even Cheryl's natural beauty and charm couldn't keep at bay the overwhelming sense that life had moved on.

One Wednesday afternoon, I waited at the school gates for her to finish. I felt like a bloody spare part, to be honest. I've always looked older than I am and as each schoolgirl came out I felt the gulf between our two lives grow further and further apart. As she approached me, a vision of blonde beauty on this wet October afternoon, her hockey stick on her back and her school uniform ironed to perfection, I felt a pang of guilt. After what I had felt when Hannah dumped me, did I have it in me to do the same to another person?

We walked and I was quiet as she told me about her day. We had spent almost every day of the summer together since we first met back in May, lying on the grass at Longford Park making daisy chains and drinking cider. I didn't even like cider, and I like daisy chains even less, but this girl was stunning, she really was.

My friend Neil had been going out with a posh girl from Chorltonville, the poshest part of an already posh part of south Manchester, and compared to where I lived we may as well have been in an episode of *Upstairs, Downstairs*. At the time I was still moping around thinking about Hannah when Neil suggested I come down to the park with him and a few schoolmates. We were stuck in the middle of revision and exams and some of the lads had chosen to relieve the pressure with a game of football every few days.

At the time it was the norm that every game of football or five-a-side had a customary crowd of girls on the sidelines watching and occasionally cheering on their boyfriends. It's no wonder so many women dislike football when they get older if this is their first experience of it. We were properly shit. But the girls kept coming along anyway, gossiping on the sidelines while we were trying out Cruyff turns and elaborate Brazilian celebrations. Fast-forward fifteen years and you should have seen the look on my wife's face when I invited her to watch me play in a charity football game last year. It was like I'd asked for one of her kidneys!

On that particular day I'd hurt my ankle and joined the girls on the sidelines. As I was sat chatting to Neil's posh girlfriend, another girl approached us. She introduced me to her friend.

'This is Cheryl, she's in my dance class and… blah, blah, blah.' I'd already stopped listening. I looked up from the damp grass at this statuesque blonde. She was stunningly beautiful and my voice quivered.

'Nice to meet you, Cheryl, I'm Jason,' I said, squinting through the bright sun as she gracefully sat herself down.

Somehow I managed to calm myself down and we started out on an afternoon of chatting and making each other laugh. As the afternoon began to wind up, I walked her home and unbelievably we kissed on the corner of her road, before I walked or maybe flew home, I can't remember now. All those bad feelings about Hannah had vanished in an instant. I felt like a new boy, well, man. I felt like a man.

It was an exciting relationship, full of sexual tension like so many young relationships at that age. That age where part of your body and brain is screaming 'Have sex now please!' and the other half is replying 'But I don't know how to and I'm scared!' We never did but almost every morning I'd walk up to her house in Urmston and we'd go out ice skating or to the cinema or just walking, holding hands. The whole relationship was like a romantic teenage montage.

But after six months, our lives were suddenly very different. Your teenage years are such a crazy age, the difference between a fifteen-year-old and a sixteen-year-old was like the difference between a 25-year-old and a 55-year-old – not a problem if you're Rod Stewart but the rest of us notice it. I'd moved on and the long summer spell was broken.

We walked to Stretford Arndale and outside Clinton Cards I took Cheryl to one side and waited for her to finish talking. Her huge blue eyes looked up at me and she moved in close for a kiss, but I stopped her.

'Cheryl, I really like you but…'

Her eyes filled up almost immediately and I felt a lump in my throat. In *my* throat, what's that about? I was the one doing the splitting up this time – surely I can't be upset both times? When Hannah dumped me I cried for days so surely if I'm the dumper rather than the dumpee, it's easier, right? Well, no, in a weird way it's not, is it? I suppose when you get dumped there's a fatalistic resignation – 'well, there was nothing I could do about someone else's decision, so que sera, sera'. But when you break it off with someone else, especially when it's only that some variables have changed and that person hasn't actually done anything wrong, you're the one making this life-changing decision, you're in control of breaking someone's heart, and you know what that feels like, it hurts like hell.

We both cried as we had one last kiss; nothing says goodbye like a snotty, salty, tear-soaked snog outside a card shop with the smell of Greggs pastics wafting past. She walked away and I watched her

disappear for ever through the glass doors between Quality Save and
Gabbotts the Butcher.

So HERE I WAS at college, young, free, newly single and surrounded
by women and it seemed my only rivals were gay men. It's the perfect
scenario. I couldn't believe only six months before I had been a
nobody at school and suddenly here I was. I'd found my groove and
I felt like king of all I surveyed. I'd have a laugh with the canteen
women and share a joke with the janitor, play football with the Irish
guys and chat about cars with the Asian lads. Girls flirted with me
and guys laughed at my jokes. I felt like the Fonz or at least a YTS
Mancunian version of him.

Loreto Catholic College, like many of the buildings from my
youth, has recently been knocked down and rebuilt as some sort of
fancy modern college. But the building I was taught in was built in
the middle of the nineteenth century at the same time as some of the
nuns that taught us were born. It was surrounded on three sides by an
imposing church, a great big Asda and Moss Side. It was bloody eerie.

Because of the eeriness of it all there were hundreds of ghost stories
about the place and you would very rarely be in the theatre or chapel
by yourself, certainly not after dark. I was less scared of the ghosts in
the place and more scared of the potential criminals who lived in and
around Manchester's notorious Moss Side. I love a good ghost story
and would often make things up about the college to scare some of
the girls backstage in Theatre Studies.

The college building lent itself to spooky stories after rehearsals in
the back office where none of the lights worked properly and one wall
was full of mirrors. I remember one story I told that scared the bejesus
out of several students.

There were four of us backstage, a lad called Stuart and two girls, Sophie and Claire. I told them that I had it on good authority, as my dad was a drinking buddy of the janitor, that underneath the ancient college building there were a series of tunnels that led all around the neighbouring area and, get this, they were haunted. One tunnel under the college led to St Mary's Church across the road and from there another tunnel led to Xavarian College in Rusholme. Back in the day, the nuns would use their tunnel to walk to church and the monks would use their tunnel to get to the same location from Xavarian. The janitor had said he never went down there because he was so scared. The story went that in 1895 a monk and a nun had had an illicit affair and the nun had fallen pregnant. Terrified of Mother Superior finding out, the nun headed down into the tunnels and killed herself. When the monk found her he too killed himself. When the bodies were discovered, the nuns buried them in the tunnels and closed them off for ever. But every so often, if you walk past the entrances, you can hear a baby cry. Then at that exact moment, right on cue, I squeezed a doll from the props room behind my back and it let out a huge cry which echoed round the theatre.

Well, that was it, the girls were up and out and Stuart was assuring me he had just been surprised but definitely not scared. As we all walked out of the building to go home, I was chuckling to myself but soon stopped when I saw my and Sophie's bus fly past in the darkening evening gloom. Left with no other option, me and Sophie decided to walk, hoping a bus would meet us on our way.

Sophie was great fun; a really funny girl. She was as tall as me with glasses and a cheeky sense of humour. We had a laugh about the ghost story and the others' reaction and we idly discussed college and family. After several hundred yards, we passed a kids' adventure playground where a few of the street lamps were out. The air stank from the fumes billowing out of the brewery a few streets away.

During the eighties this area had been ripped apart by riots. The Gooch were a notorious drug-dealing gang who were blamed for many of the gun crimes in Manchester at the time and they were named after a small street in Moss Side, Gooch Close – the very street that me and Sophie were now walking past. It wasn't called Gooch Close any more; the council had changed its name to Westerling Way to curb the violence. Idiots. I'd loved to have been a fly on the wall in the committee room.

'Ok, so we need to stop the gun crimes in south Manchester committed by the Gooch Close Gang. Any ideas?'

'I've got one, sir, you might like it. They're called the Gooch Close Gang, yeah?'

'Yes, go on.'

'Well, what about if we change the name of the road they're named after?'

Brilliant. As if there were suddenly going to be loads of gang members just roaming the streets of Moss Side, not able to find each other because the name of a street had changed, so, disorientated, they decide to knuckle down and get regular jobs.

'Yo, students!' a nasal-sounding Manc accent beckoned.

'Just keep walking,' suggested Sophie, rigidly facing forward.

'Don't ignore us, yo!' he said.

We carried on walking, not turning round, hoping that they'd get bored.

I sensed what was about to happen, I'd been mugged once before when I was eleven. Dad had sent me on my bike to the garage to get some Warburtons. As I was racing down the hill, wind on my face, bread in my hand, two guys covered their faces and stepped into the empty road.

'Give us your bike or we'll knock you out.'

Well, who was I to argue if they wanted the gold Raleigh Chopper my granddad had bought me a year earlier? That's right, the cool must-have bike of the seventies was mine, only in gold and twenty years too late. For some reason these two young muggers must've had a love of all things retro and decided it was there for the taking. I imagined their drug den full of Rubik's Cubes and them trying to get away from the police on space hoppers.

I got off the bike, handed it over and ran off. They both climbed on to the famous elongated seat and attempted to ride off, trying to control the unstably large handlebars. I eventually stopped running, sat down on the kerb and watched as these two would-be gangsters wobbled slowly up the hill, occasionally slipping off the seat and hitting their bollocks on the ridiculously placed gear stick. It dawned on me that I'd essentially been mugged by the evil version of the Marx Brothers.

As they neared the brow of the hill, a jogger came past and asked me, 'Have those two just stole your bike, son?'

'Yeah,' I said.

'Right,' he said and set off at a rate of knots.

He shouted for them to stop and they tried to pedal faster (clearly unaware that they needed to drop down a gear). This random friendly stranger caught up with them, pushed them off the bike and brought it back down to me. What a superhero. Then he just jogged off in the opposite direction. Even now I always have time for joggers; they don't annoy me like they do most people. Even when they do that jogging-on-the-spot-thing while waiting at traffic lights, I just think about my knight in shining tracksuit.

That night with Sophie, we'd have no such luck. As I turned to face the gang of five guys, the few people that were in their gardens or looking out of their windows suddenly backed away and hid from view.

'Give us your money or we'll fucking batter you,' the main knob-head said.

He obviously wasn't a good judge of a situation or aware of my working life. I was a student in the day and earned £4.50 an hour in the evening, ten hours a week, minus bus travel (when the bloody thing didn't drive straight past) and lunch. That left me with a tidy profit of just under £20, half of which I gave to my mum. So £10 between five of them didn't seem to be worth the hassle of mugging, but then again what do I know? Maybe it works itself out over time; maybe he was playing the long con.

As I handed over my money, they started to push Sophie to get her to give them some money. She was doing her best but whereas my money was simply in my top pocket, hers was in a purse inside her bag. The gang weren't prepared to wait around and grabbed it off her arm, then one of them went too far. One of the cowardly ones at the back slapped Sophie hard in the face. I moved forward.

'All right dickhead, we're giving you our money – there's no need for that!'

Whoops.

He turned on me and started to push me in the chest. 'Just take our money and go – don't hit a girl,' I said.

Most boys are brought up not to hit girls. My mum used to say it all the time: 'Don't fight with girls.' That same moral code had obviously not been passed onto to this young white lad (oh yeah, they were two white lads, two black lads and an Asian lad. I'll give them that, they were an equal opportunities gang).

As they got more agitated with our lack of funds, it got more out of hand. The good news is they'd stopped hitting Sophie. The bad news was that they'd started hitting me more. Two or three punches rained down on my face and jaw. I felt my front teeth crack and my mouth filled quickly with the thick, metallic taste of blood. My left eyelid closed over as another fist landed on my eye socket and I was knocked to the floor where for good measure a few boots were kicked against my ribs.

They ran off and I shouted something but I couldn't even think straight. Sophie was sobbing and it wasn't long before I joined her. I looked up at a window where a young woman was watching what had happened. She closed her curtain and went back into the safety of her home. I suppose the people round there had just learnt not to get involved. It wasn't worth it.

As I stumbled to my feet, the 85 bus drove past again. We got to a phone box and called the police, who picked us up and took us to the station and then home. My mum was in bits and my dad was putting his coat on, ready to head out into the night with a cricket bat. My mum bathed my face and put butterfly stitches on the few cuts I had. She was crying as she tried to use her nursing training to fix her little boy's face.

The next morning I went to the dentist to get my teeth looked at. It wasn't good news. The front four teeth were knocked back in my mouth and hanging by a thread. He did his best and managed to keep them in my mouth but he told me two of them had died and would one day need replacing. They became grey and brittle and when I returned to college the following week, the smile had literally been wiped off my face. My confidence was shot; I didn't want to talk to anyone and I certainly never opened my mouth. The few times I did talk I felt like the person I was talking to was just staring at my slowly dying teeth. Over the next few weeks I stopped going into college and even when I did I sat in Margaret's office inhaling smoke fumes and staring into space while she talked about Stanislavski.

Like I said, it's amazing how quickly things change in your life. And now I had first-hand experience that it wasn't always for the better. Cup of sugar, cup of dirt. Granddad was right. I'd had a few months of being popular, carefree in my new-found confidence and, dare I say it, cool – and now this had happened and I was lower than ever. Everyone was lovely, all my fellow students rallied round, but I could only talk to Sophie. She knew what I'd gone through and we spent a lot of time together. In the end I saw a counsellor at Victim Support in Manchester, who helped me through it.

For a good while I really didn't want to see anyone, but eventually I had to. I arrived back at the Southern a different kid. Where I had been fun and extrovert, I was now hidden inside myself. I spent most of the time in the kitchen away from the brides and families having the greatest day of their lives. Anne was understanding and had had an idea to cheer me up. She told me to come and work on a Thursday night after college when I could pot-collect for that evening's comedy club.

Chapter 17
Stand-Up

THE BUZZ COMEDY CLUB had been run for years by the very friendly John 'Agraman' Marshall, the compere and organiser of the night. If you have read other comics' books then you may have already heard of him because he gave a lot of comedians their first gig. He also gave first gigs to some right lemons and real no-hopers.

If anything, it was the occasional crap act that caught my eye at first. I'd be sweating my arse off collecting glasses and getting them washed before the next interval while some bloke on stage was telling terrible jokes with no punchlines. Then at the end of the night he'd go over to Agraman and get £150 counted into his hand. That was nearly ten times the amount I was getting. One night I dropped a huge stack of glasses to a barrage of cheers and applause and still got more laughs than some of the lads up there. But I only half watched most acts, not really taking an interest; I just wasn't in the laughing mood.

'HI, CAN WE BOOK tickets for the Buzz Club this Thursday?' a voice asked when I picked up the phone at the Southern. No one had ever booked before while I'd been there, it was just a pay-on-the-night type place. It was always packed but I never remember them turning anyone away.

'Well, we don't really take bookings as you'll be able to pay when you turn up,' I told her.

'No, we need to book, please. We've heard Peter Kay is going to be on,' she told me excitedly.

'Peter who?' I'd never heard of the lad.

That Thursday, as I approached the pub, there was a queue round the block. I got upstairs and the place was already packed to the rafters. All the seats were taken and they were letting people stand up at the back just to cram them in. I imagine Agraman was hoping none of the audience worked for Health and Safety as there were easily four hundred people in a room that held three hundred.

I still didn't get it. I'd watched loads of comedians play the club by now as I patrolled the tables. Most of them were all right but none were nearly as funny as the comics I'd watch at home with my dad. There was no one in the same league as Billy Connolly or Dave Allen or Les Dawson. I'd seen guys get standing ovations here but I'd never seen an audience so excited to see one man. The mood that was brewing was something different. It was a tough crowd for a glass collector too. I soon started to dislike this Peter bloody Kay and his army of fans making my life difficult with no floor space and their unwillingness to move as I wended my way in search of empties.

The night started in its usual fashion with Agraman unleashing some awful but well-written puns. He'd be the first person to tell you that he wasn't a comic but there was a genuine love for him in the room as this was the guy who organised it for you to see all these comedians week in week out for a fiver.

I'd just gone into the kitchen when Anne and Lorraine hurried to the top of the back stairs all giggly like schoolgirls with some fella in tow. As was my thing these days, I just carried on, lost in the washing up, not really that bothered as the booming Bolton-accented voice that was charming them so much got closer. As they reached the top of the stairs I turned to see a fairly stocky bloke in a purple shirt and black suit still making Anne and Lorraine guffaw with laughter. This quietly annoyed me as they were my audience – well, they used to be. I said hello to them in a slightly grumpy teenage way and then continued about my business of washing pint glasses for punters to dirty up again.

I was clearing a clean batch away when I heard Agraman's voice.

'Ladies and gentleman, please welcome Peter Kay!'

The noise was thunderous, I'd never heard anything like it. There were ripples in the sink water like in *Jurassic Park* and it carried on for what felt like for ever. He'd not even done anything yet and he'd already received the biggest applause I'd ever heard. After a few minutes of continuous laughter from the other room, Anne stuck her head in.

'Jason, stop being a moody bollock and come and watch this feckin' lad.'

I dried up, opened the door and was hit by a wall of noise. The laughter sent a shiver up my spine as I manoeuvred my way from various restricted view positions till I eventually saw this comedian dancing around the stage, sliding on his knees. I didn't understand the context but the audience were in bits: there were men slapping their knees and women wiping tears from their eyes. I was more worried about the carpet burns on the guy's trousers but he didn't seem to care.

My eyes widened as he asked the audience questions: 'Why do mums buy crap pop?' he said, as the room heaved.

I caught myself smiling. Oh my God, I thought, that's what my **mum does** – that Rola Cola stuff from Netto.

'That Rola Cola stuff from Netto!' he boomed. The audience lapped up every word of his slick Bolton brogue. I stood there, mesmerised by this guy who looked not too dissimilar from me – same haircut, same uneasiness in a shirt – and was blown away. I started laughing, and I mean really laughing, from the belly. I'd not smiled in six weeks and here I was properly undone. At one point I couldn't catch my breath from laughing. I listened to every word he said. Not a word was wasted. Every line was a punchline, every gag hit home with the audience. It was like he was in my brain, just pulling out pieces of information and things I knew about and turning them into jokes.

'Why can't you get out of bed on an odd number? You've always gotta wait till five past, haven't you?' he asked us.

Yes, yes, I do that. I did it this morning in fact. He told stories from his life and told us about his family, building up all the characters and colouring in the parts with lush northern language. He was like Les Dawson with a dash of Billy Connolly. He was warm and friendly and the funniest thing I'd ever seen this side of *You've Been Framed*.

I watched the audience. Not only were they laughing and clapping but they were nodding 'yes'. They were thinking, this guy is one of us, he's lived our life. But what was unbelievable was that they were all doing it; from the single geography teacher to the married Asian signwriter, from doctors to nurses and bookies to bankers. The mix was unbelievable. The warmth in the room was mainly from the broken air conditioner, to be fair, but there was something else – a communal sense that we had all witnessed something very special, that we'd be lucky to see this kind of guy in this intimate surrounding again.

I CARRIED ON working the Buzz Club every Thursday but now I was watching the acts more and more. I never took my eyes off the comics on stage. I studied everything: how they moved, how they held the mike, what they did with the stand, how they asked questions but always had a funny answer. I saw some brilliant comics up there, some you'll know and some you won't. Dave Spikey, Frankie Boyle, Steve Coogan, John Thomson, as well as other experts in their field – Gav Webster, Mick Ferry, Brendan Riley – all fantastic at working a room, milking every last idea for as many laughs as possible.

I began to chat to comedians after their sets, quizzing them on how they wrote their material and what other gigs they'd played. Comedians would come from all over the place to play at the Buzz Club. Johnny Vegas would come over from St Helens and Lee Evans would come up from London, and I saw acts from Australia, Germany, Canada and the USA. It soon became clear to me that even though I just collected pots at a rough south Manchester pub, I worked at a very special club that held a very special place in a lot of funny people's hearts.

'WHAT THE BLEEDING HELL am I gonna do?' he mumbled to himself.

Agraman was acting very strange.

It was a Thursday in June and I was getting things ready as usual for that night's gig. Having just turned seventeen, I was now allowed to help the sound guy set up the mike and equipment for the evening performance. At 7.30, half an hour before the show, Agraman had swung into the function room in a fluster. It was already half packed but it didn't stop him darting from the phone to the front door like a hornet.

'What's wrong?' Anne asked him.

'I've got two acts in a car from London who've broken down and no other acts are answering their phone.'

'Oh feck, so what are you going to do?' Anne enquired.

'I don't know, to be honest. We might have to cancel the night or give people their money back. I suppose I could ask the headliner to do a bit longer but even then I'm still going to be at least twenty minutes short.' He was in a real state.

'What about Jason?' Anne suggested.

At first I thought she was talking about a different Jason, a comedian I'd never heard of, then it dawned on me – she meant me.

'What, me?' I said, gobsmacked.

'What, him?' asked Agraman, also gobsmacked.

'Yeah, he's always telling me and Lorraine funny stories and daft things. I reckon he could do it.'

What the hell was she on about? I was seventeen. Yeah, I might have said the odd funny thing to them while washing the pots but that's because a) there was only two of them, and b) they weren't a paying audience expecting to be professionally entertained. Anyone can be funny when they're not thinking about it, when they're not pinned by a spotlight.

Agraman looked me up and down. 'Well, do you fancy a go?'

'Erm, well, I erm… I haven't really got any material ready and, er, who's gonna wash the pots?'

'Well, you're not really selling yourself to me, lad,' said Agraman. Then after a short pause, 'But I'm desperate and even if it's for novelty's sake it'll waste ten minutes.'

So that was that – the audience were sat expecting a show and they were going to get ten minutes of me. What the hell was I going to talk about? These were all adults, I was still a kid. I panicked and tried to remember something funny I'd heard or read but my mind was blank. I wasn't first up so I sat for an hour in the kitchen, hoping I was going to wake up at home and find it was all a bad dream. Then I heard Agraman on stage again explaining to the audience...

'... so they're not going to make it, but a special lad has said he'll step in. If you're regulars here then you'll have seen him moving around collecting your glasses, but tonight he's going to have a go at doing stand-up. As you know it's a tough job, so I want you to give him a chance...'

He carried on making my excuses before I even had any need for them. I walked past another comic, who asked if he was talking about me.

'Yes,' I said.

'Well, don't be shit, mate, or you'll never be able to collect glasses here again,' he said helpfully.

With those words ringing in my ears, Agraman introduced me.

'Ladies and gentleman, please welcome, all the way from behind the bar, Jason Mansfield!'

It wasn't my name but I didn't care. I walked through the heaving crowd and stepped up onto the low stage, grabbing the mike. I said hello and then started wittering on about nothing. If memory serves, it was something rubbish like, 'Aren't the people who go on *Family Fortunes* thick? The other week Les said, "Name something that's green," and this old fella said his pullover.'

A little laugh came but I had nowhere to go.

'Another time Les Dennis asked them to name a dangerous race and a woman said, "The Arabs."' I wasn't even sure this stuff was true, never mind funny.

The audience were politely smiling but there were no real laughs, not like I'd seen other acts get up there. It really was harder than I thought. My heart was jumping like a fish on a dock. I paused to think. Then the first heckle came.

'What happened to your teeth?' a bloke shouted out.

I crumbled a bit inside. I didn't have a comeback, I didn't have a joke. I just told him.

'What, this? I got mugged the other week walking home through Moss Side.'

A titter. From a female voice. It might have just been her nerves, but I momentarily recovered.

'That's not the funny bit, you tight get,' I said as she laughed some more. 'These lads attacked me from behind – well, not from behind, if you know what I mean.' More cheap chuckles, but I'd take them happily. 'The main knobhead said, "Give me your money or I'll beat you up," so I gave him my money *and* he beat me up.'

The bloke who heckled me was laughing now. I carried on.

'I mean, getting mugged is one thing but he broke our verbal contract – we had an agreement.'

I couldn't believe I was just talking about what had happened and it was getting laughs.

'The weirdest part was when I was lying on the floor, they ran away. I found myself shouting, "Oi, come back!" I could hear my brain shouting at me: "No, don't really."'

I was starting to relax. Enjoy myself even.

'One of them came back and said to another, "Get his watch."'

At this point I showed the audience my watch, still on my wrist, shining its greenish light. 'The Casio Illuminator, £4.99 at all good retailers, tells the time in three different countries. All right, so it's England, Scotland and Wales but what do you expect for a fiver?'

Wow, that was sort of like a joke (I said sort of).

'One guy rolled my sleeve up, saw the watch and said to his mate, "Nah, think I'll leave it," and walked off. I thought, you'll bloody take it, you cheeky bastard. Mugged and insulted on the same night.'

The audience had relaxed with me, no longer uncomfortable at my amateurishness. I told them about my other mugging, about the golden Chopper, about Amir Shah and his remote control watch at school, about me telling a woman who was due to cremate her husband that the oven would be piping hot. I stayed up there for fifteen minutes, and it was exhilarating. Instantly, without question, the happiest I'd ever been in my life.

As I said goodnight, the applause made me smile from ear to ear, flashing my crooked discoloured teeth at Agraman as he made his way up back onto the stage.

'Jason Mounford, everybody!'

They applauded and people patted me on the back as I went behind the bar and carried on washing glasses for the rest of the evening, beaming.

After the show had finished and the last of the audience and well-wishers had left, Agraman came over and shook my hand.

'You got me out of a scrape there tonight, lad. Here's £20.'

I couldn't believe it – £20 for fifteen minutes' work. This pot washing was a mug's game.

'Why don't you work on a tight seven minutes and I'll give you another try in a month or so.'

Has there ever been a more terrifying Santa?
With his vacant eyes and sinister white gloves,
I hope it wasn't him on my roof in chapter one.

Christmas with the
Manfords is always
a big deal. Below,
that's Stephen celebrating
with our big present in 1989, the Super Nintendo.
Above, my mum has first go and we don't get a
look in till after the Queen's speech.

Round our way –
Nettleford Road
during what looks
like a 1960s vintage
car rally.

Me posing on our
flat-pack 'twat'
(see chapter three).

Me and Colin on our street. He's helpfully wearing a
City kit with the word 'brother' on the front, as if he
always knew this picture would need to be captioned.

Our first ever holiday at Pwllheli Butlins, financed by the local loan shark and the Lord Mayor. Below, we try to rob the Pwllheli giant - we'd already nicked everything else there.

What do donkeys get for dinner on Blackpool beach? Half an hour like everyone else. Not when I'm in town, 'Giddyup'.

Me (yes in a shell suit) losing my rag with one of God's own Canadian Mounties, in Kidderminster. Even when you read about it, it won't really make sense.

My Oakwood High School photo. It was hard enough avoiding bigger boys and getting close to the nice girls without your mum ruining your chances by cutting your fringe.

My brothers went through that convict stage, whereas I look like their lawyer. The other two kids are my mum and dad's Mark II family, Danielle and Niall.

Auntie Kathleen and other family members on stage at the Little Western. There's no one on the Ryan side of the family that isn't some kind of performer. Although I can't look at that photo without thinking 'Ha! I lost my virginity on her couch'.

One of my uncles sleeping off a Friday night as we sit watching Wacaday.

Me and Dad with Barry from the manslaughter/chip fat incident (see chapter twelve). A mix of Dolph Lundgren and Alan Carr.

Me and Laura with Mum and Dad outside the Southern Hotel, the local where I started out washing pots and ended up a proper comedian.

I had to prise this clipping off my nana's wall where it's been for nearly twelve years. Good snappy headline that.

■ JASON MANFORD: Career has taken a funny turn

From pot washer to comedy clean-up

TEENAGER Jason Manford is the new City Life Comedian of the Year — after an ultimatum from his mum.

He started washing pots at Chorlton comedy club the Buzz after she told him: "Get a job, or else".

And before long he switched to performing.

Now, after just eight gigs, Jason, 18, beat many established names to win the prestigious award once claimed by TV stars Caroline Aherne and Peter Kay.

Jason, from Whalley Range, said: "I was only earning £15 a night at the Buzz and it was really hard work. Then one night a comedian didn't turn up, so I said I'd have a go."

He admits he was stunned by his award: "There were some very strong comedians — I was shocked."

Jason's mum is not the only member of the family to boost his fledgling career. He said: "I come from an Irish Catholic family so they're all

BY TANIA BRANIGAN

comedians. I get a lot of my material from my dad — his observations are really funny."

And he revealed the secret of his success: "My main jokes come fom the Manchester Evening News. I buy it every day and read it twice — once as a reader in Manchester, and then for any funny stories I can use in the act."

Cat down the pub with my dad and Stephen, now a fully paid-up member of the Manfords.

Now, we've all had bad passport photos, but who the hell is that guy and why are his eyebrows so far apart?

The best £3 I've ever spent. Me and Cat looking nervous in the passport photos we took after we found out we were stuck at Sheffield station.

Chapter 18

I'll Be There For You

THE FIRST TIME I properly fell in love it was with John Lennon's daughter.

No, not that John Lennon, friend of Paul, husband of Yoko. John Lennon the plumber from Salford.

I had become friends with a girl called Laura Lennon at college. She was pretty and blonde, and the first time I realised I was besotted with her in that way was at a choir gig for a recently departed nun. I don't tend to be on the lookout for girls at funerals, especially a nun's, but as I was midway through belting out 'Ave Maria' in front of hundreds of crying clergy I clocked her on the back row. I smiled and she smiled back.

We kept smiling all the way through the recital and at one point she even winked at me. She was sexy. We were both sixteen, she looked like not a young girl but a woman, and she obviously liked me as much as I liked her. So there in the middle of St Anne's Church, during a funeral for a recently departed woman of God, surrounded by two hundred nuns, I'm not ashamed to say, I had a bit of a semi on.

We had chatted before that gig, in and around college, but it had never dawned on me till that evening when I saw her in her black dress, her face prettily painted with a little make-up as she sang her sweet notes, that I fancied her. But it genuinely hit me, like in a cartoon when Cupid flies an arrow into someone's heart. 'Blunk', I was caught, hook, line and sinker.

Over the next few weeks we continued chatting and flirting and I could think of little else beyond Laura. As the ache and tension was becoming unbearable, I took my chance during a night out with a load of our friends from the theatre class in Manchester centre. It was getting late and everyone was starting to make moves for home when I went to the toilet and I decided to drop my house key down the loo. It was the start of something special.

As I was waiting for a bus back to south Manchester and Laura was waiting for the bus to take her in the opposite direction, back to Salford, I started my pretence.

'Oh no, my key, I've lost it,' I said, expertly mimicking a man who'd lost his key.

'Think where you last saw it,' said Laura, trying to help. But the last time I saw it it was being flushed down the toilet in a nightclub on its way to the Irish Sea. Don't ask me why I didn't just pretend I'd lost my key; maybe I was taking the method acting a bit too seriously.

'Damn it,' I carried on, shuffling awkwardly in the cold night air. 'Mum's gonna kill me if I get back and wake the whole house up.'

'Come and stay at mine if you like,' she suggested innocently.

Bingo.

We got back late to Laura's mum's house in Lower Broughton, and had a brew on her sofa while we watched a repeat of *Streetmate* on Channel 4. As Davina ran around the street, manically trying to match people up, I was trying to work out my next move. I'd done the hard part, getting her alone in her house, but what the hell do you do next? With Hannah, she tended to be the one with the moves, with Cheryl it was usually outside in a group of other people snogging, but here, at 2am, we sat pretending to watch the TV but both secretly thinking, when are we going to kiss?

As *Streetmate* finished and she flicked over to *Nash Bridges*, I was starting to get annoyed with myself that I wasn't man enough to just go for it. I was aware that I'd been over-thinking this and anything I did would feel forced and unnatural. I was trying to tell myself to be impulsive but how can you prepare to be impulsive? You either are or you aren't.

Laura turned round.

'I love *Nash Bridges*. Didn't he used to be in...'

She didn't finish her sentence as my lips met hers. I'd managed to do something so impulsive even I didn't know I was about to do it. It was as if my lips had taken over from my brain: 'You had your chance, brain. It's our turn now – watch and learn, you useless pink dickhead.'

That night, as Laura looked into my eyes and gave me a final kiss before she went up to her room and I turned in to get some sleep on the couch, I felt amazing.

LAURA BECAME the first girlfriend I properly introduced to my family. It's always nerve-wracking bringing a girl home for the first time. Luckily Laura and Mum were both Salford girls so got on straight away and my dad is happy enough once he's confirmed they don't support United.

I'd decided to bring her to the Little Western pub in Moss Side one Sunday where my nana's band had a regular gig and just threw her in at the deep end. My friend Lucy always called my Nana Ryan my 'glamorous granny'. She'd be on stage, all dolled up in a deep blue sparkly dress, maybe a black beret on the side of her head, belting out songs at the top of her voice.

I'd been coming to this pub most Sundays for as long as I could remember – I had been the scrawny kid stealing 50p pieces off the pool table and now I was an adult stopping kids doing the same to me. I was still drinking Coke rather than anything stronger; in fact I think the reason I'm teetotal now was from being in these pubs so regularly as a kid.

My nana liked a drink. Every party we had at a pub, she would always bring a present and sit it on her table for the night. It was always the same size box wrapped in 'Happy Birthday' paper and every time someone asked if she'd like it moving and putting with the other presents she'd say, 'No, don't worry, I'll give it them myself.' Of course, her real present was already on the pile – this was a box of white wine with a little tap hanging over the edge of the table, but wrapped in party paper so no member of staff was any the wiser as to how this glamorous old lady was slowly getting pissed on the atmosphere alone. My mum carried on the tradition. She has a wealth of gay pals so when they opened a village full of them in the city centre she was the first one there. She didn't like paying city centre prices, though, so that's where working at a nursing home came into its own. Every few months they'd get a delivery of supplies and occasionally a couple of catheter bags would go 'missing'. Now I'm not saying my mum still does this (just in case her bosses are reading this) but at home she would fill a catheter bag up with vodka and Tia Maria and head into town with it strapped to the inside of her thigh. Then all night she and her friends would only order Cokes, using the tap at the bottom of her trouser leg to fill up on the good stuff.

We had a laugh on those Sundays in the Little Western and even though my nana's band rehearsed and played together every week, there never seemed to be a set way of doing things. In fact, it seemed that almost everyone in the pub would get up at some point and do a number. We'd be sat chatting when you'd hear my nana's Irish accent over the top of everyone else:

'Tommy, where's Tommy?'

'I'm here, Nora.' Tommy would be coming out of the gents, buttoning up his fly.

'Ah, there he is. Everyone, welcome Tommy up, he's going to play the mandolin for us today.'

Then Tommy, whoever he was, would launch into three or four songs on his mandolin, followed by Paddy on his fiddle or Gerry on his tin whistle. It was a great craic and although they were only supposed to be on for a couple of hours in the afternoon, they'd end up playing well into the night. As a kid we'd drive home to get ready for school the next day, and we'd wind down the windows, the smell of beer in the air and the sound of the guitar on the wind, and you would swear you were in the heart of sixties Dublin, not in nineties Moss Side.

I had no reason to worry: Laura loved my family and they loved her. She got up on stage and sang a song and they were all impressed by her bravery. Just put yourself in her shoes for one minute: you're surrounded by your new boyfriend's family you've only just met and they ask you to get up and sing an Irish song in a strange pub in the middle of gangland Manchester in front of two hundred people. Well, she did it and she was wonderful. I was in love.

One evening we went to Clayton, to my Auntie Kathleen's, to babysit. I'd babysat a few times since that fateful night when I'd cried myself to sleep after being dumped, but this was the first time I'd shared that couch with a girl.

Kathleen and Dave didn't mind that I'd brought a girl and left soon after we arrived. With the baby in bed, we did what all babysitters do and groped for an hour while a game show played on the telly.

I don't want to go into too much detail. I know I have done at other moments in the book but suffice to say that that couch, where'd I'd brought my broken heart not so long ago, was now the place where a new love was about to spring forth.

God, that sounds cheesy. How the hell do you write: 'I lost my virginity on the couch when *Friends* was beginning on Channel 4'? Oh, well, I seem to have just written that so we'll go with that, eh? Oddly, for such a momentous moment in anyone's life, I don't actually remember a great deal about it. I do recall trying for half an hour to unclip her bra only to find out the clasp was on the front, so I was essentially just scratching her back for thirty minutes. I remember it, obviously, not lasting that long; the relief of getting it done was almost too much. In fact, I think I was done before the Rembrandts had finished singing 'I'll Be There For You'. Even now I get a bit of a semi on when I hear that song. Thank God I don't watch E4.

LAURA WAS THE GIRL I was going to marry and spend the rest of my life with. I was in love.

We got through college but both struggled with our A levels and ended up having to go through clearing. This is where the crappiest of the university courses get given to the crappiest of college students. We were looking for a theatre-based course anywhere in the country but we wanted to go somewhere together.

As luck would have it we found a course at Manchester Met, only a short bus ride from both our houses. Or so we thought. It was only after we'd signed up we found out that Manchester Met have a campus in Alsager, near Crewe. Crewe is well over an hour away but we were still planning on commuting so we could save money on rent.

I lasted two days. The course wasn't what I wanted to do anyway – broadcast engineering isn't really my forte. I'm not good at carrying things, and that course was mainly carrying lights, jibs, sets and sound desks – no thanks.

I knocked it on the head. At least I could stay living at my mum and dad's. Good old Nettleford Road. The house was crammed by now as my mum and dad had decided to have another child. Obviously the three of us weren't giving them enough love and attention so they had my sister Danielle, and by the time I'd given up traipsing to Alsager every day (well, for two days) my mum was about ready to give birth to my youngest brother, Niall.

So that's seven people living in a small three-bedroom house and the smallest room couldn't really be called a bedroom unless you were Dobby the house elf from the Harry Potter films. Me, Stephen and Colin were put into one room and Danielle was given the box room as a nursery. Niall was obviously in with my parents but I could sense a rumbling and the phrase 'first in, first out' was getting bandied about. I was eighteen and I think my mum and dad expected me to have moved on by now.

There wasn't a moment that I moved in with Laura; I just gradually spent more nights at her house than at mine. Like a lot of couples, it never became official; we never sat down and worked out rent or odd jobs around the house. It just sort of happened.

Laura lived with her mum, Mary, who was a tiny thing with a great sense of humour, but she could fly into a rage about the smallest of things. Many of them, it seemed, regarding me… and the kitchen cupboards. Early on I made the mistake of helping myself to a Chocolate Hobnob or four, only to get a severe tongue-lashing from the matriarch of the house. I can't say I got any better on this front and it became a constant bone of contention.

Most of the time we got on – I was the only man in the house after nearly a decade of it being these two females – but we would have stand-up rows over the tiniest thing. As is always the case, the source of these spats was much more deep-rooted. We may have been arguing about who used the last of the Lurpak and then put the empty packet back in the fridge, but deep down I think she thought I was trying to take over her house and take away her little girl, her only companion since Laura's dad had died suddenly ten years earlier.

I didn't feel like I was doing that, but I suppose with every room I decorated, or every carpet I laid down, the house was one thing further away from how it had been. I thought I was helping, but maybe with every stroke of a brush I was covering up her memories of her late husband.

Chapter 19

In It To Win It

'PLEASE WELCOME DAVE BARON.'

When I first started doing stand-up I only had eight minutes of material so I was working hard to build on it every day, buying newspapers and writing little lines on all the stories. I'd now done a handful of gigs around Manchester for Agraman and I seemed to be getting better the more stage time I got. Laura was my number one fan. She came to all my gigs and recorded me on a cheap Dictaphone I'd picked up at Argos. Some of the gigs had so few people at them when I listened back to my recording the only person laughing was her.

My number two fan turned out to be Laura's Uncle Dave. Dave Baron, I discovered, was an old-time comic on the working men's club circuit and he took a shine to me. He was a lovely fella and really funny – he did old one-liners and some funny stories and I'd occasionally go with him up to Blackpool and watch him perform.

'Good evening, ladies and gentleman, lovely to be here. I'm an unlucky so and so, I am. I went to a funeral the other day and I caught the wreath. I've been to so many funerals lately, my suit smells of ham sandwiches…'

He must have told ten gags a minute, and the audiences loved it.

I went with him to a gig at the Number One club in Blackpool once. It could easily have been what Peter Kay based *Phoenix Nights* on. It was hilariously old-fashioned but I loved it.

As I went in with Dave, carrying his suit in a bag from M&S, the doorman looked me and up and down and said, 'Tuck your shirt in, lad.'

I sat down at a table but an old couple suddenly appeared and rudely told me that I couldn't sit there because it was their table. In typical teenage fashion I replied, 'Well, it's not got your name on it.'

At which point the old fella pointed to a sign that read 'This is George and Joy's table'. You can't argue with that, can you?

Backstage there would always be a couple of other old-school comics on the bill, milling around before they went on, and Dave would proudly tell them I was a fellow comedian, even though I'd only done a handful of gigs.

'Oh, you're one of these new comedians like Ben Elton, are you? All those stories instead of proper jokes.'

I laughed it off, never once feeling I should point out that you could no longer call Ben Elton a 'new comedian' in 1999.

I might have been different from them but I learnt a lot watching those guys. Although things change with each generation, the principles are the same. Of course they weren't all using their own jokes and the odd gag was as un-PC as you can get, but their craft and their timing, honed over years of hard graft and unforgiving audiences on the old club circuit, was wonderful to watch.

When they relaxed with a pint after the show I loved hearing them swap stories about the circuit and in particular those about other comics dying on stage. I was curious. It happens at some point to anyone who ever gets on stage.

Dave told me about an old comic having a terrible time once and he was a tough fella who'd been gigging for forty-odd years. But this night he can't handle it. The audience chatted away right through his half-hour set – not at him, just to each other. Indifference is far more painful than aggression. At least with a heckle you can deal with it and get a laugh, but it's hard to have a hilarious line about people not being interested in you.

As it goes on, he is getting more and more agitated, until he's done his time and storms off the stage to little or no applause. As he's walking down the corridor to his dressing room he can still hear the chit-chat of the punters. Before he gets into his room, the club secretary passes him with the bingo cart and puts it on the stage. Then just as he sits in his room, the comic hears the chattering of the audience quieten then suddenly go completely silent.

That's it. He's livid. They are giving more respect to the bingo than they were to him. So he storms back up the corridor and onto the stage. He grabs the mike, stands in front of the club secretary and launches into a verbal assault on the crowd. 'I can't believe you bunch of bastards have given more respect to the bingo than you gave to me. I've been doing this job man and boy and you didn't even have the common courtesy to give my act a chance. Well, the lot of you can fuck right off. Look at you, you bunch of fucking sad old bastards…' Before he can finish, the club secretary leans over and whispers into his ear, 'Calm down, Alf, the bingo's not started yet – we were just having a minute's silence for a barmaid who died last week.'

They were tough gigs in those working men's clubs, not like the easy ones I was playing. I'd been spoilt really; after the Buzz Club I played a student gig in Fallowfield at Scruffy Murphy's. The compere Toby Hadoke brought me on and I did my eight minutes to a great response. At that point I genuinely thought stand-up comedy was the easiest job in the world. And it can be, when you're in the zone, the crowd are up for it, and you're at a good time in your life. It can be a piece of cake.

If I thought I was in the zone at Scruffy Murphy's, I realised I wasn't even close when I watched the headliner that night. It was the second time I'd seen him and I was still in awe of what he could do to an audience.

'Let's hear it for Peter Kay...'

After he'd finished the gig I went over to say hello. We went for a kebab up the road at Abdul's and talked about comedy and our lives. We had lots in common, from our Irish families to working dead-end jobs. An hour later I was crying with laughter into my doner meat.

He gave me a lift back to Laura's house in Salford and came in for a cup of tea and some Jaffa Cakes. I don't remember Mary telling him off for eating half a packet of them but I think she was a bit star struck.

I told him I had entered the City Life Comedian of the Year competition and asked if he had any tips, seeing as he'd won it two years previously.

'How many hours a week do you work?' he asked.

'About forty-five all in,' I replied.

'And do you want to be a full-time comedian?'

'Yeah, course I do.'

'And how many hours a week do you think a good comedian works?'

'Erm, I don't know. I suppose twenty minutes a set, three times a week, so an hour.'

He looked at me, clearly disappointed.

'Treat comedy like you treat your work now. Work on it for forty hours a week, whether that's writing or reading or ringing up for gigs. If you wanna be taken seriously you've gotta take it seriously.'

And d'you know what? He was right.

Laura came with me to the first heat of the competition. It was at the Buzz Club so I'd copped lucky with a home fixture. The heat was my seventh ever gig and I went on after the competition's favourite, a character act called Jackie Valentio.

He was hilarious, singing, doing impressions and telling great gags all in the space of eight minutes. He even had time to interact with the audience. He tore the roof off the place and the crowd went mad. I got on stage and looked at the audience. I could see what they were thinking: 'How's this guy gonna follow that? He looks like a fat Michael Owen.'

So that was my first line. I did sort of look like a fatter version of Michael Owen. The audience laughed and listened to my other jokes about being mugged and I managed to scrape through to the final in second place behind Mr 'Goodtime' Valentio.

The final took place at the Dancehouse Theatre in the city centre and was full to bursting with about four hundred people. It was the biggest audience I'd played to, even if you'd put all my other audiences together. I had a party of about twenty people for support: my mum, dad, brothers, Lucy with some of her friends, and Laura had brought her mum and her Uncle Dave.

I was on again after Jackie Valentio, backstage I'd found out he was actually a comic and actor called Archie Kelly, who later went on to play Kenny in *Phoenix Nights*. He was as hilarious backstage as he was on stage and I started to think, if I could get second or even third then that would be one hell of an achievement.

I was in the wings of the theatre waiting for a funny Scouse comic called Chris Cairns to finish his act. He'd done really well and I looked along the front row to see one woman wiping away a tear. I was nervous, almost sick with worry, and as I went on to do my ninth ever gig, this friendly Scouser wished me luck. Damn it, he was funny *and* nice.

As I did my gig, I could see my dad looking around the room, watching the audience's reaction, Laura was beaming and Lucy looked proud. Bar a couple of word fumbles and dirtying my trousers that were 'clean on', I couldn't have wished for a better gig and I went off to a lovely round of applause.

After the break, Archie Kelly was putting his Jackie Valentio wig on and readying himself for winning the competition and its £150 prize. He went on and did some impressions, which did really well, then a song about Princess Margaret scalding both her feet in the bath that time, then he went to chat to some of the audience. He picked the wrong woman.

Sometimes it just happens like that. I've done it myself. You end up talking to the one person on the front row who really doesn't want to chat and has absolutely nothing to say that you can make jokes about, it's called a 'comedy cul de sac'. The worst thing is, it's not even their fault, it's yours. The normal part of your brain tells you to leave it and move on but the comedy part tells you to keep going until you find something you can get a laugh out of.

For Jackie Valentio that night, his chosen victim was giving him nothing and he ended up spending over two minutes of his allotted eight trying to cultivate funnies from this woman. His other six were fantastic, though, so we all still presumed he'd done enough to win.

As the winners were being announced, we were all stood at the side of stage. Chris Cairns, the friendly Scouser, whispered to me that I'd won it but I wasn't convinced. There were at least four other acts who were better than me that night, Chris being one of them. He came third. Jackie Valentio came second. And the winner was...

'... Jason Manford.'

I went back onto the stage and collected my prize, the most money I'd ever had in one go, and when I looked up I could see all my friends and family were standing up, cheering.

This was it. It really was. I'd made it.

Chapter 20

'You Can Stick It Up Your Arse'

'LOOK, JASON, you need to work out what you want to do.'

It was a wet Wednesday night at the Southern and I'd turned up late again. Anne had me cornered and was giving it to me with both barrels.

I'd gone on to win another competition for the *Leicester Mercury* and if I'm totally honest I was getting a bit full of myself. With the security of making thirty to fifty quid a gig I started to think I could turn up late for work at the Southern. Anne certainly agreed with this character assessment. She thought my 'career' as a comedian was going to my head. There were four or five people working the bar but I would often let them down at the last minute because a gig had come up in Plymouth and I had to go. She had quite a scary voice when she was really angry.

'You can't keep leaving me with no notice. It's not fair on the other staff members.'

The kid in me came out and I tried to be pretty nonchalant about it.

'Well, whatever, really – if you wanna sack me, just sack me.'

God, I was a little shit at times.

It got heated, she said I wasn't showing her enough respect and I told her she didn't appreciate the work I did put in (those glasses didn't wash themselves, you know).

In the end I stormed out. I think I may even have said those immortal words: 'You can stick your job up your arse.' I don't know why I said it, I don't know why I was so rude, but I had just turned eighteen and was on stage most nights making people laugh; I felt indestructible.

Even on the way home, when I realised I'd left my coat at the pub, I was too proud to go back and get it. You can't, can you? Not after you've told someone to stick something up their arse, you can't sneak back in and say, 'Sorry, I forgot my jacket.'

I'VE WALKED OUT of a lot of jobs over the years. That summer I got a job at CIS Insurance in Manchester city centre. It was a call centre job giving people car insurance quotes over the phone. I worked my arse off there while doing gigs whenever I could in the evening. I'd spend all the time between phone calls reading the newspapers and writing jokes.

There are not many good jokes about car insurance, but you couldn't tell the fella who sat next to me that – he was always using them to clinch deals. There was one gag he used to do relentlessly. Whenever a caller said to him, 'Can I get a motor quote, please?' his eyes would light up at the opportunity. 'Yes, of course, madam. "Bruuum, bruuum." That's a BMW!'

He'd look at me, silently laughing, and I'd give him the awkward smile you do when someone thinks they're hilarious – you know, that really wide smile where you raise your eyebrows and lift your head back, nodding a little as if to say, 'Yeah, good one, mate.'

I hated it. I hated choosing what tie to wear in the morning and I hated chatting about my weekend by the water cooler. I had the same sandwich every day from the sandwich shop across the road and at least once a week on the bus back to Laura and her mum's house I would sit in recently chewed chewing gum and have to put my trousers in the freezer overnight.

I had to fit the gigs in as best I could and the managers, to be fair to them, let me leave early on days I had to get a train to Southampton or Aberdeen or wherever. After travel and accommodation to these far-flung places, I was earning less money than I was sat on my arse in this office making people's Ford Escorts fully comp.

One afternoon I got a call from a gig booker in Truro, in deepest Cornwall. He'd had an act pull out and asked if I could go down there and do it. I totted up the numbers: after travel, B&B and food I worked out I would be £72 down. I also needed to take the rest of the day off to do it, which meant I was losing £6 an hour too. So off I went to let the manager know that I needed to go and lose nearly £100 in Cornwall.

The manager wouldn't let me go. There'd been a spate of gastric flu and we were short-staffed and if I went it would leave the customers with queues of over twenty minutes on hold. I accepted her decision: if I was going to make the gig I'd have to leave at 11.30 to make the train and it was nearly eleven o'clock now.

At 11.28 a call came through – a woman who had been cut off by another member of staff and had had to hold on for a lifetime again before she got through to me.

'Good morning, CIS Insurance, Jason speaking, how can I help you?'

'I have been on this phone for over an hour and all I want to do is insure a fucking Cinquecento third party fire and fucking theft.' She was in full flow but I wasn't listening, my mind was wandering. I could feel the stage lights warming my face and hear the people of Truro's laughter ringing in my ears; I could see their little smiley faces light up when I came on stage to tell them some of my jokes and thoughts.

'... some absolute dickhead cut me off and now I seem to have come through to an even bigger dickhead...'

I could hear the applause at the end of my set and could see the people coming to chat to me at the bar afterwards and tell me how funny I had been.

'... are you listening to me, you little shit? It's an N-reg and it needs insuring now...'

I calmly took my headphones off and placed them on the desk. I grabbed my wallet and phone, and put my coat over my cheap George at Asda suit. I got up and walked serenely to the end of my block of desks and then towards the lift, hoping that no one would ask me where I was going. As I left I could still here the woman's tiny distant voice ranting away in the earpiece, like an angry Borrower.

I got in the lift, got out at the ground floor, walked out of the front doors and never went back again. The warm daytime air woke me up and I couldn't believe what I'd just done. It felt brilliant. I recommend to anyone in a job they hate to just walk out. I know you can't always afford to and it may be a while before another one comes along, but that first free afternoon you have off after a lifetime at the same desk is the best feeling in the world.

Chapter 21
Vienna – Edinburgh – Salford

IT WAS THE SUMMER of 2000 when Peter Kay rang me, as he did from time to time, to check how my comedy career was going. And apart from losing £100 in Truro every so often it was going pretty well. But I'd had enough of call centres and still wanted to go to university to study and was waiting for clearing to come around again so I could apply. Peter had done a HND course in Media and Performance at Salford University and he couldn't speak highly enough of it.

I rang the university and asked them for an audition, but because of my woeful A-level results they declined to even see me. I was devastated. I was working all the hours God sent at these crappy jobs and the rest of my time was spent writing and gigging, but I was a long way off breaking even. I was as poor as a student but without the benefit of having a qualification or getting a lie-in every day.

That summer me and Laura and the rest of her family were invited to her cousin's wedding in Austria. It was the first time I'd ever been abroad so I was going to need a passport. Well, actually, no, I'd been to France with school when I was thirteen but for some reason I'd not needed a passport for it. It was a three-day European Awareness trip. The idea was you get to know a little bit more about Europe. I imagine you're thinking we spent whole days in galleries and museums, looking at wonderful works of art and ancient artefacts from the dawn of

European civilisation. Well, no. We spent half a day in Brussels looking at the European Courts. We bought some chocolate, had a quick look at a statue of a boy having a piss then spent two days at EuroDisney: proper culture. I think the teachers enjoyed it more than we did in the end, apart from Miss Bloom who got her tits felt up by an odd Spanish man in the queue for Space Mountain.

So I set off with my brother, Stephen, to our nearest passport office in Liverpool to get one. I'd borrowed just enough money from my mum to pay for the train fare, the pictures and the passport itself, with not even a spare 40p for a can of Lilt, so this had to be a slick affair.

We arrived at Old Hall Street and got in the smallish queue to get my photos taken – you know the one, where no matter how you are looking on the day it makes you look like you're on day release. It was one of those machines that lets you take as many pictures as you want until you're happy, or so I thought. I started messing about, trying to entertain my brother with daft faces, pulling my favourite Les Dawson gurns. My brother was wetting himself and even though there was a bit of a queue gathering, we were both in stitches.

On my fifth photo attempt I leant really close to the screen and opened my eyes wide. I didn't smile or pull any face, I just stared coldly at the camera. I looked like a serial killer. I showed my brother and he had a good chuckle; then I heard a robotic American voice say: 'Photographs printing.'

The machine started to whirr and print my photo, but it wasn't me, it was my evil-looking twin. My brother was in convulsions on the floor as he knew I didn't have any extra money to pay for another set. I was gutted. If they wouldn't accept them I'd have to go all the way home and explain to my mum that I needed another thirty quid to get me back to Liverpool another day. She'd go spare. The machine finally stopped blow-drying the photos and my brother took them out, composing himself before having a good old look. You could hear his laugh from the top of the Liver Building, but I wasn't laughing. This was money I didn't have, I was already well into my overdraft, and I was only getting a free ride on this wedding trip because someone else had dropped out.

I was just contemplating Mum's reaction when my brother, through his tears, had an idea. A ludicrous idea, an idea so crazy it might just work.

I waited in the queue to be seen by a passport clerk. As my number was called, I had a quick look at my picture and readied my face.

'Yes, sir?' the clerk asked as she looked up at me.

I was leaning right into the glass, my eyebrows raised and my eyes wide open in a mad stare, not smiling and with nostrils flared.

'Just a passport, please, love,' I said in a slightly Mr Bean type voice. I don't know why I'd changed my voice too but I felt it suited my new slightly crazy-looking face. My brother was hyperventilating in the corner somewhere.

Somehow it worked and we travelled back to Manchester with my passport in hand. Stephen couldn't wait to show it to Colin and my dad. Dad had a little chuckle, as did Colin, but Mum saw through the comedy to the real effect this was going to have on my life.

'What are you going to do when you go through customs?' she asked.

'What you on about, Mum?'

'Well, it looks nothing like you. You're not going to be allowed in to other countries unless you pull that face.'

As I entered passport control at Salzburg airport, my laughter had dried up as I raised my eyebrows for the fifth time that day and attempted to get into a country looking like a Manc madman. My mum's words went round and round my head.

'And that's a ten-year passport, you dozy sod. You're gonna be pulling that face for a decade.'

WE LEFT the wedding party early as me and Laura were flying to another new country where they were waiting to see my passport. We were due at the Edinburgh Festival, where I was in a Channel 4-sponsored competition called So You Think You're Funny?, a competition that had helped launch the careers of comedians like Peter Kay, Lee Mack and Dylan Moran.

If you've never been to the Edinburgh Festival, then please, this summer, instead of two weeks in Majorca, just go – it's brilliant. Thousands of impromptu shows and plays, films and presentations. There's no atmosphere like it on earth.

It was our first experience of it and Laura and I were instantly hooked. Not even staying at a dingy youth hostel in the centre of town in a room with a German man who smelt of wet grass and a geriatric Geordie woman who sang in her sleep could stem our enthusiasm. As you walk down the Royal Mile there are hundreds of performers trying to sell you their show, people dressed up and randomly thrusting leaflets in your face, saying things like, 'Shakespeare on a Bouncy Castle, 2pm at the Dog and Sporran, mate.' That was a surprisingly good show, actually.

Every time I go there's a double act on the Royal Mile that always make me laugh. It's a man and a woman; the woman has more piercings in her face than you could count and can be seen pulling and hanging items of various weights from a clip in her lip or her nose.

Meanwhile the guy is sat behind her playing the bongos. I always wonder if they split their takings 50–50. That would seem unfair; he is quite literally not pulling his weight in that partnership. Maybe his dad owned the van or something, I don't know.

The final featured seven comics and was hosted by Graham Norton, who we got to meet backstage before the show. He was lovely in his gorgeous dressing room full of flowers and fruit and mirrors with lights around them. We were in the dressing room next door, which even Anne Frank would have complained about: seven of us squeezed into a small toilet cubicle as we prepared to go on stage and answer the competition's question, So You Think You're Funny?

If that was the question, the answer from me was 'Well, I thought I was, yeah, but now I'm having second thoughts.' An Australian chap won and a brilliant Scottish comic called Des Clarke came second. There was no third place so I sort of counted myself and the other five as joint third (in fact I used to put 'joint third' on my comedy CV when sending it out to clubs and no one batted an eye).

I went home with Laura, feeling like a loser. Not just because I was on a night bus but because it was the first competition final I hadn't won. All right, I'd only won two, but that's still a pretty good hit rate. And I don't count the BBC comedy heats, which I didn't even get close to winning after a fatal mistake on the night.

Peter Kay was hosting that one, and it was at the Frog and Bucket in Manchester, a fun if slightly rough comedy club with floral wallpaper that smells of broken dreams and chip fat. Many acts have started their careers there and later on I would go back time and time again for some fantastic gigs. It was run by a guy called Dave Perkins, a cigar-smoking, Crombie-wearing, gangster-looking bloke, who was always very nice to me, thank God. He reminded me a bit of Arthur Daly in

Minder but he was built like Ray Winstone in *Sexy Beast*. I remember him coming over to me one night and shaking my hand.

'Well done, son,' he said.

'Thanks, Mr Perkins,' I replied.

As I took my hand away, my wages of £60 were in my palm. Even though I'd earned the money fair and square, and it was the amount we'd agreed before I went on stage, he still, for no apparent reason, managed to pay me in such a way that it felt underhand and slightly dodgy.

The night of the BBC heat, Laura's Uncle Dave had given me a pep talk.

'You've only got four minutes this time, so why not tell a couple of old gags before you start your own stuff – get them onside with a few sure-fire winners.'

It seemed like a good idea and he gave me a couple of one-liners from the magical pot of pub jokes he had in his brain.

As Peter introduced me, I was debating what gag I should do, so I went with the shortest:

'So this dyslexic walks into a bra...'

I was confident it would get a titter or two but it got nothing but an awkward, uncomfortable silence. I looked round and the audience were avoiding my gaze. I carried on into my act, stunned, like a boxer who thought he was going to spend the first few moments of the round just hopping from one foot to the next but ends up getting a great big fist in between the eyes.

At the end of my bit, I'd won the audience over and I got a good reception but I still couldn't understand why that old pub gag hadn't got a bit more of a response. Even if it was a groan or a heckle, I could've dealt with it, but to just stare at me was weird.

Laura came over.

'Why did you do that?' she said.

'What?'

'That dyslexic joke,' she replied.

I shrugged. 'Why not? I thought it was funny.'

'It was. When Peter did it.'

It turned out that moments before Peter Kay had introduced me on stage, he'd told a few old pub gags to warm the crowd up. And as my luck on that night would have it, the last gag he told before I went on was about the same unfortunate dyslexic.

It must've looked so odd to the audience. They didn't know that I'd been watching Peter from behind a fire door where no sound could penetrate; I'd just about heard my name but I'd not heard a single bit of his act. Literally the last gag he told and the first gag I told were identical. I always wanted to be like him, but not that much.

A few days later he rang me. I thought I was about to get it in the ear for my comedy faux pas, but actually he was ringing to help me out again.

'You fancy going to Salford Uni?' he asked.

'Yeah, I'd love to, mate. Why?'

'I've rung them – you start in September.'

I'd told him about me getting knocked back so I couldn't believe what he was saying.

'Oh my God, that's fantastic! What about Laura?' I thought I'd push my luck.

'Yep, her as well. You've got to audition but you'll piss that.'

And he was right. I did have to audition and I did piss it. We were both signed up and started Salford University in the September and as it was so close to Laura's house, we didn't even need to stay in student halls, which I'm sure Mary was chuffed to bits about.

Chapter 22

Bert and Ernie

THINGS WERE LOOKING UP and the gigs were starting to roll in. I still wasn't being paid a living but I was getting valuable stage time and a good array of gigs. From little sweaty student pubs to village art centres, I was building up my act and getting more and more confident on stage. Agraman was really helping me out, giving me gigs at all the venues he ran and even letting me be the guinea pig at some new ones.

One such gig was at Manchester University student union. I arrived at seven, an hour before the gig was due to start, and found another act in the bar – a tall chap from Cannock with kindly eyes, not unlike the BFG, called Steve Edge. I can honestly say Steve instantly became the funniest guy I'd ever met. We sat down in the corner of this dingy bar and he told me about his family and his crappy flat in Salford.

'It's rough where I live – the other day I got a taxi home and as he turned the corner near the block I actually said the words, "Just here, mate, next to where that settee's on fire."'

He really made me laugh and the hour before the gig just flew by.

The student union ents officer eventually came to show us to the room we would be performing in, but there were two quite big problems. Firstly no one had bothered to advertise it to the student population so there was no audience, and secondly the room was double-booked with the karate club.

As we walked in the ents manager's face was a picture: there, ten yards from where we were stood, were nearly sixty guys in white pyjamas and multi-coloured belts all 'haaaiyyyaaaaa'-ing in unison. I looked at him and his face had gone the colour of their robes. He couldn't even talk, devastated. They were all looking up at the sensei, who was stood on our stage, barking out directions.

'Punch, kick, punch, punch, kick.'

Steve turned to the worried-looking manager, raised his eyebrows and said, 'Tough crowd, eh, mate?'

I laughed for days afterwards at the timing of the line. It was exquisite.

By the time Steve gave me a lift home later that night, I knew he was going to be my best mate for ever. It's hard making new friends as a grown-up; you always think, I've got enough mates now, there are no more interview spaces, but every so often someone special comes along and you thank your lucky stars that fate allowed you to meet as your life is a richer, fuller place with them in it.

To be honest I needed the friends. Since I'd been going out with Laura, me and Lucy had grown apart. I don't know if it happens with a lot of platonic friendships at that age but we found it difficult being friends when the other one was in a relationship. It's hard to explain the friendship to your new partner and then it was difficult to hear about how great Lucy's new guy was without feeling, I don't know, jealous maybe? And with me at university and Lucy finishing college, we stopped hanging out.

I'd met a few people at university. I had plenty of pals but hadn't really met a genuine 'friend'. Laura, on the other hand, was in her element; she'd made loads of friends and was out every night with them while I was gigging as much as possible. I didn't drink so I very rarely joined her. It was weird; for the past couple of years we'd been with each other almost 24/7 and now I was only seeing her when either one of us climbed into bed from a night out.

Me and Steve had started writing a sitcom together. We found each other funny and had a few ideas for a show. We decided to go away on a writing weekend to Oxford, away from girlfriends and families, somewhere we could have a laugh and hopefully write the next *Only Fools and Horses*. I told Laura I was going away, gave her a kiss goodbye and off we went.

We arrived in Oxford on a Friday evening at a B&B that Steve had booked us into for fifteen quid each, and when we got there it was easy to see why it was so cheap. You know those B&Bs that are essentially someone's house and you feel like you're intruding on their lives and ruining their weekend because you want a shower at 10.30 but they turn the immersion heater off at nine? Yeah, well, it wasn't even as good as that.

I walked up the crumbling concrete steps and through the door and was transported back fifty years, with dusty patterned carpet at my feet and a smell of must in the air. I felt like Nicholas Lyndhurst in the opening episode of *Goodnight Sweetheart*. While Steve parked the car I checked us in. The owner seemed jolly enough.

'Have you come for the flower festival? It's very busy.'

'Erm, no, not really.'

'Oh well, you were lucky to get the last room.'

'You mean two rooms? We booked one each.'

'Erm, no, it came through as one booking, a Mr and Mrs Steve Edge. Are you Mr Edge?' As he said that, my new husband came through the door with his man bag wrapped round his tight white T-shirt.

'Hey, there's a flower festival on – we'll have to pop in and have a look.'

Me and the proprietor just stared. I could hear the cogs turning in this old man's head. This was a man who, like his house, was still living in the 1950s. He thought he knew what he had here, but he'd got the wrong end of the stick. As far as he was concerned he had two options: he could either banish us from his establishment or he could move with the times and turn a blind eye to whatever goes on behind closed doors, as long as he gets his thirty quid.

I saw it dawn on Steve's face that the man thought we were lovers. He explained about the two-room booking but the fact remained that there was only one room left and we had to have it.

To compensate, Steve went into overdrive.

'Well, nowt wrong with two friends sharing a bed – look at More-cambe and Wise or Laurel and Hardy.'

'Or Bert and Ernie,' I chucked in to help him out.

'Well, I think Bert and Ernie were in separate beds, but yes, I get your point, two straight guys just kicking back, enjoying each other's company.'

'You're making it sound worse now, mate,' I whispered.

The owner went into his own sort of overliberal overdrive.

'Well, whatever gets you through the night, chaps. It's no concern of mine what grown adults get up to once the door's closed.'

'No, we're not...'

'As I said, thanks for choosing to stay at the Shine Inn. We're open to anyone – nobody judges anyone here.'

He kept talking. We both wanted him to stop but he just kept going.

'I always say to my wife, live and let live. I don't care what anyone's into as long as they don't shove it down my throat...'

We grabbed our keys and made our way to our room. We had a chuckle about the mix-up as we opened the door, but then we stopped dead. In the corner of this Victorian-themed room was something that concerned us both: not the bed that we were going to have to share – we could get over that – but past the bed and under the window was the bathroom. Well, I say bathroom, but it wasn't in a different room. Within the four walls of our bedroom were a shower, sink and toilet. This guy had taken the en-suite to the next level.

That night we slept alongside each other, very much like Eric and Ernie. I even smoked a pipe. When we woke with a wall of pillows between us instead of under our heads we were happy that we'd got through our first night in bed together with no awkwardness. Then we looked at our bathroom suite and had to toss a coin for first use.

Steve had first dibs. As I sat outside the door on the floor playing Snake on my Nokia, the owner came up the stairs and we locked eyes for a few seconds. He was obviously one of those people who didn't like an awkward silence and had to fill it with something even if it created more awkward silences.

He looked at the door and then down at me in my boxer shorts and A-Team T-shirt.

'Lovers' tiff, is it?' he enquired.

I just sighed. 'Yeah, if you want, mate.'

WHEN STEVE dropped me off at Laura's, she was upstairs, alone. I couldn't wait to tell her that this guy thought me and Steve were gay and about the toilet in the room. The one thing me and Laura shared was the same sense of humour; we made each other laugh all the time, it was the centre of our relationship. I went into our room and she was crying. My heart sank.

'What's up, sweetheart?' I asked.

'I need to talk to you.'

Oh God, I thought, not this again. I'd been broken up with once already in my life, but I was an adult now, and this was the girl I was planning to spend the rest of my life with. I sat down and prepared to take it like a man. This time I wasn't going to cry like a girl, or a baby, or a baby girl.

'Go on then, what is it?' I asked.

She handed me a Clearblue test. I didn't even need to look. I knew what was happening.

'I'm pregnant and it's not yours.'

Chapter 23

When the Rain Starts to Fall

I'M ONLY MESSING, it was mine – I just thought it'd make that chapter end a lot more dramatically. I'd even like you to go back again and imagine the *EastEnders* drums after she said it.

I was half in shock and half over the moon, to be honest. OK, I might only be nineteen but my mum had had two by that age. If anything I was a late starter. I was never one of these guys who was terrified of fatherhood. I think parenting suits a younger couple, all that running around in the park and staying up till all hours changing nappies. I don't fancy that when I'm an old man. The only nappy I want to be changing by then will be my own.

We hugged and worked out how to tell our parents. I wasn't too concerned about mine: for one they wouldn't have a hypocritical leg to stand on and my mum had just had another baby herself. I was more worried about telling Mary and Laura's family but we'd been together a few years and we weren't kids any more.

The plan was I'd finish the year at university and then get a job in an office or a call centre to support them both. We started looking at flats and baby seats and cots; we had everything circled in the Argos catalogue before I'd even told my nana.

We went to the doctor's and they did all the tests. We were six weeks already. I say 'we', I mean Laura obviously. I went on stage a few nights later and just thought, sod it, I'm gonna tell the world.

'So, I'm going to be a dad, everyone.'

The crowd cheered and it felt fantastic.

Our parents were great and everyone was really supportive. They could see we were in love and I genuinely couldn't wait. Every day was like Christmas Eve. I put my ear to Laura's tummy each morning hoping to hear something or feel a kick from my son or daughter, but it was much too early for any of that.

Laura was a bit more cautious and tentative about the whole thing at first. She told me to calm down on countless occasions and I tried, I really tried, but I was in Mothercare weeks before our three-month scan, working out if our student loan would pay for one of those fancy three-wheeler buggies that all the cool dads were pushing around.

Maybe I got carried away. Maybe I just wanted it too bad.

One night we were lying in bed, laughing as usual over something or other. I was planning on turning Mary's room into a nursery and shipping her off to an old folks' home – the usual things sons-in-law say behind their mother-in-law's back. I looked at Laura as she laughed and at that moment I couldn't have loved anyone any more.

'Thank you.'

'What for?' she said.

'You know what for – for this, for giving me this, this baby,' I said, tears filling my eyes.

'You daft sod, you won't be saying that when it's 3am and you've got poo under your fingernails.'

'I will, I bloody will, I promise. You will never once hear me complain about baby poo under my fingernails.' We laughed and fell asleep in each other's arms. I had a smile so wide I thought my face would rip.

A few mornings later, I woke up to an empty bed. The sun slipped through the gap in the curtain and the dust danced in the beam. I yawned, smiled and stretched my arm to the other side and felt nothing. I rolled over to see where she was. But there was nothing. Her pillow was cold. So was my leg. I could hear crying coming from the bathroom. As I pulled the covers back, I realised what had caused the tears.

I felt like we cried for weeks, just the two of us in that room, mourning a child that we never knew, would never know. People offered their condolences but with the occasional moment of clarity it seemed so ridiculous.

'I'm sorry for your loss.'

What loss? We never saw them, or held them, or heard them cry. The only person that had died was someone I'd created in my head. It was the strangest, most upsetting feeling of my life. I can't even describe it properly, but my immediate feeling was that this was all my fault. I'd built it up so much and not even considered Laura's feelings. I didn't know if she was worried or excited about having a child. I selfishly just couldn't wait to be a dad.

We hardly left the house for weeks, I just held Laura on our bed – and when we did I would get sick of hearing the same things from people.

'You can always get pregnant again.' That's hardly the point, is it? You wouldn't say that if your kid was ten, would you? I know I'm being silly comparing a foetus to an actual child, but honestly that's how it felt. Maybe I'm not being silly, maybe that's how you should feel. It would be a pretty cold heart that said, the day after, 'OK, love, let's have another try then.'

A few weeks later and I felt like I couldn't cry in front of Laura, even though every time I saw her I was reminded of what I'd put her through, what I'd caused. I felt like I had to be strong for her so I didn't cry when I was with her, and soon, I stopped crying altogether.

Laura's friends rallied round her and took her out every night to take her mind off things, but I didn't have anyone. I'd only just met Steve so I couldn't lumber him with this. Lucy was in Newcastle at university, ironically doing midwifery, and anyway I'd not spoken to her properly for months. My parents were great but they had two babies in the house and I couldn't bear to see any kids at that time. It's crazy now when I look at my little brother Niall to think I could have a son or daughter that age. It's also terrifying to think how different my life would've been.

While Laura was out getting drunk with her university friends, I was trying my best to get on with things. I had a few gigs in the diary but I wasn't in the mood for making people laugh; I don't think I even smiled during those dark months.

I did a gig for my family, which was not a good idea. Don't ever do a gig in front of people that have changed your nappy and don't mind telling you about it. It was a charity gig for a hospital ward that had looked after my nana.

As my uncle introduced me on to the stage, I knew my heart wasn't in it. There's nothing worse than seeing a comedian on stage who doesn't want to be there. An audience can sense it. My jokes felt hollow and pointless. Of course most comedians' jokes are hollow and pointless, but there was no magic spark, and it just felt mechanical. I didn't want people to laugh, I didn't care if they laughed or not. I did about three minutes and no one was listening anyway so I put the mike down on the floor and just left.

It's not something people think about, I suppose. How is a comedian supposed to make people feel good when he doesn't feel good himself? Well, some comedians can channel it and still create gold. Tony Hancock was a manic depressive and created some of the funniest comedy I've ever heard, but he ended up drunk and alone, eventually committing suicide. His suicide note read: 'Things just seem to go too wrong too many times.' I think we can all relate to that.

I'm not saying I was anywhere near suicide, of course. God, no, I don't even know how to work the oven. But I was in a dark place and couldn't see a way out. I thought after I'd got mugged I'd felt bad, but it didn't compare to this. I was angry with the world, everything annoyed me. Laura came in drunk one night at 4am and I was just sitting up in the darkness, wide awake, waiting for her, like a bloody weirdo.

'What fucking time do you call this?' I was fuming. I'd created a world in my head where this girl who I loved with all my heart had lost our baby and now didn't care. I blamed myself and I blamed her, I blamed everybody and everything, I couldn't make sense of it. Why would anyone take this off me? Why couldn't I have what a million people have by accident every day?

But Laura did care. She cared more than she was letting on. We stopped spending time with each other and, for a while, stopped sleeping in the same bed. When we did see each other it was fleeting, as if we thought that if we avoided each other the inevitable wouldn't happen.

One night I came in from another terrible gig where I'd called a completely undeserving audience member a 'fat fucker' because he'd got up to go to the bar while I was talking, and had lost the audience again. The club owner told me to leave and said he wouldn't be booking me again, but I couldn't have cared less. Comedy was by wankers, for wankers. It was for people who had nothing to say beyond spouting their stupid jokes. There's more to life than telling a room full of people a stupid story with no consequence or point. And who the hell were these people who didn't have enough imagination of their own to come up with some funny ideas themselves that they had to pay someone to do it for them? I began to hate it.

My last gig, and at the time I really felt like it was my last gig, was a Christmas show for the *Daily Sport*. I mean, already you're thinking, wow, Jason, that sounds like a classy do. Well, it gets worse: I was the comic booked to do twenty minutes of stand-up to a group of pissed-up journalists who spend their day writing daft news stories to belie the fact that their paper was essentially little more than a porn mag.

I wasn't the only act on the bill, although I was the only comedian. I was to follow a well-known 'variety act' called Mr Methane. Now if you've never heard of this guy, then put this book down for two minutes, log on to YouTube and type in his name, then come back.

OK, what did you think? Yeah, dog shit? Well, this audience thought he was hilarious. He stood on stage in his green superhero outfit and farted the National Anthem into the microphone for twenty minutes. To this crowd, it was up there with Tommy Cooper and Bob Monkhouse; they were crying with laughter. I was standing at the back of the room, looking on in horror. I knew two things: one, this was the worst thing I'd ever seen on stage (and I've seen Phil Collins live), and two, I was definitely not using the same microphone as that dirty bastard.

I was nineteen and felt too good to be there: not a good character-istic in a comedian. I was rude and obnoxious and I hated every person in the room and hated every second I was on stage. I actually tell a story in my show now about a heckle that happened on this night.

Because I was so young, this one guy shouted, 'Where's your pubic hair?' and his mates fell about laughing as if it was the funniest thing they'd ever seen since a man trumped 'Don't Cry for Me Argentina' about five minutes earlier.

Now, in my stage show I say, 'So I said, "In your wife's teeth,"' which is a brilliant response. But it never happened. It's one of those responses the French call *l'esprit de l'escalier*, or 'the wit of the staircase', a smart response you only think of on the way out when it's too late to be of any use. We've all done it: someone says something, you can't think of anything to say back, but an hour later in the car you're replaying the scene in your head and it comes to you, the perfect retort. Well, the good thing about being a comedian is that when we retell the story we can get rid of the hour in between and make it all seem like one moment.

What actually happened was he heckled, they laughed at me, I got angry, threw the stinking mike on the floor and walked off. It would be the last gig I did for almost two years. Now I knew what it was like to die on stage.

I got home to Laura and felt like a walking ball of rage, that at any moment I could snap and say or do something I'd regret. Stinking of smoke and curly fries, I got into bed.

'It's changed me,' she whispered.

'What has?' I said.

'This thing, this thing that happened to us, it's changed me.' I could tell she'd been crying for hours.

In all the anger and depression and the feeling sorry for myself, I'd not even thought that she would still be upset. She'd seemed so carefree, like it was a burden lifted and she could go back to enjoying the last few months of her teenage years. But of course, that was her mechanism for dealing with it. We'd not spoken about it for months. I thought I was being there for her, by holding her when she cried, but I realised I was never there at all, neither of us were. We'd gone somewhere else to protect ourselves.

I turned the light on and looked at her and my heart was empty. I loved her more than anything in the world but just looking at her made me remember. She was looking at me in exactly the same way. I held her again and we fell asleep, silently sobbing in each other's arms. It would be the last time.

The next day I left.

Laura had cornered me in the kitchen while I was washing up.

'It's not working, Jace.'

'I know.'

'I think we keep reminding each other of it.'

And she was right. Every time I looked at her I pictured myself in a park with a faceless child running and laughing in the warm breeze. But that wasn't going to happen now. I would never have left if she hadn't have told me to; I knew I didn't have it in me. But the relationship had collapsed under the weight of itself and Laura had done the hard part and set us both free.

Chapter 24

University Challenge

I DON'T KNOW if you've ever lived in student accommodation in inner-city Salford but it's essentially a mix between a prison and a holiday camp. With ten-foot walls surrounding the perimeter and guarded by two security men in what would quite easily pass for a gun turret, Castle Irwell was where I would spend a lot of my student life, in a flat I shared with ten other student lads with a shared bathroom and rats the size of Yorkshire terriers.

The only difference between my room here and the one I had at home was that it had a sink in it. The sink in the room always struck me as odd. Although it was useful, it was very rarely used for the strict purpose it was intended.

Nobody likes getting up in the middle of the night to go upstairs to the loo, so the Castle Irwell management had very handily left us one in our room within easy reach of the bed. More often than not you could pretty much lean out of bed and with the trajectory correct, bang that stuff right down the plughole. You couldn't have a poo though as that would come out of your deposit.

While I'm on weeing in sinks, I may as well tell you everything. At our house on Nettleford Road, our toilet was in a separate room from the bathroom so very occasionally you'd be bursting to go and find the door was locked.

'Who's in there?' I would shout, hoping above all hopes that the next word didn't come back as the answer:

'Dad.'

My worst nightmare. With anyone else you could at least wait till the end and then duck straight in and relieve yourself but with Dad it was different. He took forever in the first place and you had to give it at least twenty minutes after a Dad dump, it was like a wall of stink. Those times when I just couldn't wait for Dad to finish reading the sports pages of the *Daily Mirror*, I would pop next door to the bathroom and relieve myself in the sink, obviously washing it down with running water and a bit of Listerine (I'm not a monster).

I even had previous away from home. One night I was staying at my friend's house (I won't embarrass him by naming him) and in the middle of the night I'd gone to use the loo but the light was on and someone was already in there. I was desperate. Hopping from one foot to the other, I had no option – I'd have to go downstairs and wee outside in the garden. I ran down as fast as I could but couldn't find a key to let myself out. In a mad panic (you know, when you think you've held it in that long that something inside might burst and break) I spied, in the gloomy darkness, the kitchen sink. I climbed up on the sides using cupboard door handles to hoist me up, knelt down, pulled down my pyjamas and let rip.

Seconds into my pee session, there was a click and the kitchen striplighting blinked into life. I looked up in horror to see my friend's mum looking at me in exactly the same way.

'What the hell are you doing?'

I looked down at the jet of yellow leaving my body, like I also didn't know, as if to say, 'Yeah, what the hell am I doing?' To make matters worse, nobody had done the washing-up that night and the sink was full of dishes and mugs from that evening's tea. I never got to stay over again and a week later they were the first people on our street to get a dishwasher.

One of the good things about student accommodation is that you, if you'll forgive the cliché, meet friends for life. It's similar to kidnap victims who stay in touch as only they know what they went through and no one else would understand. My fellow kidnap victim was Stuart. A big strapping lad from Chesterfield, he was the most northern bloke I've ever known. The night I met him he was stood at a closed KFC drive-thru shouting through a crack in the glass, 'Give us us foods, give us us foods.' He was one of those people who didn't know how funny he was. Which always made it all the funnier.

There was the night we went up Saddleworth Moors to make a horror film we'd written as part of the course, and he nearly got us arrested. We got up to the top and there was 'Do Not Cross' tape all over the place, like there'd been some sort of crime. We didn't know what to make of it, but we had to get this film finished and edited by the end of the week so there was no way we were driving back up here again in the middle of the night. We just wanted to get it done and get back to civilisation.

As we stepped over the tape and onto the moors, we set up the lights and camera and started rehearsing through the script, which was basically, 'I don't really like it up here, Edward, it just seems so sinister… Edward? Ed? EDWAAAAARRRDDD!'

You know, that sort of thing.

It was pitch-black and there was no one around for miles, which was the reason we nearly shit ourselves when a bloke and a dog came running across the moors screaming, 'Whoa, Whoa. What do you think youse are doing up 'ere?'

'We're filming, pal,' Stuart replied.

'Never mind "pal", it's officer to you.'

As he came out of the darkness, I ducked behind the camera and left things to Stuart.

'Have you lot got a death wish?'

'No, officer,' said Stuart. 'Why?'

'Two words, son.' The officer looked at Stuart as if he'd never seen the news. 'Foot and mouth.'

Stuart looked incredulous. 'That's three words, officer.'

We got a police escort back to Castle Irwell and were banned from visiting the Moors until the mad cow outbreak was over. Cannes would have to wait.

I ONCE NEARLY killed Stuart. Genuinely too. But even that was funny. One of our flatmates had a course project where he planned to release a thousand helium balloons into the Salford sky. I can't remember why now, but the long and short of it was we had a hired helium gas canister in the flat for a fortnight.

Now bored students will have fun with anything, but a genuine gas canister knocks spots off a stolen traffic cone any day of the week.

For days we would sit around the flat sucking helium out of balloons and talking. I don't care who you are, a squeaky helium voice is always funny. I bet even the Queen has a little suck on a 'Happy Birthday, Philip' balloon once in a while and chats to Charles in a high-pitched voice. There's only two people who don't like helium: Joe Pasquale and Ashley from *Coronation Street*, because if they had a go on it, only dogs would hear them.

Stuart had been away in Chesterfield for the week and missed all the fun. Most of us had sore throats and terrible chests as constant helium abuse is bad for you, and we were pretty much overdosing. He came in and saw the canister in the kitchen and nearly wet himself with excitement.

'Oh bloody brilliant, can tha let us have a go?' he said in his still deep and slow Derbyshire accent.

He positioned his mouth over the opening of the high-pressure canister. I tried to shout out and stop him in my helium-addled stupor but just wasn't quick enough. We had been putting the helium into balloons and sucking it out of those, but he was about to release the gas into his lungs at huge pressure.

'Stu…'

BANG.

All sixteen stone, five foot eleven of Chesterfield's finest flew across the room into the cooker. Pans of beans and empty Pot Noodles juddered as he clutched his chest and his face went bright purple like Violet Beauregarde in Willy Wonka's factory. Me and a few other students looked over, helpless; it all happened so fast. Stuart was wheezing for oxygen as he struggled on the dirty kitchen floor. Was this it? Was our friend going to die here? Would I be done for possession?

'Stu, mate, are you OK?'

His eyes bulging out of his face and his face flashing through various blues like a police siren, he looked up at me like a drowning man.

In a slow, high-pitched helium voice, he screamed, 'You fucking bunch of bastards, I could have died!'

The seriousness of the situation mixed with the cartoon sound of his high-pitched voice was too much. Every one of us were on our knees, crying. With laughter.

'Why didn't you tell me, you set of wankers! I can't breathe!'

The angrier he got, the higher the pitch went and the more we rolled about laughing. We tried to tell him to stop as our stomachs were hurting so much, but even as his anger subsided, the force and amount of gas that he'd inhaled meant he kept his high-pitched voice for well over twenty minutes.

WHILE I WAS AT university I was only actually in three full days a week so on my other two days my dad had managed to get me a job as a logger. I know this conjures up images of me in a garish check shirt, chopping down mighty redwoods in the forests of British Columbia, but nothing could be further from the truth. I was a logger at Manchester Crown Court. You know when you watch *Ironside* and there's what appears to be a typist sat just below the judge, going at it hell for leather recording everything as everyone talks away? Well, she is in fact a stenographer: they're highly skilled and very expensive. So for most court cases they instead used a logger – someone who tapes the proceedings and makes relevant notes to accompany the recording. Someone not skilled at all and ridiculously cheap: the perfect job for a student and former North West Comedian of the Year.

Now it probably sounds quite exciting, doesn't it? And yes, some court cases are terrifically exciting, but of course those are the cases where it usually warrants the expense of a stenographer. A logger ends up with the cases about someone's garden being three inches into a neighbour's or someone robbing a pan set from John Lewis.

Having said that, there was often much unintentional entertainment to be had from the hearings. In that way my sense of humour hadn't really moved on from the classroom – and possibly still hasn't. Sometimes during plea and direction hearings they would connect us using a video link direct to the prison to save time and money. The court would assemble and over the live TV link the clerk would ask the prison officer, for example, 'Have you got Smith there?' and the defendant would then enter their plea. Often the prison officers and prisoners couldn't see the courtroom or the judge. It usually ran smoothly, apart from one morning when a German defendant was due for sentencing.

The overworked clerk didn't even notice the name: it was just another defendant on a long list. He spoke to the prison.

'Hello, officer, have you got Kuntz there?'

The prison officer came back in a flash in a strong Scottish accent: 'This is Strangeways, pal, we've got fucking hundreds.'

I logged it down, of course.

ONE OF THE PERKS of working in the courts is that with so many adjournments there is lots of downtime. These breaks in the corridors outside the court could be just as amusing as the cases themselves. There was once this little scally who was due to be sentenced for some violent crime. His own mother had turned him in, and the little toerag was all tears in the dock as the judge called a short adjournment to consider his sentence. We all trooped out of court and as soon as we got outside the little sod turned to his mum and screamed, 'This is all your fault, you grassing bitch.'

There was a smartly dressed bloke sitting next to me in the corridor. He nudged me.

'Have you heard him, going on like that?'

'I know,' I whispered. 'It's his mum as well.'

'His mum? He needs a bloody good hiding. These kids today have no respect, have they? World's going to bloody pot.'

'Tell me about it,' I said. 'Who are you defending?'

'I'm not a lawyer, I'm next up in the dock.'

'Sorry, mate, I thought you were one of the barristers. What you up for?'

'Murder.'

A LOT OF PEOPLE think the judiciary are out of touch with the real world but I think this view is unfounded. Most of the judges I sat with were as sharp as knives and embraced new ideas and technology. I mean, sometimes accidents can happen. One judge, who shall remain nameless for legal reasons, obviously, endeavoured to sort out a dispute over a new drink product called 'Celebrity Juice'. In all innocence he typed this into his laptop and was as surprised as the rest of us when various pornographic sites came up as well as clips of Keith Lemon. The jury had to be discharged.

Finally I'll let you into a secret here. One of the reasons judges and barristers wear wigs and gowns is so they won't get recognised in public, and it works, as the following illustrates. One well-known, very efficient judge was once walking across Crown Square in Manchester. On the bench he was the epitome of judicial dignity, but off duty he was just a little old man in a raincoat. A fellow logger and I were walking in the opposite direction. She was a quite attractive young girl, and as the two passed, the judge, being a friendly soul, gave her what he thought was a friendly smile. My co-worker was in a bit of a bad mood so instead of the 'Good morning, judge' he was expecting, he got 'Fuck off, you dirty old bastard.'

I was quite shocked, to tell the truth. 'You know who that was, don't you?'

'No idea. I couldn't care less.'

'No, it was Judge Dread.'

She paled visibly. 'You're joking, aren't you?'

'I'm afraid not. You've just called one of the most senior judges in Manchester a dirty old bastard.'

AFTER LAURA AND I split up not only did I stop looking for gigs but I stopped looking at girls. It'd been such a heavy relationship towards the end, I just couldn't bring myself to be with anyone. For months I just got on with my work at uni and occasionally went out with Stuart and a few friends. Of course, because I wasn't looking for girls and had no interest in chatting anyone up, I suddenly became hot property. It's an odd phenomena which I wish I'd known about when I was fourteen, but the less a bloke looks like he cares about sleeping with a girl, the more the girl wants to sleep with him.

The odd girl would come over and some really odd ones would come over too. One night I got chatting to this proper Manc girl in a club on Deansgate. She was all right looking and very flirty but I just wasn't that bothered. The less bothered I became, the flirtier she got. When I got up to go, she couldn't believe I was leaving. It'd obviously never happened to her before, but we swapped numbers and I said I'd call.

I didn't call but she called me and a few days later I was going to her house in Benchill, one of the roughest council estates in south Manchester. I couldn't believe I was seeing a girl only three months after breaking up with Laura. I'd promised myself that I was going to stay single.

This girl had a really strong Manchester accent. Even Frank Gallagher of *Shameless* would have had to occasionally ask, 'Sorry, what did you say then, love?' I sat in her living room and waited for her to get ready: we were going out to the cinema for the night. The doorbell went and she opened the front door and in walked the biggest, hardest-looking bastard you've ever seen in your life. He must have been approaching seven foot, had to duck his massive melon-shaped head as he came in, and had the bulk of Hagrid from Harry Potter. But the most terrifying thing about him was this huge glass eye, almost double the size of his normal eye. A huge scar ran from the centre of his forehead to the edge of his cheek, completely through his eye, like that character from *The Lion King* – you know, what's his name? Scar.

'You two boys have a chat while I get ready,' the girl said as she returned upstairs without even telling me who this was.

'So have you known Katie long?' I asked after a bit of awkward silence.

'All her fucking life, son, I'm her dad,' he growled.

'Course you are. Well, er, it's nice to meet you.'

'I wish I could say the same,' he said as he turned the TV on and completely ignored me.

Of course, now I have daughters myself I can completely understand where this guy was coming from. I mean, mine are only two years old but my wife is always trying to match them up with boys of the same age.

'Oh, is this your boyfriend?' she'll say as another toddler wanders over.

No, you're not their boyfriend, I'm thinking, so back off. I've been your age – I know what's going through your mind. Take your little yogurty smile somewhere else.

As I sat there, uncomfortable in every way on the worn-out sofa, I scanned the room for clues on what the hell I could chat about to this hairy, scary man.

I spotted a Manchester United mug. 'So you support Man United then?'

'Nope, not really.' He carried on watching *Countdown*; his working eye was watching Richard Whiteley but his glass eye was at a different angle and seemed like it was transfixed on me.

As the ticking music for the thirty-second Countdown Conundrum started, it felt like it was timing down my life. Inside I was praying for Katie to get ready faster and come downstairs. I'd only known her for about an hour if you added it all up, and she seemed nice enough, but no woman was worth this.

I tried to watch the telly but then heard myself speak again. 'Overlarge,' I said.

'You what?' He turned round for the first time. 'What did you just call me?'

'No, it's the answer,' I replied, pointing at the screen. 'The Countdown Conundrum.'

'Oh right, yeah.'

It seemed to work and he cracked a little but after a few moments of reflective thought he stood up and came over, towering above me as I sat on the sofa. I heard myself gulp.

'You fucking my daughter?' he growled.

Not yet, I thought, but managed not to say it out loud.

'You do not go near her bedroom, you do not have sex in this house, and if you break her heart and she cries I will track you down and you'll be fucking sorry you ever met her.'

I was already pretty sorry. As a threat it worked, because even if she had wanted to have sex with me she couldn't as my penis had crawled back up inside my body like a terrified puppy. I had heard about dads like this but this was the first time I'd met one. At the time

I thought he was a complete knobhead but now, as a father of three girls, he's my hero.

Moments later Katie came downstairs and we went to the cinema to watch *Exit Wounds* with Steven Segal (he was starring in it, he wasn't sat next to us at the Showcase on Hyde Road). I didn't enjoy it, mainly because it could have been a biopic of Scar Dad's life and it was as if I could feel every kick and punch the film offered up raining down onto my own body.

So where do you think I ended up only seven hours after the warning of a lifetime? Of course, I was having sex with his daughter in her room – you know, the one he forbade me from ever going near. I had protested but once you're back at a girl's house and the only two answers to the question 'Shall we have sex?' is a 'yes' or 'no', a man will always say 'yes'. The trick is to make sure you don't get to that point where your options are that limited; you need a reason behind each answer.

'Shall we have sex?'

'No, because we're on the number 109 bus from town and the driver's looking at us.' That sort of thing.

But against my will I dragged her up the stairs to her room and she'd made me take my clothes off and lie in the bed – I was really a victim in all this. No means no unless a nineteen-year-old lad says it to a semi-naked nineteen-year-old girl. I won't go into detail as I'm a gentleman, but suffice to say, I was brilliant.

Halfway through our session (although I can't be sure on it being exactly halfway) I heard the sound of a loud diesel van pulling up outside. Katie froze.

'Shit, it's my dad.'

Those four words struck fear into me so hard, I let out a noise of such whimpering weakness that I'm still ashamed of myself. My courage left me, climbed out of the window, shimmied down the drainpipe and then, alongside my bravery, left town on the 109 bus. Just as I felt I couldn't feel any more afraid, the front door opened and the first of his heavy feet climbed the stairs.

'Katie, are you in?'

'Yes, Dad,' she shouted back.

'What the bloody hell are you doing?' I whispered frantically. 'Don't tell him you're here.'

'It'll be fine, he'll have had a drink.'

Brilliant. Not only was he the hardest man I'd ever seen who probably cut out his own eye just to prove it, he was now as pissed as a fart. My whole body had turned to jelly, except my penis, which for some reason was still holding out hope that we were somehow going to get through the last few pages of the *Karma Sutra*.

'Quick, stand there,' she said, pointing to the wardrobe.

'I'm not getting in there, he'll hear me moving about.'

'No, not in,' she said hurriedly, walking me to the spot. 'Just stand next to it.'

She got back into bed as her dad knocked and walked into the room. I was stood stark bollock naked behind the wardrobe as he asked her about her night. I could hear him talking, slurring his words as he told her about some bloke he'd had a fight with at the pub.

As he stepped forward to show her his bloodied knuckles, I was sure he could hear my heart beating; if not he'd definitely feel the vibrations. If it wasn't my heart he could hear beating in my chest like a pneumatic drill, surely he could hear my arse squeaking as it went from 50p to 5p. As he showed her his hands, his eye rested on me, standing naked in his daughter's room, underneath a Take That poster. I froze even more than I had done earlier. I felt my eyes lock onto the cyclops psycho as the fight or flight question kicked in. How far would I get in the middle of this Wythenshawe council estate with no clothes on? I like to think it'd be like that scene in *Terminator* – 'Give me your clothes, your boots and your motorcycle' – but it'd probably end up like a scene from *Confessions of a Window Cleaner.*

I was waiting for the rage to start. I held my breath for an eternity, picking what bits of my body and face I would protect. But it never came. Maybe it was the eye of the storm, I thought, but then I realised the eye that was looking right at my naked body was the glass eye. He couldn't see me.

Eventually he turned and left. I can't tell you how relieved I was. I smiled over at Katie who looked back at me smugly. Then I thought to myself, hold on, she was so sure of where I should stand in the room, and was so right about it, she must have done this before. I was half expecting to look down and see two well-worn foot marks on the light pink carpet.

IT WAS APPROACHING the end of the university year and stand-up felt like a distant memory. I still didn't feel like getting off my arse and ringing anybody for gigs, and there was certainly nobody ringing me. I'd got a job in a pub near university, the Old Pint Pot, and was happy enough plodding along. You may or may not have had those moments in life where everything is fine; not great, not crap, just OK. You don't think about the future and you don't think about the past, you just get through each day, just living.

One evening in the pub in walked a girl I recognised instantly, but at first couldn't put a name to her face. I went over and chatted to her but still nothing came to my mind and she wasn't giving me any clues.

You know when you do that thing where you recognise someone so you start asking leading questions, hoping they'll finish off the sentence and fill in the missing information?

'Wow, you look great! I've not seen you since, oh man, when was it now?'

'College.'

'That's it, college, and how's what's her name?'

'Alison, yeah, she's fine.'

'Alison, of course, your erm… best friend.'

'My sister.'

'Yeah but I bet she's like a best friend.'

Then it clicked. It was Roz Norbury. She had been one of the fittest girls at school and here she was chatting to me. Of course we'd all evened out now. I was no longer a misshapen young boy and she was no longer an out-of-reach goddess. She'd turned a bit grungy, which is why I couldn't initially place her – darker make-up and hair – but she was still absolutely stunning. We seemed to hit it off immediately and by the end of the night I had her laughing, and her telephone number.

Finally, after months of feeling rotten, things were starting to look up. Someone who had once been out of reach now wanted to go out with me. I tried to be grown up with her, so we went out a few times to Angelino's restaurant in Chorlton, an Italian place where the owner would come to your table and talk to you for half an hour even though you had a mouthful of tagliatelle. He had this cod Italian accent which he would lose when he thought you couldn't hear him.

'Okaai, I get you de soup of ze day, madam, eeza no problem.' He looked and sounded like Super Mario but the second he was in the kitchen you would hear this rough Manc accent from behind the door. 'Oi, knobrash, table fourteen is waiting for his Carbonarrrrraaaaa.'

We had a lovely time, it was a fun relationship, but there was one thing stopping it lasting a lifetime. She was mental. Not properly mental – I wasn't afraid that one day I'd find myself tied to the bed with my ankles nobbled – just high maintenance, occasionally a little insensitive and often hard work.

I'm sure you're reading this now thinking, well, why did you stay with her for four months? (Which would be amazing if you did as I haven't told you how long it lasted.) But the reason I stayed with her is because, well, firstly she was so hot and I felt that if I did break up with her the fourteen-year-old me would be very disappointed in the nineteen-year-old me. But secondly, at the time, she was a little damaged: her parents were going through a separation, her twin sister had gone to university and she was living with her dad who was a bit down in the dumps. Also her dad was a lot nicer than the last dad I'd had a confrontation with: he had two eyes, no scars and, as far as I know, not even a hint of a criminal record.

I spent a lot of time at her house mainly arguing over nothing. We'd argue then have sex, argue, sex, argue, sex. It was a fifty per cent perfect relationship. I'm not an argumentative person so often I'd just let her decide what was right and wrong and just go along with it. But strangely, and you're going to think I'm really odd here, I started to fall for her. Maybe it was because she was that sexy girl from school, or maybe because I was looking for another relationship to make things right after I'd failed so badly at my last one.

It's always awkward that first time you decide to tell someone you love them – one of you has to bite the bullet and just go for it. Some people are scared of it, like it'll ruin what they have. Some people say it too soon. But Roz was never going to say it to me, I knew that. So I felt like I had nothing to lose: either she could say 'I love you too' or she could get scared and run away accusing me of 'moving too fast' or whatever bollocks people come out with under the pressure of that situation. How on earth any man or woman in a relationship can get scared of three little words is beyond me. But some girls can get really freaked out by it. I mean, considering it's us guys who are the ones with the reputation for being commitment-phobes, we don't seem to mind; even if you say 'I love you' on a first date we don't worry. Mainly because we're not listening. But also because maybe we don't hold that phrase in such terrifyingly high regard. Of course it's important, but lots of things are, like chips and Nando's and Call of Duty: Black Ops.

It's different for girls, though. If a bloke says 'I love you' too early then he's at risk of being instantly dumped. 'That's it, Brenda, he loves me so he can sod off. He's too needy and clingy, I'm going to go back out with Darren– at least he's got the decency to call me a stupid bitch once in a while and treat me like shit.'

It's funny, once you're older and married, people say it every day and it starts to have less gravitas than that first time – it slowly wears away through use. You say it while your partner is getting the milk out of the fridge: 'Ah, you making a cup of tea? I love you' or 'Have you cleared that cat shit up? I do love you.' I'm not saying you love your partner any less, I just mean those words, they should be used sparingly otherwise they become habit rather than instinct; it becomes second nature. I was once on the phone complaining to BT about something or other. 'Well, I'm not happy about it, but I suppose I'll have to live with it. OK, fine, yeah, goodbye, love you.' I was utterly raging, but because I'm so used to ending phone calls in that way, it just popped out.

One evening, as we sat on the sofa watching Hugh Grant acting like Hugh Grant in *Notting Hill*, it suddenly occurred to me that true to form, I was falling in love with Roz. I don't know why – a few minutes earlier she'd bollocked me for not wanting to go out that night with some of her pals as I wanted to stay in and just be with her. Maybe it was Stockholm Syndrome, the psychological phenomenon where a kidnap victim has positive feelings towards their captor.

I spent half an hour building up to the moment I was going to tell her this momentous thing. I knew we weren't going to be with each other for ever but I just wanted to tell her that for these few months she had, in her own odd way, improved my life. OK, we argued; all right, she wasn't interested in my stand-up; she even took the piss out of me when I made her a mix tape using mainly the hits of Lionel Richie; but there were some great times as well. I can't remember them now but I'm pretty sure there were.

'I love you,' I croaked.

There was silence. Maybe she hadn't heard me, but there was no way I was going to say it again. I let it linger in the air just as on screen Julia Roberts was standing in front of a guy asking him to love her. Well, I was just a guy, letting a girl lie across his lap while drinking a cup of tea, asking her to not let this silence last any longer.

A few minutes after I'd said it, there was still no reply. I decided to cough a little. Still nowt. So I thought, sod it, I'm going to say it again. I've already said it once, I may as well go for it.

'Roz, I love you.'

Without turning round, she took a slurp from her mug and replied, 'Ah, that's nice.'

Nobody wants that. I think I preferred the silence, to be honest. There is only one reply anybody wants from 'I love you' and that's 'I love you too.'

I WAS STAYING at my Nana Manford's house in Withington over the uni summer holidays as there was no room at my parents' house for me. Occasionally Roz would stay over there but you and I both know you can't have sex in your nana's house, even if she probably won't hear you above *Heartbeat*. The other weird thing was that I was actually staying in my dad's old queen-size bed, which now, decades on, was broken down the middle. Each night we'd start on opposite sides of the bed but gradually through the night we'd end up lying with our faces pressed against each other in the centre. There was no spooning in this bed; we were like two knives in a cutlery drawer lying side by side.

Me and Roz broke up in a unique way. One thing that used to infuriate me about her was that I was always the one who would ring her and instigate some activity – restaurant, pub, cinema, etc. She would never ring me, and I mean never. Can you imagine *never* receiving a phone call from your girlfriend? It drove me crazy. One afternoon I rang her and quite clearly said, 'Ring ME later and we'll go to the cinema.'

I made it pretty obvious the onus was on her to ring ME. But she didn't and I stubbornly refused to ring her and then a week passed and then another, and with both of us refusing to ring each other, we gradually just forgot about the other. In hindsight, I don't think I'd fallen in love with her. I was just desperate for someone to fall in love with me again and thought that that was the way to hurry it along a little.

Chapter 25

I Can See Clearly Now

MY SECOND YEAR at university started without much pomp and ceremony. I'd also started another job, which you'll be surprised to hear I hated. It was in an outbound call centre where, alongside hundreds of other drones, I rang people to see if they'd had an accident in the last three years. Yes, I was one of those people, one of those bastards who, just as you're sitting down for your tea, rings you to see if they can make some money out of you. It was soul-destroying, but it paid £6 an hour, which is obviously the exact price of my soul.

I mixed that with uni but I wasn't really loving that either. I felt a bit aimless. A few people told me to get back into stand-up but I just didn't want to. You need to really want to do stand-up comedy, an audience can sense a comic who doesn't want to be there and it's not nice for anyone. Also I couldn't shake the memory of those last few disastrous gigs. When a man farting 'Fur Elise' is getting bigger laughs than you, it's time to pack it in.

But I still found myself attracted to the stage and I joined the Theatre and Arts Society where they let me direct a couple of shows, *Bugsy Malone* and *Dracula*. The Theatre Society was full of lovely, attractive girls and we became a bit of a gang with nights out at various events, including every student's favourite, the Traffic Lights evening. If you've never heard of it, this is where everybody goes out and puts on a sticker that's either red, amber or green: red means 'Stay away I've got a partner', amber means 'Maybe' and green means 'I'm a bit of a slag'.

When we arrived at the club I was the only one with a red sticker; every single person was prominently displaying a green one. Of course it makes sense – why the hell would anyone come to what is essentially a night for pulling and before they've even chatted to a girl already have told them they're not interested? Well, that was me. I sat down, had a Coke and watched the cat and mouse game of seduction.

The music was pumping through the room as much as the adrenaline. Guys were spotting girls from across the floor, clocking their green sticker and heading over for the next stage. A brief chat, a drink or two bought and drunk, a group dance, a fun dance and then a close dance and that was it, they left together for a night of passion, both their nights sorted. They came, they saw, they conquered and then probably came again. It seems so simple when you're watching from a distance.

'It's funny isn't it?' a girl's voice said, 'They go to all this effort to get with someone then end up sat in the corner having no fun at all with a red sticker on their chest.'

I looked up and through the haze of the smoke machine, I saw this vision of beauty that's hard to describe. You know in *Snow White* when you read the words 'her skin was white as snow, lips as red as blood, hair was as black as ebony' and you think to yourself, that sounds like one weird-looking girl. Well, it's not weird, it's beauty personified. It was Cat, dark hair, pale perfect skin and rosy lips. She smiled.

'I suppose so, yeah,' I said.

Not the most imaginative opening sentence to use on the prettiest girl you've ever seen, but not the worst.

Cat had recently joined the Theatre Society, I'd seen her around but this was the first time we'd actually spoken. She was the only other person in the room who also had a red sticker on. I looked at mine and realised straight away that she'd presume I had a girlfriend. Damn it, why hadn't I gone amber? I needed to let her know that I didn't have a girlfriend, but I wanted to be subtle about it.

'I don't know why I'm even wearing one, I've not even got a girl-friend.' I think that did the trick.

'Well, why are you wearing one then?' she asked quizically, a little crease of skin appearing in the centre of her forehead, the first thing that broke her porcelain complexion.

'I don't know really, I suppose to put people off chatting me up.'

She laughed. 'Oh, you're that much of a catch, are you? You've got to put people off you?'

'No, I don't mean… I didn't mean that, I just mean… oh, I don't know what I mean. Why are you wearing one?'

'Well, I've got a boyfriend, that was the reason they said to wear one.'

Gutted. Not the answer I was hoping for. Not even thirty seconds in to our first conversation and our relationship was over. I'd already started to work out how attractive our kids were going to be, and she'd pulled the rug from under my feet.

'So why isn't your boyfriend here?'

'He's at Old Trafford, watching the football.'

I felt myself bristle. I hated him. I didn't even know who he was but not only had he nabbed my Snow White before I'd had even the chance to meet her, but he was a United fan. Bastard.

I chatted to her for the rest of the night and despite what I knew I could still feel myself falling hopelessly for her. As two green stickers became one all over the dance floor, we made our way out of the club. 'Summer of 69' played mutedly in the background as I walked her past Burger Brian's burger stand to the taxi rank. A fellow student was being sick only metres away, so it really was rank.

The taxi came quicker than I wanted it to, and she got in it.

'Thanks for the nice chat, it was good to get to know you, Jason.'

'Yeah you too, Cat, hope we can do it again some time.'

'Come on, love, close the door, it's fucking freezing,' her Salford taxi driver demanded, ruining the moment; if there even was a moment.

I stood and watched her drive away, doing that thing where inside you're willing them to turn and wave, as if it's some sort of confirmation that they like you back. Like a mantra playing in your head: 'Come on, come on, come on, turn, turn, wave, wave back to me, go on.' Just as the taxi went round the corner, she turned. And waved. I waved back. Result, I thought as the student next to me carried on vomiting.

I thought about her non-stop for days. I convinced a girl in the office to show me her timetable so I could 'accidentally' bump into her in the hallways and act all casual. I accepted every invitation for nights out that I knew she'd be on and then acted surprised when I saw her. 'Oh, no way, I didn't know you were going to be here!' She always seemed pleased to see me and never talked about her boyfriend and of course I never asked. I'd spotted them once arguing in the student union bar. He was decent-looking, I suppose, pretty well built and had a white bit in his dark hair, like Dicky Davies. They were arguing over something or other and I started to imagine it was because of me. I had no idea why it would've been about me but it was my daydream and I'll do what I want with it.

We became friends over the next few weeks, meeting up in the cafeteria at lunchtimes. We were flirty but never over stepped that unwritten boundary. We would go on group nights out and not leave each other's side, and as people walked past us I would always think to myself, 'I wonder if those people think we look like a couple?'

I'd tell all her friends how much I liked her and then say, 'But please don't tell her,' knowing full well that one thing women can't do is keep secrets from their mates. I knew it'd filter through. It's one little trick us fellas have up our sleeves from time to time. You think we don't know how you work, but we know bits.

One afternoon, as I was walking through the musty corridors of the old glue factory that was my university building, I heard Cat arguing on the phone somewhere close. I tracked her down and did that weird silently-mouthing-your-words thing you do when trying to talk to someone who's on the phone. 'Are you OK?' I asked, over-enunciating the words.

She hung up. Close to tears.

Bingo!

She had to go to Derby that night to see her sister in a play and her boyfriend wouldn't drive her because he was going to play snooker with his mates. I've never met anyone under forty who plays snooker but he obviously liked it more than he liked keeping his girlfriend happy. She would have to spend a few hours on the train by herself and was contemplating not going at all.

'Well, I don't drive, but I'll keep you company,' I offered.

As we left Piccadilly station, I couldn't believe my luck. She was a popular girl so even when I did spend time with her, she always had other friends around, but now I had her to myself for a whole night.

We went and watched her sister perform *A Midsummer Night's Dream: The Musical* or something; I can't remember now because I was watching Cat all night. She laughed throughout. It was a sexy laugh, like an uncontrollable girlish giggle, and I'd made it my mission these past few weeks to hear it as often as possible. It dawned on me that it was the first time in over a year I'd actually wanted to make anyone laugh.

After the show we stood at Sheffield station waiting in the freezing cold for our connecting train back to Manchester. We waited, and we waited some more. We were the only two people on the platform and it slowly became apparent that maybe this train wasn't coming. After checking the timetable, it was confirmed. Cat had got her times wrong and we were stuck in Sheffield with no way of getting home.

Cat went to check her bank balance at the hole in the wall but I didn't bother. I'd had pretty much no money for over a year now. In fact, I was well into my overdraft and had a couple of credit cards maxed out too. I was working all the time, and I'd got my student loan, but I'd crept into the red and decided I'd stay there.

We had two options: we could stay in a Travelodge (my idea) or get a taxi home (her idea). I couldn't sell the Travelodge idea enough. We'd get a twin room obviously, but just the very idea of sleeping so close to her was exciting enough.

In the end we opted for a taxi. For £60 he would drive us the hour journey over the Pennines back to civilisation. Before our journey home I put £3 in a passport photo machine they had at the station and grabbed her inside the booth. She sat on my knee and we squeezed in. I could smell her flowery perfume and feel the coldness of her smooth cheek as she pressed her face to mine. As I waited for the pictures, still buzzing from our closeness moments ago, Cat's phone rang. My heart sank. It was Dicky Davies. She told him she was OK and was on her way home. I could hear him apologising and her forgiving him and I tried to block it out as we got into the back of the minicab.

I could feel a wave of sadness creeping up on me as I sat in the back, watching the Yorkshire houses winding down for the night. My forehead was pressed against the cold glass and I had the row of four pictures in my hand. I looked down at us both laughing and knew right then that I was in love. I know I've told you I was in love before, and maybe I was, but this felt different. This was a painful love because this was a love that I couldn't have. My heart ached and I couldn't bear it.

I spent half an hour in silence, hoping she would break it and tell me how she was glad she'd spent the evening with me. I stared at the picture and tried to build up my confidence to say something, but the words wouldn't form in my mouth. Eventually a little bit of bravery kicked in.

'I had a really nice time tonight and I feel like we've got even closer. I know you've got a boyfriend but he should've been here for you tonight, I think you're too good for him and I...'

I turned round to face her, moments away from telling her I loved her. I remember how hard it was when I was going to tell Roz but maybe that's because I didn't. This time it felt easy, it felt natural, it felt true and, although the variables on this relationship were vast and complicated, I just had the uncontrollable urge to tell her.

But she was asleep. Head flopped down on her chest, lolling up and down as we drove across the Pennines. I looked out and saw Manchester below, a carpet of orange street lights as far as the eye could see. I caught the driver's eye in the rear-view mirror.

'Unlucky, mate,' he said in his half-Indian, half-Yorkshire accent.

I held her hand as she slept, and watched her, willing the driver to take his time getting us home. We arrived back at her student house and she got her bag, said goodbye and made her way inside. The taxi driver turned the car round and she came back out. 'Thanks for coming with me tonight, it really meant a lot.' It was gone 2am and she still looked beautiful, her face lit by the yellow glow of the street lights.

'That's OK, it meant a lot to me as well.' I smiled.

'Do you want to come in for a cup of tea?' she asked, smiling.

I thought about it, about what could or might happen if I did go in for a cup of tea, about how bad she'd feel if something happened while she had another man in her life and how bad I'd feel at... well, no, actually, I wouldn't have felt bad at all to be honest, but I still didn't.

'No, it's OK, I'm really tired, I best go,' I said reluctantly.

She kissed my cheek and went in the house. As we pulled off I clocked the driver's face in the rear-view mirror again. He was shaking his head and rolling his eyes.

'You fucking dickhead, mate, you were in there.'

IN THAT SECOND YEAR, me and Stuart moved into a small ground-floor flat across the road from our campus. It was pleasant enough and made us feel a little bit more grown up. It was a newish flat and we were surrounded by other students and young professionals. Stuart used to go home every weekend and during the holidays, so a lot of the time I was left by myself, but it didn't bother me too much.

Three nights before Christmas I was in my room in a pair of boxers, trying to relax as I took Rochdale to the FA Cup semi-final on Championship Manager, when I heard a noise. I got up and walked slowly to the door. I could hear people chatting quietly; it sounded like they were in the living room. I creaked open my door and could hear two voices – at first I thought it might be Stuart but dismissed this as it was so close to Christmas and he would have rung to tell me if he was coming back. I turned my light off and through the crack of the door I watched these two shadowy figures move round the flat like lightning. I was frozen to the spot as one of them walked right past me into our small kitchen and helped himself to some Cadbury's Chocolate Fingers I'd left on the side. Then he took all the carrier bags from under the sink, walked back into the living room and started putting all my CDs into them. I watched them open the back door and, with 'Every Little Helps' emblazoned on the side of their swag bags, they made off.

I was shaking like a leaf by now but managed to ring the police, who were there in no time at all – if you're like me and 'no time at all' means an hour and a half. I sat in the empty living room staring at the space where an eight-year-old 22-inch telly used to be. I mean, who steals off students? It's like mugging a tramp. They'd taken all the presents from under the tree, all the DVDs and all but one of the CDs. Still in its case by itself on the shelf was *The Best of Neil Diamond*. These burglars had no class. I went and had a look in the garden, being careful not to disturb any evidence. I'd seen *CSI*, I know how it works. As I got to our broken back gate, I noticed they'd dropped something on the floor. It was the DVD of *It's a Wonderful Life*, which would make quite a romantic end to this little story, but the case was empty as the actual disc was inside the DVD player that they'd just nicked.

THE LIFT in my spirits that falling for Cat had given me seemed to slip away in the run-up to Christmas. It felt like an impossible situation. Agraman had rung a couple of times to offer me a gig, God knows why because the last few he'd seen me at weren't particularly great. I dodged his calls and got through Christmas as best I could. At that age, with no mates around and no girlfriend, Christmas can be a bit crap. I hung out a bit with Lucy but she had a new boyfriend so I was a bit of a spare part at the Kellaway house. Sat alone in the flat, I thought about ringing Cat but felt a bit of a loser in doing so. I'd put in her number a few times but never gone through with actually calling. Then I got sacked by the Rochdale board after losing the support of the fans and that really put me on a downer.

I was working every day at the outbound call centre. Not just ruining people's tea now, I was spoiling their Christmas too. It was life-sapping work. Each day I had to ring hundreds of numbers. For every fifteen people shouting at me and calling me names, I would find one person who had actually had an accident at work. The managers were happy with me – I was making them money – and I took every shift I could.

'We're going to be open till five on Christmas Eve, does anybody want to work it?' one of the managers shouted from the top of the room. Not one hand went up. 'It's time and a half.' Slowly about a dozen hands went up, including mine.

I figured I would only be on my tod anyway so I may as well be getting paid. There's something about time and a half, double time and time in lieu that makes people do crazy things. We love it, it's like free money.

Come Christmas Eve, I settled down to work my five-hour shift. Bits of tinsel were on each computer screen and a Motown Christmas CD was playing in the background. I made about thirty phone calls and didn't have one bite, although I was called a 'heartless bastard' fifteen times and one woman actually called me a 'rude Grinch'. An hour before my shift ended, a number came up on the screen like any other number. The computer rang it and I waited for my answer, ready with my sales patter. Now usually one of two things happened: if nobody answered, either it would go to an answer phone or the company's computer system would cut you off after a minute or so and dial the next number. Occasionally there was a glitch and it didn't cut out, no matter how long it rang. We tended to view these as a little unexpected treat – a break in which to daydream or scan the sports pages. This number just rang and rang. Minutes went by. I was actually timing it – five, six, seven minutes. What the heck was wrong with this phone? After twelve minutes of ringing, it clicked.

'Hello?' It was an elderly voice. 'Is that you, Barbara?'

'Good evening, sir, this is Jason calling from Accidents Finance. Can I ask, have you had an accident at work in the last three years?'

There was a long silence and then the old man sighed.

'Sir, if you've had an accident I can help get you the money you deserve. There is over six hundred million pounds' worth of compensation, and some of it could be yours.' I said that last bit like a voiceover guy on a game show with a little pause between 'could' and 'be yours'.

'Son,' the man said, not angry, just dispirited. 'I'm sixty-two and registered blind and disabled.'

My heart sank and I felt rotten. I'd wasted nearly fifteen minutes on this guy and wasn't going to get any bonus.

'OK, sir, well, I'm sorry I interrupted your afternoon. Merry Christmas.'

As I went to press the 'hang up' button on the screen, he said, 'Are you happy doing this, Jason?'

How the hell did he know my name? Oh yeah, I told him at the beginning of the phone call but I was still shocked, like any worker when a customer uses their real name even though it's on their name badge.

'I'm sorry, what?'

'Are you happy, lad? With your life? Doing this?'

This had never happened before. I either made a sale, got abused or they just hung up; never once did anyone actually talk to me.

'Erm, I suppose so, Mr...' I checked the screen. 'Holmes.'

'You know just now, I was upstairs, and this phone is downstairs. It took me so long to get down but the phone just kept on ringing so I thought it must be my daughter. I've not spoken to her for a few months you see and I was very excited.'

'I'm sorry about that, Mr Holmes. I was just doing my job, sir.'

'How old are you, lad?'

'Twenty.'

'And this is your job? Phoning people up at home, ruining their day just so you can make some man in a suit some money?'

'I suppose.'

'And you want to do this for ever, do you?'

'Not really.'

'Shouldn't you be at home with your family or a girlfriend, enjoying Christmas?'

I scoffed at the thought 'I haven't got a girlfriend, sir.'

'You're better than this, Jason lad, much better.'

'Am I?' I was looking at the guy sat next to me, rolling my eyes at this nutter on the phone. 'How do you know?'

'I can tell it in your voice, the fact you're still talking to me and not badgering the next person on your list. What do you want to be, son?'

'Nothing.'

'Nothing? Are you joking? Nobody wants to be nothing, lad. What did you want to be when you were a child?'

I smiled to myself, remembering. 'A dog. I wanted to be a dog.'

He laughed. 'A bloody dog!? Come on, what do you want to do with your life, what have you enjoyed doing?'

'Well, I did a bit of stand-up comedy a while ago, that was fun for a bit.'

'And what happened? Were you any good?"

'I was OK. Won a few competitions but I, well, I just didn't feel like it any more, stopped enjoying myself.'

'Oh dear, that is sad, son. Poor you.'

'I know.'

'Twenty years old, your whole life ahead of you with two working legs and a couple of decent eyes as well, I bet? Must be a tough life.' An element of sarcasm entering his voice.

'Sometimes it is, yeah,' I said, but as the words left my mouth I didn't believe it myself.

'Son, listen to an old man. You're probably going to be the only person I speak to this Christmas, so do me a favour.'

'OK.'

'Hang up this phone, put your coat on and go and enjoy your life. We're not here for ever.'

The manager was stood over me now, tapping his watch, looking incredulously at the clock on my computer screen as it passed the half-hour mark.

'I should go, Mr Holmes.'

'Promise me, Jason, son, have a Merry Christmas.'

'Merry Christmas.'

As I got off the phone the manager tapped my shoulder. 'That better have been some sale, mate. You've been on for ages.'

I stood up, grabbed my coat and walked straight past him.

As I hit the cold December air, I chuckled to myself, shaking my head in disbelief that I'd taken some random blind stranger's advice and quit my job. I suppose just because you have no sight doesn't mean you can't see. I walked home from Salford Quays to my mum and dad's, looking forward to getting up at 5am and opening presents with the rest of my family. I took my phone and checked the voicemail.

'Jason, Merry Christmas, it's Agraman, the human anagram. I've a gig on in January at the Buzz and some comics have let me down. I was just wondering, as you've not done it for so long, if you fancied it. I can't offer much, £25, but you can bring a guest if you like.'

I rang him back and took the gig. I was a comedian again. Now I needed a guest.

'Hello?'

'Hiya, it's Jason. Just wanted to say have a Happy Christmas.'

'Oh, thanks. Yeah, you too, have a good one.'

'You spending it at home or with Dicky Davies?'

'Who? Oh, you mean Andy? Well, me and Andy kinda split up a couple of weeks back so I'll be at my mum's,' Cat said.

I don't know if you've ever seen a grown man do a run and then click his heels like in a film, but if you'd been on Seymour Grove that Christmas Eve at 5.30 then that's exactly what you'd have seen.

'Good.'

'Good? How's it good?'

'Oh, well, no, I didn't mean good as in good, I meant it as in good for me.'

She was laughing at my panicky explanation. 'Oh, how so?'

'Well, the thing is, I like you, a lot, and, well, I'm single and you're single, it just seems like the timing is right. Will you go out with me, please?'

Why the hell did I say please? I was losing myself to the silence at the other end of the phone, I changed tack.

'Listen, I've got a comedy gig in a few weeks – you could come and watch me if you like?'

The pause got longer, so long in fact I had to take the phone from my ear to check I hadn't been cut off. The wind was growing bitter and was slapping my face as I moved the phone back just in time.

'No, Jason, I can't.'

Can't what? Come to my gig, or go out with me? I knew she was all I wanted, the only person in the world who could make me happy.

'Can't what?' I asked with trepidation.

'I can't go out with you. I'll come to your gig but I can't go out with you, I don't want to go out with anyone.'

'OK, no worries.'

'And we're such good friends, I wouldn't want to ruin that.'

Argh, the classic!

'Oh, I see. Not to worry, I understand.' I didn't. 'I'll just have to get used to the idea that we'll never go out with each other I guess.'

She chuckled that girly laugh I'd fallen in love with. 'Jason.'

'What?'

'I didn't say "never" did I?'

Chapter 26
Christmas 2010

25 December 2010, 5.30am

I wake up and it's freezing. My wife is sleeping next to me, her pregnant mound moving rhythmically with every breath under the duvet. I slide out of bed and into my slippers, and quietly move onto the landing to get ready. I can hear Mum snoring away next to my dad in the spare room like a juggernaut hitting the wrong gear going up a hill. My brother Colin is asleep on the crappy sofabed in my office and my ten-year-old brother Niall is top and tailing with my twelve-year-old sister Danielle on a semi-deflated airbed on the landing, leaving their real bed empty in case Santa needs a rest. My twin daughters are fast asleep in their cots in the nursery. The house is full but sleeping.

I put on an old A-Team T-shirt to keep me warm, the timer for the heating won't kick in for another couple of hours.

'If you're cold, wear a jumper,' I hear myself say on a regular basis.

I go to the bathroom to brush my teeth, noticing that the tube is almost empty and will need replacing once the shops open after Christmas, but the thought only stays in my head as long as the water stays in the sink.

I move gently downstairs, smiling at the tinsel and decorations that flow down the banister as the light from the outside decorations floods the hallway. Outside, the roofline of the house is full of multi-coloured bulbs and the tree out the front is done up in over 2,000 fairy lights. It took ages and cost a few hundred quid but when my daughters saw it and said, 'Wow' for the first time in their lives, I decided it was worth it, even if a taxi driver the previous week had said, 'Bloody hell, who lives here? Liberace?'

I walk towards the kitchen past a wall of Christmas cards and photos stuck on with Blu-Tack. Among the usual pointless ones from barely known neighbours that simply say, 'To number 23, Merry Christmas, from all at number 74,' are the special ones from family and friends: 'Merry Christmas from Uncle Brendan and family… from Uncle Gary… from Nana Manford… from Lucy and all the Kellaways… from Peter and the family.'

I sit in the lounge and flick the switch that brings the Christmas tree to life. I look round at the piles of presents for the girls. There's at least forty each and I know that I am only responsible for about three of them – the rest are from members of my huge loving family. I stand up, take a bite from the mince pie, glug down the sherry and take a chunk out of the carrot that our girls left out for Father Christmas the night before. They're too young to know what's going on but I figure you've got to start these family traditions early.

I make a brew and look out the patio doors at the white snow that covers our back garden. It's the first white Christmas I can remember, and the evening before me, Stephen and Colin had taken our parents' latest dog, Nikita, for a walk to the park where we'd ended up having the biggest snowball fight ever. Nikita is a fluffy white samoyed. She's like the Paris Hilton of dogs. All three of us grown up, with partners and families of our own, running around Longford Park like we were ten, crying with laughter. We even threw snowballs for the dog to catch. Each time she caught one in her mouth it would disappear and she'd turn round to us as if to say, 'All right, Gandalf, where's me bloody ball?'

We'd done the rounds, dropping off presents at Nana's and cousins' houses, even though on the news they'd told us not to drive 'unless absolutely necessary'.

As I pour my Cheerios, I chuckle to myself as I remember a little tradition we used to have as kids. Every day of the year we had Scott's porridge oats for breakfast but on Christmas morning we would have a choice from one of those Kellogg's Variety Packs: it was like a pre-Christmas-presents present. The one in 365 days bowl of Coco Pops was like no other taste; we were like the kids from the advert with huge grins on our faces as the milk turned chocolatey.

As I sit waiting for the heating to kick in, I ponder my luck. I've had a difficult few weeks with no one to blame but myself. I've left yet another job but this one was a bit more high profile than walking out of Burger King, instead of eight or nine customers watching the action, over 5 million people watched me go. I chastise myself again, as I've done every day for the past month and a half, until a noise wakes me from my introspection.

The family are awake.

Footsteps and cries of 'Merry Christmas' shake the house to its foundations as I pop the kettle on, lower in some toast and grab a can of Carling from the fridge for my dad. Any other day you'd be called an alcoholic but when it's celebrating Jesus's birthday, all social norms go out of the window. 'C'mon, have a drink, it's Christmas. Enjoy yourself, Nana, have a wrap of whizz – it's for Jesus.'

My brother Stephen rings at just after 6am to wish everyone a Merry Christmas and my whole family flock to the living room to begin opening presents. My daughters are tearing at wrapping paper like there's no tomorrow and my parents are helping them. I look at my smiling wife as she piles their presents up and I feel like the luckiest man on earth. I think to myself, I will never cancel Christmas for these girls, even if I have to go back to ringing people to see if they've had an accident in the past three years or washing glasses at a wedding. I sit in the corner with a black bin bag, collecting the wrapping paper that's flying around the room, thinking to myself, I only stopped wrapping some of these presents four hours ago.

'Your turn, Jay,' my mum says.

I grab my three presents. The first one is soft, and I do a look of mock disappointment as I realise it's socks. But I'm soon beaming as they read 'A girl's first love is her daddy'. I give my daughters a kiss even though they are oblivious to it and engrossed in an In the Night Garden Ninky Nonk train set. My second present is from my mum and dad. It's small and hard and I know exactly what it is. It's the same thing they've given me every Christmas for over twenty years.

'I wonder what this could be?' I smile as I read the inlay card to my dad's homemade comedy tape. This annual gift is the only reason I own the North West's only tape deck and these days the tape doesn't feature my comedy heroes, but my contemporaries: Michael McIntyre, Frankie Boyle, Sarah Millican, Jimmy Carr and Peter Kay.

'Cheers, Dad.'

'Last present,' Cat says, smiling mysteriously as she pushes the biggest box in the room across the wooden floor. 'It's from all of us, your whole family.'

'You're really hard to buy for,' Mum adds. 'What do you give to the guy who's got everything?'

'Antibiotics,' Dad says without looking up from his granddaughter's new toys.

I rip open my present, the eight-year-old me tearing at the Christmas wrapping. And like with all presents, you get a glimpse of a word or a picture that excites you into pulling at the last bit of Sellotaped ribbon, I spot a few letters, 'LEXT', in big yellow block capitals and my smile grows till it fills my face. I start laughing, a lump forming in my throat as I open the rest.

'No way, guys! I've not thought about this for years,' I say.

'No idea when you're going to play with it with another baby on the way,' my mum says.

'I'll mind it for you!' says Colin.

'No chance, mate. As soon as I finish writing this bloody book I'm going to play with my Scalextric every day.'

Acknowledgements

Right well, I'd like to thank myself for writing it, cos it was well hard. But I would also like to thank my dad for helping me along the way, his brain was like an external hard drive for my own memory. Mum, Stephen, Colin, Uncle Gary and Uncle Brendan for coming out for a few drinks and reminding me of some really bonkers stories, some of which are in this book, some of which can never ever be told to another living soul. I'd really like to thank Andrew at Ebury for being both on my back and also pretty relaxed about the whole thing, he's got a good way of making ideas seem as if they were my idea. Thanks to my agent Lisa for roughly the same and for also being the first person to believe that I could do it. Thanks to my three daughters for sharing the breakfast table with my laptop for the last twelve months and the biggest thank you to my wife Catherine, who I could not live without, and has helped me make the most out of my life.

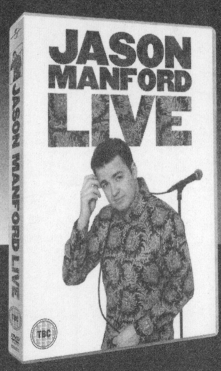